Masculinity
and
Femininity

Cross-Cultural Psychology Series

SERIES EDITORS

Walter J. Lonner
Western Washington University

John W. Berry
Queens University

Many of the basic assumptions contained in standard psychology curricula in Western universities have been uncritically accepted for many years. The volumes in the **Cross-Cultural Psychology** series present cultural perspectives that challenge Western ways of thinking in the hope of stimulating informed discussions about human behavior in all domains of psychology.

Cross-Cultural Psychology offers brief monographs describing and critically examining Western-based psychology and its underlying assumptions. The primary readership for this series consists of professors who teach, and students who take, the wide spectrum of courses offered in upper-division and graduate-level psychology programs in North America and elsewhere.

EDITORIAL BOARD

Books in this series:

1. **Methods and Data Analysis for Cross-Cultural Research,** Fons van de Vijver and Kwok Leung
2. **Health Psychology in Global Perspective,** Frances E. Aboud
3. **Masculinity and Femininity: The Taboo Dimension of National Cultures,** Geert Hofstede

Masculinity and Femininity

The Taboo Dimension of National Cultures

Geert Hofstede

With
Willem A. Arrindell
Deborah L. Best
Marieke De Mooij
Michael H. Hoppe
Evert Van de Vliert
Jacques H. A. Van Rossum
Johan Verweij
Mieke Vunderink
John E. Williams

CCP

Cross-Cultural Psychology

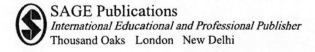

SAGE Publications
International Educational and Professional Publisher
Thousand Oaks   London   New Delhi

For information:

 SAGE Publications, Inc.
2455 Teller Road
Thousand Oaks, California 91320
E-mail:order@sagepub.com

SAGE Publications Ltd.
6 Bonhill Street
London EC2A 4PU
United Kingdom

SAGE Publications India Pvt. Ltd.
M-32 Market
Greater Kailash I
New Delhi 110048 India

Printed in the United States of America

Library of Congress Cataloging-in-Publication Data

Main entry under title:

Hofstede, Geert H.
    Masculinity and femininity: The taboo dimension of national cultures / by Geert Hofstede with Willem A. Arrindell ... [et al.].
    p. cm. — (Cross cultural psychology ; v. 3)
    Includes bibliographical references and index.
    ISBN 0-7619-1028-X (cloth : acid-free paper)
    ISBN 0-7619-1029-8 (pbk. : acid-free paper)
    1. Sex role—Cross-cultural studies. 2.
Masculinity—Cross-cultural studies. 3. Feminity—Cross-cultural
studies. I. Arrindell, Willem A. II. Title. III. Series:
Cross-cultural psychology series ; v. 3.
    HQ1075 .H63 1998
    305.3—ddc21   98-9074

98 99 00 01 02 03 04   8 7 6 5 4 3 2 1

Acquisitions Editor:	Jim Nageotte
Editorial Assistant:	Fiona Lyon
Production Editor:	Sanford Robinson
Editorial Assistant:	Karen Wiley
Typesetter:	Danielle Dillahunt
Cover Designer:	Ravi Balasuriya
Indexer:	Molly Hall
Print Buyer:	Anna Chin

CONTENTS

SERIES EDITORS' INTRODUCTION

The comparative study of thought and behavior across cultures has been one of the most interesting and productive developments in psychology during the past quarter century. We believe, as do many others, that psychology can mature into a valid and global discipline only to the extent that it incorporates paradigms, perspectives, and data from an ever-widening circle of both cultures and ethnic groups. That was the general guiding philosophy behind the **Cross-Cultural Research and Methodology** series that was started in 1975, in which 20 volumes were published. Like the CCRM series, this new series offers books describing and critically examining Western-based psychology and its underlying assumptions. Most of the basic assumptions contained in standard psychology curricula in the many universities of the highly industrialized Western world have been unchallenged. The volumes in this new series present cultural elements that challenge Western ways of thinking in the hope of stimulating informed discussions about human behavior in all domains of psychology. Books in this series are written for use as core texts or as supplements, depending on the instructor's requirements. We believe that the cumulative totality of books in this series will contribute to the development of a much more inclusive psychology and will lead to the formation of the interesting, testable hypotheses about the complex relationships between culture and behavior.

As series editors, we are fortunate to have an international panel of experts in cross-cultural psychology to help guide us in the selection and evaluation of manuscripts. The 14 members of the editorial board represent 11 different countries and many of the domains within psychology.

Many books relevant to cross-cultural psychology have appeared during the past 25 years. One of the defining publications was Geert Hofstede's *Culture's Consequences: International Differences in Work-Related Values.* Published in 1980 by Sage, as a volume in the Cross-Cultural Research and Methodology series, that book has influenced many people and has been a factor in a large number of research projects. In *Culture's Consequences,* Hofstede explained how he developed ways to measure the now-familiar four values of Individualism, Uncertainty Avoidance, Power Distance, and Masculinity. He provided considerable data to support the validity and usefulness of these sociocultural dimensions. Hofstede's tour de force has had an almost unparalleled influence on cross-cultural research. Transcending the workplace, or managerial attitudes and values, these four dimensions have been used by many researchers to explain such things as macroscopic (cultural) and microscopic (individual) characteristics and variables, clinical syndromes, and the nature of interpersonal interaction among people from different cultures.

One of these dimensions, that of Individualism, was the focus of a later book in the CCRM series (Kim, Triandis, Kagitçibasi, Choi, and Yoon, 1994).[1] This new book addresses in more detail the Masculinity dimension. The idea of treating Masculinity (and reciprocally, Femininity) as an important and researchable dimension of human values is at once both quite acceptable and logical as well as perhaps the most controversial (or delicate, or misunderstood) of the four dimensions— hence the appropriate subtitle, "The Taboo Dimension." Hofstede did his characteristically excellent job of designing the book. Bringing together different pieces of the puzzle in the form of various chapters by individuals who have done research on this dimension, this edited book is a valuable addition to the cross-cultural literature. Like *Culture's Consequences*, it will guide many researchers in dozens of societies as they attempt to understand how culture and the phenomena of psychological masculinity and femininity interact. Now, nearly 20 years since the publication of his seminal book, we are pleased to be part of this continuity of scholarship that looks into important ways to understand sociocultural processes.

—*Walter J. Lonner*
—*John W. Berry*

NOTE

1. Kim, U., Triandis, H. C., Kagitçibasi, C., Choi, S.-C., and Yoon, G. (Eds.). (1994). *Individualism and collectivism: Theory, method, and applications.* Newbury Park, CA: Sage.

PREFACE

This book fits Sage's Cross-Cultural Psychology series like a bead in a string. It builds on my 1980 book *Culture's Consequences* (Volume 5 in the Sage Cross-Cultural Research and Methodology series), and it is a partner volume to the reader *Individualism and Collectivism* edited by Kim, Triandis, Kagitçibasi, Choi, and Yoon (Volume 18 in the Sage Cross-Cultural Research and Methodology series, 1994).

Unlike its partner volume, however, the present book is as much a monograph as a reader. Four large chapters by me carry the main line of the argument; eight shorter chapters by invited contributors support and illustrate it. This is a consequence of the different developments in the study of individualism/collectivism and of masculinity/femininity. Individualism/Collectivism and Masculinity/Femininity were twin dimensions in *Culture's Consequences*, derived as independent (orthogonal) factors from the same country-level factor analysis of work goals.

Those two dimensions, along with two others (Power Distance and Uncertainty Avoidance), derived in different ways, were proposed as anthropological distinctions between societies, affecting sociological and psychological processes within those societies. The Individualism/Collectivism distinction was eagerly picked up by cross-cultural psychologists. It correlates with national wealth, opposing wealthy to poor countries. It also opposes Western to Asian countries. It continues to do so after these Asian countries have developed economically, although to a diminishing extent. The dimension provided a useful framework for the growing community of Asian psychologists in their dialogue with a psychological discipline developed entirely in the West. Since Harry Triandis took the initiative in 1986, there have been symposia on Individualism/Collectivism in the biannual congresses of the International Association for Cross-Cultural Psychology. In 1990, there was even a special conference on the topic alone, organized by Uichol Kim in Seoul, Korea, and preceding the IACCP Congress in Nara, Japan. Papers presented at this conference were the source of the Sage reader *Individualism and Collectivism*.

Masculinity/Femininity was just as important an anthropological distinction in my 1980 book as Individualism/Collectivism, but it did not correlate with national wealth and did not oppose the West to Asia. There were masculine and feminine national cultures in Asia, Europe, and the Americas. Psychologists from feminine cultures like Sweden, Portugal, Thailand, and Costa Rica were unlikely to rally to symposia or conferences with colleagues from masculine cultures like Japan, the United States, Mexico, or Germany. Also, in some countries that I had identified as masculine, the dimension was judged politically incorrect.

In the 1992 IACCP Congress at Liège, Belgium, I convened a symposium about research connected to the Masculinity/Femininity dimension. This was followed by similar symposia in Pamplona, Spain, in 1994, and in Montréal, Québec, Canada, in 1996. Six of the eight short chapters in the present book are based on contributions made at one of these symposia. Three of the six had in the meantime been published elsewhere, and they have been reprinted with permission and with minor editing. The five other short chapters have been rewritten or newly written for this book. My own four chapters were outlined in a long working paper titled *Masculinity, Religion, Gender and Sex* presented in Montréal, but they have been considerably elaborated.

Profound thanks are due to the nine contributors of the eight chapters, who were supportive and fast, and who put up kindly with my editorial interferences. Among the ten of us are three women and seven men, representing a variety of disciplines (clinical psychology, cross-cultural psychology, developmental and sports psychology, social psychology, education, marketing, and sociology). What will strike any reader is the predominance of authors from the Netherlands—six of us were born in that country. This was not a deliberate selection by a Dutch editor; all but one of the other Dutch contributors already had done their research before I even discovered their existence. Among the countries with a pronouncedly feminine national culture, the Netherlands probably has the largest concentration of social scientists accustomed to expressing themselves in the English language. In the same way that Asian researchers recognize the importance of the Individualism/Collectivism dimension, the Dutch are turned on by Masculinity/Femininity differences.

As an editor, I have been more strict than most reader editors. The chapters by others were selected for their synergy and cross-fertilization. Their common element is that they all refer to, and make use of, the Masculinity/Femininity dimension in *Culture's Consequences*. Part I is devoted to a definition of the dimension, its validation in different studies, and methodological questions. Part II relates the dimension to gender issues and gender role gaps in different national cultures. Part III reviews contributions on the relationships between Masculinity/Femininity, religion, and sexuality, domains where the dimension is highly relevant but to which it has rarely been applied. A name index and a subject index provide easy access for users.

Although this is only half my book, I want to dedicate it informally. The dedication is to my teachers, especially those at the two secondary schools I attended during the difficult years 1939-1945. Having more time to reflect since I became an emeritus, I increasingly recognize to what extent my intellectual capital was formed during those years, and how our teachers fed our interests in culture, cultures, history, languages, and ideas. The teaching profession in the Netherlands and elsewhere is sometimes considered to be in a crisis, but to all teachers who read this, I want to testify the gratitude of a student who benefited from his teachers' lessons over a lifetime—and there are many like me.

There is another teacher, Maaike Van den Hoek, my partner and complement for 43 years in interests, skills, gender role play, sex, religion, and cross-cultural experiences. Without you, *douce amie*, I am only half a person, but it takes a whole person to write meaningfully about femininity and masculinity.

Geert Hofstede
Velp, the Netherlands

PART I

MASCULINITY/ FEMININITY AS A NATIONAL CHARACTERISTIC

1

MASCULINITY/FEMININITY
AS A DIMENSION OF CULTURE

Geert Hofstede

In this first chapter, Masculinity/Femininity (Mas/Fem) is introduced as one of five empirically derived dimensions of national cultures. The dimension, opposing ego-goals to social goals, was found in a factor analysis of work goals across the subsidiaries of a large multinational corporation in 40 countries. The label "Masculine/Feminine" was chosen for theoretical reasons that were empirically supported. Country Mas/Fem scores correlate with the results of a number of other studies; together these produce a picture of the implications of the dimension at the level of general norms, the family, the school, the workplace, politics, and ideas. Mas/Fem should not be confused with Individualism/Collectivism, nor should the cultural distinction be confused with differences in individual personality. Research on the implications of Mas/Fem continues. Two common problems are that different respondent categories may need different ways of measuring and that Mas/Fem differences are sometimes hidden behind other influences,

3

such as differences in national wealth. Mas/Fem differences have deep historical roots and are unlikely to disappear in the future.

A CASE OF VIKING
CULTURE SHOCK

At 3:30 p.m. on a Friday afternoon in June, Barry Kline sailed into the office of Ove Rasmussen in downtown Copenhagen. Barry was manager of human resource development for Nanny Brow Inc., a major multinational food corporation. Ove was human resource manager of the Danish subsidiary.

Barry came straight from the airport, carrying a clothes bag and a heavy leather briefcase. He had just flown in from Minneapolis, Minnesota, where the corporate headquarters was located. He had, in fact, made an appointment with Ove for 9:00 a.m. that morning, assuming that he would land at 7:15. Because of a mechanical defect, his plane had been grounded in Minneapolis for 7 hours and arrived as many hours late. He had jumped into a taxi and hurried to the office.

At the time, Barry was spearheading a new Performance Improvement Program across all the subsidiaries. He had counted on a day of briefing with Ove and on seeing the other managers of Nanny Brow Denmark early in the next week.

"Man, you must be dead tired," said Ove when he had heard Barry's story. "Have some of our strong coffee." Barry pretended to feel fine and burst into the essentials of his new program, which he knew very well by now. Ove listened carefully, made extensive notes, and asked pointed questions. Barry felt pleased.

At 5:05 p.m., Ove excused himself, dialed a number, and said something in Danish. "That was my home," he said. "I got permission until six." The discussion continued. At 6:05, Ove got up and asked, "Shall I drop you off at your hotel? I have to put the children to bed. My wife has a council meeting; she is in politics."

In the car, Barry proposed to continue the discussion on Saturday. Ove said, "I promised to take the children to the zoo. Why don't you come and join us? We'll keep business until Monday."

Barry muttered something about still wanting to work on his presentation to the general manager. The two men parted uneasily at the hotel.

In spite of his fatigue, Barry slept badly. What was wrong with Ove Rasmussen that he did not understand the need for putting in an extra effort? Barry's first explanation was that Ove had a low work ethic and hated to work overtime, but during international staff meetings, Ove had always shown himself to be a hard worker. A second explanation was that Ove disliked corporate headquarters imposing unsolicited programs on him and had seized the opportunity to resist, but he had looked genuinely interested. A third ugly possibility was that Ove simply disliked Americans—but then why would he work for a U.S. multinational?

In fact, Ove's goals in life in this story obviously differ somewhat from Barry's. He sometimes attaches different priorities. Family comes before work more often, and under more circumstances, than for Barry, and he is not ashamed of that. This difference will have something to do with Ove's and Barry's personalities, but more to do with the different national cultures in which they were born, grew up, live, and work.

DIMENSIONS OF
NATIONAL CULTURES

My household definition of "culture" is "the collective programming of the mind which distinguishes the members of one group or category of people from another" (Hofstede, 1980,[1] p. 260). "Culture" is a fuzzy concept. At least two meanings are frequently confused: (a) culture in the narrow sense of "civilization" and its products, and (b) culture in the anthropological sense of broad patterns of thinking, feeling, and acting, which includes much more than "civilization" alone. My definition obviously refers to the second meaning.

In *Culture's Consequences* (Hofstede, 1980), I collected empirical evidence of differences in culture (as defined above) among 40 nations in the modern world. The differences found do not imply that everyone in these nations shares the same mental programming. In fact, what I considered to be "national cultures" were *dominant* mental programs, those shared by the majority of the middle classes of these countries. I justified this choice by the argument that the middle classes serve as the stabilizing element in national societies (Hofstede, 1980, p. 95).

Mental programs can include a lot of things, from religious beliefs, food preferences, and aesthetic choices to attitudes toward authority; I have distinguished them into symbols, heroes, rituals, and values, in which symbols are the most specific and values the most general (Hofstede, 1991, p. 7ff). I defined "values" as "broad tendencies to prefer certain states of affairs over others" (Hofstede, 1991, p. 263). Cross-national patterns in mental programs can be more easily distinguished at the general level of values than at the more specific levels of symbols, heroes, and rituals (summarized under the label "practices"). My research on national culture differences was therefore based on the study of values, self-scored by matched samples from the populations of the nations studied.

The message of *Culture's Consequences* is that the cultures of the 40 countries could be positioned on four, largely independent, dimensions:

1. Power Distance (unequal versus equal),
2. Uncertainty Avoidance (rigid versus flexible),
3. Individualism/Collectivism (alone versus together), and
4. Masculinity/Femininity (tough versus tender).

The number of countries studied was later increased to 50, plus three multicountry regions (Hofstede, 1983, 1991). After continued research, a fifth dimension, Long/Short Term Orientation, was added (Hofstede, 1991, Chapter 7; Hofstede & Bond, 1988).

THE MASCULINITY/
FEMININITY DIMENSION

This book is devoted to the results of research about the dimension of masculinity versus femininity, abbreviated as Mas/Fem. Masculinity stands for a society in which men are supposed to be assertive, tough, and focused on material success; women are supposed to be more modest, tender, and concerned with the quality of life. The opposite pole, Femininity, stands for a society in which both men and women are supposed to be modest, tender, and concerned with the quality of life (Hofstede, 1991, pp. 261-262).

The Mas/Fem dimension was originally identified from a section in the values questionnaire that asked for the importance to the respondent, in an imaginary ideal job, of 14 work goals: challenge, (living in a) desirable area, earnings, cooperation (with colleagues), training, (fringe) benefits, recognition, physical (working) conditions, freedom, (job) security, (career) advancement, use of skills, (relationship with) manager, and personal time (for personal or family life). The questionnaires were answered by matched samples of employees in different national subsidiaries of the IBM corporation around 1970. These samples represented very narrow and specific slices from the national populations, but they had the advantage of being extremely well matched—same company culture, same jobs, same education levels, and only minor differences in age and gender composition—but with different nationalities. The surveys in IBM were held twice, with an interval of about 4 years; only those questions were retained for analysis for which the rank orders of country mean scores remained stable over this period (Hofstede, 1980, chapter 2). The number of respondents per country for either survey round for the initial 40 countries was at least 50; in the later extension to other countries, this limit was lowered to 20 (Hofstede, 1983). The validity of the IBM samples for conclusions about national societies as a whole was not a matter of assumption: It was tested by correlating the country scores obtained against a host of other measurable characteristics of the countries, collected by other researchers for other purposes and unrelated to IBM.

The answers to the 14 "work goals" questions were scored on 5-point scales, with answer categories from 1 = *of utmost importance* to 5 = *of very little or no importance*. The country answer scores were a stratified mean across seven occupational groups (every group carrying equal weight) and averaged for the first and the second survey round. The occupational group mean scores had been standardized across the 14 goals first. Standardizing is a mathematical operation in which each score in a set (in our case, a set of 14) is replaced by a z score, that is, its deviation from the common mean of all (14) scores divided by the common standard deviation. Standardizing the scores for each group eliminates differences between groups in response set, that is, the tendency to score *any* question higher or lower, regardless of its content. Standardizing

TABLE 1.1   Factors Found in an Analysis of Mean Scores on the Importance
of 14 Work Goals Across 40 Countries

Factor 1 *Individual/Collective*	Factor 2 *Social/Ego*
Positive	**Positive**
Personal time	Manager
Freedom	Cooperation[a]
Challenge[b]	Desirable area[a]
Desirable area[b]	Security
Negative	**Negative**
Training	Earnings
Physical conditions	Recognition
Use of skills[a]	Advancement
Benefits	Challenge[a]
Cooperation[b]	Use of skills[b]

SOURCE: Hofstede (1980, p. 241).
a. First loading.
b. Second loading.

also eliminates differences resulting from a greater or lesser use of the
extreme answer categories from one group to another.

With 14 goals and 40 countries, the answers to the "work goals"
questions produced a 14 (variables) × 40 (cases) matrix. This matrix was
subjected to a varimax factor analysis with orthogonal rotation. This is
a heuristic statistical device that allows a search for the smallest possible
number of independent underlying factors. *Factors* are new variables
able to explain a maximum amount of the total variance in the original
matrix in the simplest, most parsimonious way.

The work goals matrix produced two such factors, of which the first
was labeled Individual/Collective and the second Social/Ego. The first
accounted for 24% of the total variance of the country means, the second
for 22%. The distribution of the 14 goals over the two factors is shown
in Table 1.1.

Goals marked with superscript letters a and b are related to both
factors, but more to the one marked with an "a." The first factor opposes
goals that stress the person's independence from the organization to
goals for which the person has to depend on the organization. The
second factor opposes goals that stress a concern for people, inside or

TABLE 1.2 Masculinity Index (MAS) Values for 50 Countries and Three Regions

Score Rank	Country or Region	MAS Score	Score Rank	Country or Region	MAS Score
1	Japan	95	28	Singapore	48
2	Austria	79	29	Israel	47
3	Venezuela	73	30/31	Indonesia	46
4/5	Italy	70	30/31	West Africa	46
4/5	Switzerland	70	32/33	Turkey	45
6	Mexico	69	32/33	Taiwan	45
7/8	Ireland	68	34	Panama	44
7/8	Jamaica	68	35/36	Iran	43
9/10	Great Britain	66	35/36	France	43
9/10	Germany	66	37/38	Spain	42
11/12	Philippines	64	37/38	Peru	42
11/12	Colombia	64	39	East Africa	41
13/14	South Africa	63	40	El Salvador	40
13/14	Ecuador	63	41	South Korea	39
15	United States	62	42	Uruguay	38
16	Australia	61	43	Guatemala	37
17	New Zealand	58	44	Thailand	34
18/19	Greece	57	45	Portugal	31
18/19	Hong Kong	57	46	Chile	28
20/21	Argentina	56	47	Finland	26
20/21	India	56	48/49	Yugoslavia	21
22	Belgium	54	48/49	Costa Rica	21
23	Arab countries	53	50	Denmark	16
24	Canada	52	51	The Netherlands	14
25/26	Malaysia	50	52	Norway	8
25/26	Pakistan	50	53	Sweden	5
27	Brazil	49			

SOURCE: Hofstede (1991, p. 84).

outside the organization, to goals that enhance the person's ego but do not imply a concern for others.

The first factor became the basis for the Individualism/Collectivism (Ind/Col) dimension, the second, after reversing the positive and negative poles, for the Mas/Fem dimension. The factor analysis produced scores for each of the 40 countries on either factor, varying between approximately −2.5 and +2.5. The factor scores on the first factor were used as the basis for calculating the country Ind/Col score, IDV,[2] and the factor scores on the second factor for calculating the country Mas/Fem score, MAS.[3]

Table 1.2 shows the MAS values for the extended set of 50 countries and three multicountry regions (Arab countries, East Africa, and West Africa). Masculine are, for example, Japan, Germany, the United States, Great Britain, Mexico, and the Philippines; feminine (low on MAS) are the Nordic countries (Denmark, Finland, Norway, and Sweden), the Netherlands,[4] France, Portugal, Costa Rica, and Thailand. Unlike Ind/Col, Mas/Fem is unrelated to wealth; both among the masculine and among the feminine countries, some are rich and others poor.

WHY THE LABEL
"MASCULINE/FEMININE"?

Since *Culture's Consequences* appeared in 1980, I have been criticized several times for the label I attached to this dimension. The criticisms came more from countries whose cultures I had identified as masculine than from those I had called feminine, and more from men than from women. Let me explain my choice of the label.

The four dimensions were arrived at by an analysis of *country mean scores*, an "ecological analysis." They explained differences in answers on values questions between one country and another, not between one person and another. They belong to anthropology, not to psychology. For such differences to appear across as many as 40 countries, there should be fundamental underlying reasons. Each of the five dimensions reflects a basic and enduring anthropological fact about a national society: that society's specific answer to a general problem with which any human society has to cope.

What problems for human societies are general enough to qualify for worldwide relevance? Power Distance is associated with the problem of human inequality; Uncertainty Avoidance with the unpredictability of the future, which in the last resort is the problem of coping with death; and Individualism/Collectivism with the relationship of individuals with groups, which is the problem of the cohesiveness of society. The new dimension of Long/Short Term Orientation deals with the problem of choosing between Virtue and Truth (Hofstede, 1991, Chapter 7). What fundamental problem is behind the fact that societies differ in their choices of social versus ego goals?

Study of work goals *by gender* have shown again and again that other things being equal, men tend to stress ego goals more and women tend to stress social goals more (Hofstede, 1980, pp. 272-273; see also Chapter 5 of this book). The balance between ego goals and social goals in an individual is influenced by that individual's gender. Gender differences in values have been popularized by Deborah Tannen (1990), who showed the difference in female and male discourse in the United States: more "rapport talk" for women versus more "report talk" for men. Tannen argued convincingly that the genders have their own ways of thinking, feeling, and acting. One can speak of "gender cultures" (Hofstede, 1989, and Chapter 5 of this book). The Mas/Fem dimension is the only one of the five that produces consistently different scores for female and male respondents (more ego for the males), except in very feminine countries; it is the only dimension associated with the values that play a role in the differentiation of gender cultures.

Thus, the fundamental problem behind the emergence of this dimension must be the duality of female versus male, nature's number two law (after the duality of life and death), which governs procreation and thus the perpetuation of society (Hofstede, 1980, p. 262). The biological differences between women and men are universal, but the social differences are society specific. Mas/Fem does not primarily concern the visible roles in society, such as men going out to work and women staying at home to care. These roles are to a large extent determined by economic factors. Mas/Fem concerns first of all the emotional roles in the home. In some societies, men specialize in ego-boosting, and women in ego-effacing, roles. In others, the emotional roles are more equally divided, with men also being oriented toward ego-effacing goals.

My interpretation of the meaning of the first four dimensions was given a theoretical base in a classic study, originally written in 1954, by two Americans, sociologist Alex Inkeles and psychologist Daniel Levinson. On the basis of a broad survey of the English language literature on "national character," they suggested that the following "standard analytic issues" qualify as common basic problems worldwide, with consequences for the functioning of societies, of groups within those societies, and of individuals within those groups:

1. relation to authority,
2. conception of self, and
3. primary dilemmas or conflicts, and ways of dealing with them.[5]

From the dimensions I empirically found 20 years later, Power Distance obviously deals with relation to authority; and Uncertainty Avoidance, or rigid/flexible, which also included ways of control of aggression, relates to primary dilemmas or conflicts. Both factors from the "work goals" analysis, Individual/Collective and Social/Ego, relate to the conception of self. About the conception of self, Inkeles and Levinson wrote, "Pervading the overall conception of self will be the individual's concept of masculinity and femininity . . ."; later, following psychologist Abram Kardiner, they referred to "the self characteristics, such as modes of impulse control and social adaptation, by means of which the individual strives to achieve a secure, meaningful position in society and a correspondingly meaningful inner identity" (Inkeles, 1997, pp. 47-48). Inkeles and Levinson thus split "conception of self" into two dimensions, one related to the individual's position in society (Ind/Col) but the other to her or his concept of masculinity and femininity.

The emergence of a Social/Ego factor in the analysis of values across countries shows that there are *between-country* culture differences on the same values that play a role in *within-country* gender culture differences. Psychologists sometimes assume the roles, values, and behaviors of the genders in all societies to be similar. Because most English-language publications on gender issues are produced in the United States, the dominant gender role model in the psychological literature is American; gender roles in other countries, if different, are supposed to develop toward the U.S. model. This assumption is not only made by Americans. The emergence of a Social/Ego factor in national culture differences suggests fundamental reasons why gender role patterns vary and will continue to vary, even among "Western" countries.

The actors in the case with which this chapter opened differ in values related to the Mas/Fem dimension. Barry Kline shows more ego orientation, and Ove Rasmussen more social orientation. As Table 1.2 shows, the United States scores masculine (62, rank 15) and Denmark very feminine (16, rank 50).

Although I thus think that the label "Masculine/Feminine" is justified, this does not mean that, for example, trainers who believe the label will shock their audience could not choose their own interpretation. They might call it "Ego/Social" or "Assertive/Nurturant," for example. I once received a letter from a doctoral candidate involved in a survey across different national subsidiaries of a U.S.-based multinational. He had omitted the Mas/Fem questions from the Values Survey Module because "company management will not allow me to ask for masculinity or femininity." This strikes me as naive on the side of this researcher: He could have explained to the company's managers that the actual survey questions were asking for such politically correct things as the importance of careers, or of cooperation between colleagues. Omitting the dimension meant throwing the baby away with the bath water. By leaving out questions on which U.S. respondents have been shown to differ substantially from those in some other developed countries, this doctoral candidate condemned his own research to myopia. The anecdote shows, however, the strength of the taboo, and therefore of the underlying value, in that particular country.[6] Taboos are signals par excellence of deeply seated values (see Chapter 12).

INTERPRETING THE MAS/FEM DIMENSION: RELATIONS WITH OTHER DATA

In the previous section, I argued that differences among countries in their people's relative priority given to social versus ego goals are rooted in different roles and values of the genders. The Mas/Fem dimension therefore implies much more than the answers on 14 "work goals" items, and its relevance stretches beyond IBM subsidiaries. "One important point that anthropologists have always made is that aspects of social life which do not seem to be related to each other, actually are related." (Harris, 1981, p. 9). The IBM scores are just one manifestation of a Mas/Fem cultural syndrome at the country level. Other aspects of differences among countries on the Mas/Fem dimension can be found by correlating the IBM scores with conceptually related data from other sources. The pattern of correlations shows the construct validity of the dimension and allows one to trace its complex implications. In this way, we can arrive at the most complete possible picture of the Mas/Fem syndrome.

A large part of *Culture's Consequences* was devoted to this kind of validation, not only for Mas/Fem but also for the three other dimensions: Power Distance, Uncertainty Avoidance, and Ind/Col. Validations were both quantitative and qualitative. Quantitative validations are of two kinds: comparisons with country mean scores for other cross-national surveys (Hofstede, 1980, pp. 326-327) and comparisons with indicators measured at the country level (such as per capita Gross National Product; Hofstede, 1980, pp. 328-331).

Correlations With Results of Other Surveys

MAS correlated significantly, and more than the Power Distance Index (PDI), Uncertainty Avoidance Index (UAI), and Individualism Index (IDV), with a variety of survey results (Hofstede, 1980, pp. 299-309; Hofstede, 1991, p. 108). Examples include the following:

1. A correlation with the values of students, measured across 17 countries with L. V. Gordon's Survey of Interpersonal Values. Students from masculine countries claimed more need for recognition but less benevolence.

2. A correlation with the life goals of management course participants, measured across 12 countries by an exercise of IRGOM, the International Research Group on Management. Participants from masculine countries scored higher on "assertiveness" but lower on "service."

3. A correlation with an index of "permissiveness" toward things like joyriding, soft drugs, accepting bribes, prostitution, divorce, and suicide, calculated from the European Value Systems Study for representative samples of the public in nine countries. The public sentiment in masculine countries was less permissive than in feminine ones.

4. A correlation with the choice between higher salaries versus shorter working hours, from a public opinion survey in nine European countries. Masculine countries preferred higher salaries.

5. A correlation with the preference for larger or smaller enterprises among the public, from a survey across six European countries. Masculine countries preferred larger enterprises.

Since *Culture's Consequences* appeared, other correlations with survey data have become available. Important is a .56***[7] correlation between MAS and a value cluster "Mastery" in the responses by schoolteachers from 23 countries on Shalom Schwartz's Value Survey (Schwartz, 1994, p. 109). "Mastery" values (ambitious, capable, choosing own goals, daring, independent, successful) were more important to teachers from masculine than from feminine countries. In the responses to the same survey by students from 22 countries, "Mastery" correlated .39* with MAS. None of the other Hofstede indices correlated with "Mastery."

Correlations With Country-Level Indicators

Examples of country-level indexes correlating with MAS follow.

1. Geographical latitude (either North or South, measured for the country's capital city), correlated −.31* with MAS across all 40 countries in *Culture's Consequences* (pp. 305, 330). Latitude correlated .75*** with IDV and −.65*** with PDI, but in a multiple regression, MAS made a substantial contribution and came second after IDV. Geographical latitude is related to temperature: In Chapter 7, Van de Vliert has established relationships between MAS, temperature, and domestic political violence.

2. In *Culture's Consequences* (p. 308), I had already found that MAS (and none of the other Hofstede indices) correlated significantly (−.81***) with the mean percentage of the Gross National Product of 15 donor countries spent on development aid to poor countries in the period 1967-1976. Using data from the *World Development Report 1996* (World Bank, 1996, Table 37), I find that for 1994 the same correlation across now 20 donor countries was −.78***. The range is from 0.15% for the United States to 1.05% for Norway. Masculine countries spend (much) less on aid than feminine ones.

3. Gender segregation in higher education (the extent to which women and men study different subjects) correlated weakly (.28*) with MAS across all 38 countries for which data were available, but much more strongly (.56**) across 18 wealthy countries. In feminine countries, women and men more often choose the same curricula, especially after the countries have reached a certain level of economic prosperity.

4. In *Culture's Consequences* (p. 306), I had found that the share of women in professional and technical jobs correlated negatively with MAS, but only if expressed as a percentage of all working women, and only across 16 wealthy countries. Women as a percentage of all professional and technical workers in 38 countries, wealthy and poor, correlated weakly negatively with PDI and positively with GNP per capita. The *Human Development*

TABLE 1.3   Key Differences Between Feminine and Masculine Societies

Feminine	*Masculine*
General norm	
Dominant values in society are caring for others and preservation	Dominant values in society are material success and progress
People and warm relationships are important	Money and things are important
Everybody is supposed to be modest	Men are supposed to be assertive, ambitious, and tough
Both men and women are allowed to be tender and to be concerned with relationships	Women are supposed to be tender and to take care of relationships
Sympathy for the weak	Sympathy for the strong
Small and slow are beautiful	Big and fast are beautiful
Sex and violence in the media are taboo	Sex and violence in newspapers and on TV
In the family	
Both fathers and mothers deal with facts and feelings	Fathers deal with facts and mothers with feelings
Both boys and girls are allowed to cry but neither should fight	Girls cry, boys do not; boys should fight back when attacked, girls should not fight
In school	
Average student is the norm	Best student is the norm
Failing in school is a minor accident	Failing in school is a disaster
Friendliness in teachers appreciated	Brilliance in teachers appreciated
Boys and girls study same subjects	Boys and girls study different subjects
At work	
Work in order to live	Live in order to work
Managers use intuition and strive for consensus	Managers expected to be decisive and assertive

Report 1996 (United Nations Development Project [UNDP], 1996), with recent data from 47 countries, finds women as a percentage of all professionals and technicians correlating $-.60^{***}$ with PDI, $.52^{***}$ with GNP per capita, and $-.44^{***}$ with MAS. In a multiple correlation, MAS makes a substantial contribution (multiple correlation coefficient $R = .71^{***}$). In large Power Distance countries, men hold more strongly to these jobs, and more so if the culture is also masculine.

TABLE 1.3 *Continued*

Feminine	Masculine
Stress on equality, solidarity, and quality of work life	Stress on equity, mutual competition, and performance
Resolution of conflicts by compromise and negotiation	Resolution of conflicts by letting the best "man" win

In politics

Feminine	Masculine
Welfare society ideal	Performance society ideal
The needy should be helped	The strong should be supported
Permissive society	Corrective society
Preservation of the environment should have highest priority	Maintenance of economic growth should have highest priority
Government spends relatively large proportion of budget on development assistance to poor countries	Government spends relatively small proportion of budget on development assistance to poor countries
Government spends relatively small proportion of budget on armaments	Government spends relatively large proportion of budget on armaments
International conflicts should be resolved by negotiation and compromise	International conflicts should be resolved by a show of strength or by fighting
A relatively large number of women in elected political positions	A relatively small number of women in elected political positions

In prevailing ideas

Feminine	Masculine
Dominant religions stress the complementarity of the sexes	Dominant religions stress the male prerogative
Women's liberation means that men and women should take equal shares both at home and at work	Women's liberation means that women should be admitted to positions hitherto occupied only by men

SOURCE: Developed from Hofstede (1991, pp. 96 and 103).

Besides these quantitative validations, there is qualitative validation in comparing countries that differ strongly on Mas/Fem but less on the other dimensions. In this book, Chapters 8 (Van Rossum) and 9 (Vunderink and Hofstede) describe comparisons between matched U.S. and Dutch groups that represent qualitative validations of a Mas/Fem difference.

The various validations allow one to put together an integrated picture of what a dimension, in this case Mas/Fem, stands for. A country's norms for the meaning of masculinity and femininity are transferred to the young child in the family, further developed and confirmed in school, in the workplace, in political life, and even in the prevailing religious, philosophical, and scientific ideas. Key differences between masculine and feminine societies in all these areas have been listed in Table 1.3.

For each line in Table 1.3, there is some external validatory evidence. The picture is not complete. I have compared the work of assembling it to the archaeologist's job of restoring an ancient work of art from the shards found in an excavation. Pieces are missing, and the end result contains a dose of subjectivity. The table shows opposites. It is a didactic device to make the issues clear, but it does not mean that the situation in a country needs to correspond to one of the opposite statements—it can be somewhere in between. Not every statement in Table 1.3 applies necessarily to every country for which its MAS score would suggest so. The table is an overall picture across more than 50 countries and shows trends, but every country is unique, and specific historical and other compelling conditions cause exceptions for which the table does not account.

MISCONCEPTIONS ABOUT WHAT
MASCULINITY AND FEMININITY STAND FOR

In the psychological literature, the Mas/Fem distinction is sometimes confused with the distinction between individualism and collectivism. American authors have considered feminine goals as an expression of collectivism; on the other hand, I saw a Korean master's thesis in which goals that I found to cluster with the collectivist pole of Ind/Col were supposed to belong to masculinity.

The dimensions of Ind/Col and Mas/Fem are statistically wholly independent because they are based on orthogonal factors. The difference between them is that Ind/Col is about "I" versus "we": independence from versus dependence on in-groups, especially on the (extended) family. Relationships in Ind/Col are basically predetermined by group ties: "Groupiness" is not feminine but collectivist. Mas/Fem is about ego enhancement versus relationship enhancement, regardless of group ties. The biblical story of the Good Samaritan, who helps a Jew in need—someone from an enemy ethnic group—is an illustration of feminine and not of collectivist values.

Femininity is not the same as *feminism*. Feminism is an ideology taking different forms in masculine and feminine cultures; there is masculine and feminine feminism (see Chapter 5). The first is about access of women to jobs hitherto taken only by men; it is about competition between the genders. The second is about a redistribution of roles inside and outside the home; it is about complementarity between the genders and it implies "men's lib(eration)" as much as "women's lib."

The issues with which masculine feminism deals with are not necessarily related to the Mas/Fem dimension at all. Mas/Fem is rooted in the power balance between father and mother *in the home*; what happens outside the home depends largely on other influences. The sharing of power in society in general, including by women, depends largely on Power Distance.[8] The legal position of women and their access to jobs depend primarily on the level of economic development of a country; its level of individualism also plays a role.[9] We will see below that often it is only after controlling for these other influences that we can detect differences related to the Mas/Fem dimension.

IS MAS/FEM ONE
OR TWO DIMENSIONS?

Sometimes the objection is made that Mas/Fem should be seen not as one bipolar dimension but as two unipolar dimensions, "masculine" and "feminine." Bem (1974), using the two-scale Bem Sex Role Inventory (BSRI) questionnaire, could divide U.S. students into four groups: masculine only, feminine only, androgynous (scoring both masculine and feminine), and undifferentiated (scoring neither). This was an analysis based on comparing the answers of individuals, that is, *at the individual level*. Our Mas/Fem dimension was found in an ecological analysis, that is, *at the country level* (Hofstede, 1980, pp. 28-31). An individual can be both masculine and feminine at the same time, but what I found is that a country culture is either predominantly one or predominantly the other. When one moves to a higher level of analysis, the number of factors found normally gets smaller: At the level of country means, "more people with masculine values" is statistically so strongly correlated with "fewer people with feminine values" that this becomes one single dimension. The same is true, in fact, for the Ind/Col dimension: There, too, an individual can be both individualist and collectivist, but a country culture is either predominantly one or the other.

MEASURING MAS/FEM:
NO ONE INSTRUMENT
FITS ALL POPULATIONS

A problem in the measurement of all five dimensions of culture but particularly in the measurement of Mas/Fem is that different respondent groups may need different ways of measuring, because the issues related to the common underlying syndrome are not the same for all categories of respondents. The 40 IBM subsidiary populations studied in *Culture's Consequences* were exceptionally homogeneous as to their work situation, which led to a shared perception of the various work goal items, even across countries. This perception, however, is not necessarily the same for other, non-IBM populations. What this means is that for different populations, different survey items (from among those conceptually related to the dimension) may have to be chosen in order to replicate the results.

Hoppe, in Chapter 2, illustrates this point very clearly. He replicated Hofstede's values research on elites from 19 countries. Using Hofstede's Values Survey Module formulas (Hofstede, 1982a, 1982b), he found significant correlations between his elite country scores and Hofstede's IBM country scores for three dimensions (.69*** for IDV, .67*** for PDI, and .64*** for UAI), but not for MAS (a nonsignificant .36). In IBM, the MAS scores reflected, among other things, the combined importance of "advancement" and "earnings," because across the IBM country subsidiaries these were positively correlated: In the IBM system, promotions and earnings went hand in hand. For Hoppe's elite respondents, country mean scores for the importance of "advancement" and of "earnings" were, if anything, negatively correlated: In countries where respondents focused more on advancement, they would focus less on earnings, and vice versa. The same problem has surfaced in a comparative study of the work goals of students in eight countries, four of them in Eastern and Central Europe (Hofstede, Kolman, Nicolescu, & Pajumaa, 1996). Within all countries, both "earnings" and "advancement" are rated as more important by men than by women, yet for these non-IBM populations, one cannot meaningfully add the country scores for these two goals in a MAS index formula, because they would cancel each other out. It turns out that in these cases, "advancement" more than "earnings" expresses what the Mas/Fem syndrome stands for. "Earnings" in some countries is more interpreted as the means for physical survival than as a measure of success. We had to look for other items that could replace "earnings" in the MAS formula;[10] using the new formulas, Hoppe found a correlation coefficient between his elites and IBM of .83*** (and .90*** for UAI, .76*** for PDI, and .72*** for IDV). Unfortunately, there is still no guarantee that the new formulas will work with all new populations and for all times.

This is evident in a replication of Hofstede's values research with a population of about 10,000 male, commercial airline pilots in 20 or more countries for which data were collected in the period 1993-1997 (Merritt, in press). This project will bypass Hoppe's study as the largest replication to date. As I am writing this, work on it is still in progress, and new data continue to come in. Using Hofstede's Values Survey Module 1982 formulas, Merritt so far has found significant correlations between pilots' country scores and IBM scores for PDI and IDV but not for UAI and MAS. In the latter two cases, she could replicate the IBM scores fairly closely by replacing some of the items in the formulas. In the case of MAS, for the pilot population "advancement" and "earnings" country scores seem to intercorrelate positively, as in IBM, but the mean importance of the other MAS items "job security" and "cooperation" varies across countries hardly at all (they are high everywhere). These replications illustrate that although the underlying syndrome can be seen as universal and permanent, the measuring instruments have to be adapted to the population and probably also to the spirit of the times.

MAS/FEM DIFFERENCES AS
A SECONDARY INFLUENCE

Mas/Fem is the only of the four initial Hofstede dimensions that is entirely unrelated to national wealth: There are just as many poor as there are wealthy masculine, or feminine, countries. Many forms of external data, however, that can be used for validating the culture

TABLE 1.4   Number of Significant Contributions to Multiple Regression
With External Indicators, for Four IBM Indices

Order	PDI	UAI	IDV	MAS	Total
Zero	16	20	20	9	65
2nd	6	3	3	9	21
3rd	—	2	—	1	3
Total	22	25	23	19	89

SOURCE: Data are from Hofstede (1980, pp. 326-331).
NOTE: PDI = Power Distance Index; UAI = Uncertainty Avoidance Index; IDV = Individualism
Index; MAS = Masculinity Index. MAS appears significantly more frequently as a second- or
third-order correlate than the three other indices, χ^2 = 8.2 with 1 degree of freedom, p < .01.

dimensions are at least partly dependent on wealth. This is even more
the case for country-level indicators than for survey data. In these cases,
it is often necessary to control for wealth (separate wealthy from poor
countries) before any relationship with MAS can become visible. The
correlations with country-level indicators shown above provide examples of this (gender segregation in higher education, percentage of
women in professional and technical jobs). More examples will be
found in Chapters 3 (Arrindell) and 5.

Because of these potential correlations of external data with wealth, I
have always included a measure of wealth (per capita GNP for a year close
to the time the data were collected) when correlating external data with
my culture indexes. Only if any of the culture indexes explains more
variance than wealth per se is it meaningful to use a cultural explanation. This is the philosophical principle of parsimony (Occam's razor).

Across 40 countries, IDV correlated .82*** with per capita GNP, PDI
−.65***, and UAI −.30* (Hofstede,1980, p. 331). Because of their wealth
component, IDV, PDI, and UAI show more correlations with external
data than MAS. MAS often appears as a significant *second-order* correlate. This is demonstrated in Table 1.4, which draws on the summary
tables of external correlations in *Culture's Consequences* (pp. 326-331).
These tables contain 65 cases in which a multiple regression has been
calculated between an external indicator and all four indices. Table 1.4
counts the number of significant first-, second-, and third-order correlations. Whereas the four indices in total appear with about equal
frequency (between 25 and 19 times each), MAS comes significantly
more often in second or third place, after one or two of the other indices

(10 times). This means that it takes a somewhat more sophisticated research approach to find the full implications of MAS differences than it takes to validate the other three indices.

MAS came after IDV or PDI several times. An example is Traffic Death Rates (Hofstede, 1980, p. 207). Across 14 countries, these were found to be negatively related to IDV, but, secondarily, positively with MAS. Traffic is safer in individualist, wealthy countries, but more so if these countries are also more feminine.

A case of a secondary correlation with MAS after PDI, not published before, deals with the choice between maintenance of economic growth and preservation of the environment (referred to in Table 1.3). It uses two questions from a survey of representative samples of the populations of 24 nations (Dunlap, Gallup, & Gallup, 1993). Table 1.5 shows these questions and answer percentages for the 20 countries appearing both in the Gallup and in the IBM set.

On question 1, priority for the environment or for economic growth, a majority of respondents in 21 out of 24 countries chose the environment. The percentages per country correlated significantly (but weakly) with the Power Distance Index (−.42*), but not with per capita national income. On question 2, willingness to pay higher prices for protecting the environment, a majority in 17 out of the 24 countries chose to pay. The answers to the two questions were not significantly intercorrelated (.34, not in the table). The percentages willing to pay were correlated significantly with PDI (−.60**), with MAS (−.48*), and with IDV (.40*), but again not with per capita national income. PDI and MAS together produced a quite strong multiple correlation, $R = .69***$.

This is a very interesting result. It illustrates the difference between a "value as the desirable" and a "value as the desired" (Hofstede, 1980, pp. 20-21; Hofstede, 1991, pp. 9-10). Question 1 is a typical statement of the desirable: choosing between virtue and sin but without consequences for the respondents' personal behavior. The question is noncommittal. In the statistical analysis, it is only weakly related to PDI, showing that in large Power Distance countries more people are accustomed to leaving decisions about the environment to the authorities. Question 2 touches the desired: what people are prepared to do themselves. In this case, the answer levels in the countries are much more significantly linked to the culture indices. The first relationship is still with PDI: Where Power Distances are larger, fewer people are prepared

TABLE 1.5   Answers by Representative Samples of the Populations From 20
Countries on Two Questions About Protection of the Environment

1. With which of (the following) statements about the environment and the economy do
you most agree? (a) Protecting the environment should be given priority, even at the risk
of slowing down economic growth; (b) Economic growth should be given priority, even
if the environment suffers to some extent.
2. Increased efforts by business and industry to improve environmental quality might
lead to higher prices for the things you buy. Would you be willing to pay higher prices
so that industry could better protect the environment, or not?

Countries in Order of MAS	Percentage Answering "a" to Question 1	Percentage Answering "Yes" to Question 2
Japan	57	31
Switzerland	62	70
Mexico	71	59
Ireland	65	60
Great Britain	56	70
Germany (West)	73	59
Philippines	59	30
United States	58	65
India	43	56
Canada	67	61
Brazil	71	53
Turkey	43	44
South Korea	63	71
Uruguay	64	54
Portugal	53	61
Chile	64	64
Finland	72	53
Denmark	77	78
The Netherlands	58	65
Norway	72	72
Product moment correlation with:		
PDI	$-.42^*$	$-.60^{**}$
IDV	.17	$.40^*$
MAS	$-.23$	$-.48^*$
UAI	$-.15$	$-.32$
LTO[1]	$-.15$	$-.13$
GNP[2]	.31	.30
Multiple correlation with PDI and MAS	$.46^*$	$.69^{***}$

SOURCE: Data are from Dunlap, Gallup, and Gallup (1993, Table 14).
1. Long Term Orientation Index, across 10 countries.
2: 1994 per capita Gross National Product according to *World Development Report 1996* (World
Bank, 1996).
$^*p < .05$. $^{**}p < .01$. $^{***}p < .001$ (one-tailed).

to get personally involved by paying more for their products on behalf of the environment. The second correlation is with Masculinity: In more masculine cultures, fewer people are prepared to pay for the environment, in line with the statement in Table 1.3.

The combination of large Power Distance and Masculinity also played a role in the explanation of attitudes toward biotechnology in the countries of the European Union, in a study performed by the Institute for Research on Intercultural Cooperation (IRIC), which I cofounded in 1980 (Van Baren, Hofstede, & Van de Vijver, 1995). Biotechnology is an area that raises severe environmental concerns in many people. The IRIC study analyzed national differences in attitudes on this subject across 14 countries, on the basis of information collected by the EU survey system Eurobarometer. The Eurobarometer questions could be summarized empirically into three clusters: Knowledge of Biotechnology, Biotechnology as a Promise, and Biotechnology as a Threat. "Threat" questions referred to the degree to which research into different applications of biotechnology should be controlled by governments, because of their risk to human health or to the environment, or because of their ethical implications. The national level of perceived threat in the EU countries was strongly associated with Power Distance and Masculinity, in the sense that respondents in large Power Distance, masculine cultures perceived less threat. The explanation of this is the same as in the previous paragraph: The larger the Power Distance, the more people refer such issues to the judgment of the authorities; the stronger the Masculinity, the less people are concerned about environmental issues anyway.

Some of the lines in Table 1.3 were inspired by multiple regressions of MAS together with, but after, the Uncertainty Avoidance Index UAI.

The percentage of Catholics across 29 Christian countries as well as across 17 wealthy Christian countries (Hofstede, 1980, p. 209). Catholicism combines strong Uncertainty Avoidance with masculine values, more so than most Protestant churches; see Chapters 11 and 12. As will be shown in Chapter 5, the percentages of women in parliaments and as government ministers across 22 developed democracies are negatively correlated with first UAI, then MAS, which also implies that there are fewer women in these responsible positions in Catholic Christian countries. The association between Mas/Fem and religion will be extensively explored in Part III of this book.

Maximum speeds allowed on motorways in 14 developed countries. These are positively correlated with both UAI and MAS (Hofstede, 1980, p. 207). Uncertainty Avoidance implies stress and hurry; Masculinity implies "fast is beautiful."

The combination of *weak* Uncertainty Avoidance with masculine values, across 22 countries, correlates with Need for Achievement, as measured by McClelland (1961) in a content analysis of children's readers from around 1925. *Culture's Consequences* cites this as an example of the cultural limits of motivation theories (pp. 324-325). This relationship will be referred to further in Chapter 10.

ORIGINS AND FUTURE OF MAS/FEM DIFFERENCES BETWEEN COUNTRIES

The IBM studies found that countries with a shared history usually showed similar score patterns on the dimensions. Examples are the "Latin" pattern of large Power Distance and strong Uncertainty Avoidance in countries descended from the Roman Empire and the "Chinese" pattern of large Power Distance but weaker Uncertainty Avoidance in countries with a Chinese majority. For the Mas/Fem dimension, there are some evident clusters. The feminine Nordic cluster (Denmark, Norway, Sweden, Finland, Netherlands) shares the influence of the Hanseatic League, an association for peaceful trade (Hofstede, 1991, p. 104). For the Netherlands, citations from travel reports by foreign visitors as far back as the 16th and 17th centuries show the Dutch as caring for their poor and sharing responsibilities in the family between husband and wife. In Latin America, there are both clusters of masculine countries (Mexico, Venezuela, Colombia, Ecuador) and of feminine ones (Panama, Costa Rica, El Salvador, Guatemala) that probably derive from different combinations of native and immigrant cultures.

Although this suggests that Mas/Fem differences have ancient roots, it does not explain what these roots are. The correlations of the Masculinity Index with various ecological indicators are not conclusive and explain at best only a small part of the variance in MAS (Hofstede, 1980, p. 294). The most interesting relationship is with population growth. MAS is negatively correlated with the number of children per family (leading to population growth) for the wealthier countries, but positively for the poorer countries. This, however, looks like a consequence rather than a cause of Mas/Fem differences; I will come back to it in Chapter 5.

The historical resilience of Mas/Fem differences means that these differences are likely to continue in the future. There is no sign of convergence of country cultures in the direction of more masculinity,[11] nor in the direction of more femininity. Bridging such differences will remain an essential part of intercultural cooperation, as Barry Kline and Ove Rasmussen experienced in the case with which this chapter opened.

OTHER CONTRIBUTIONS IN PART I

The three other chapters in this part validate the Mas/Fem dimension in different ways, each across a number of countries.

In Chapter 2, Hoppe describes his survey of elites from 19 countries, using among other questions those from Hofstede's Values Survey Module 1982. He shows how the Mas/Fem dimension was validated, provided that he took into account that some of the questions meant something else for these high-level respondents than for the employees in Hofstede's original IBM research. From his point of view as an executive development trainer, he then looks at the meaning of the country differences along the Mas/Fem dimension for leadership across national borders.

In Chapter 3, Arrindell tests a hypothesized negative relationship between MAS and happiness (subjective well-being), assuming that the focus on welfare in feminine countries should have positive effects. Using existing data from 32 countries, Arrindell shows that the expected relationship is modified by national wealth. Femininity is associated with well-being in wealthy countries. Among poor countries, where well-being is rated lower overall, it is the masculine ones where people rate themselves relatively happier.

In Chapter 4, De Mooij, a consultant in international marketing, offers a wealth of fascinating and entirely new validations of all four Hofstede dimensions in general, and of the Mas/Fem dimension in particular, against data from three different consumer surveys, covering 16 European countries. This work opens new perspectives for predicting consumer behavior across borders.

NOTES

1. Besides the integral 1980 hardcover edition, there is an abridged 1984 paperback version that omits most of the statistics and part of the literature reviews.

2. The formula used was IDV = 50 + 25 × (factor score). Country IDV values varied between 12 (Venezuela) and 91 (United States).

3. The formula used was MAS = 50 − 20 × (factor score). In later replications of the research, the fact that IDV and MAS were derived from factor scores was a problem. Adding new cases is possible (see Hofstede, 1980, p. 299), but it is cumbersome. Consequently, in the scoring guide for the Values Survey Module 1982 (VSM 82; see Hofstede, 1982), I designed simple approximation formulas, calculating IDV and MAS from unstandardized mean scores for only four goals each. The formula for IDV used the scores for personal time and desirable area versus those for physical conditions and cooperation; the formula for MAS used the scores for advancement and earnings versus those for security and (again) cooperation. In 1994, a new Values Survey Module was issued (VSM 94; see Hofstede, 1994) with partly new items and new formulas.

4. In this book, this country will always be called the Netherlands, although its common name in English is Holland. Technically, Holland is only the Western part of the Netherlands (2 out of 12 provinces). For the population of the Netherlands, the common English name "Dutch" will be used. Dutch, therefore, is not the same as German.

5. See Inkeles and Levinson (1969, pp. 447-452), republished in Inkeles (1997, pp. 43-51).

6. For a similar case, see Chapter 4 of this book. Chapter 12 discusses the meaning of the taboo at a more basic level.

7. Throughout this book, * stands for a significance level of $p < .05$, ** for $p < .01$, and *** for $p < .001$. In cases where the expected direction of the correlation is explicit, one-tailed tests are used; otherwise, two-tailed tests are used.

8. This is illustrated by a .78*** correlation between PDI and gender differences in the affective meaning of self-concepts, found by Best and Williams (see Chapter 6).

9. Williams and Best (1990b, p. 91) administered a test of "modernity" in gender role conceptions, the Kalin Sex Role Ideology measure, to about 100 students from each of 14 countries. The overall country modernity scores they found rank correlate .54* with IDV and .52* with 1987 GNP per capita (calculation by author).

10. This has happened in the 1994 version of the Values Survey Module (VSM 94; see Hofstede, 1994).

11. In a popularized version of a Dutch doctoral thesis, Vennix and Bullinga (1991) suggest a "masculinization" of Dutch society since the 1970s. What they mean is that while women's role in Dutch society has changed considerably since the demographic shift of around 1965 (see Chapter 5), men's role has changed less. Surprisingly, these authors use the results of research inside the United States to argue for what this means for *Dutch* society. They do not seem aware of differences between nations, and their concept of "masculinity" obviously differs from the one I use in this book.

2

VALIDATING THE MASCULINITY/ FEMININITY DIMENSION ON ELITES FROM 19 COUNTRIES

Michael H. Hoppe

This chapter is based on the author's (1990) comprehensive follow-up study of Geert Hofstede's *Culture's Consequences* (1980). The study's main purpose was to test the construct validity of Hofstede's four-dimensional model with a set of 19 countries whose respondents differed markedly from Hofstede's. In contrast to Hofstede's sample of IBM employees, Hoppe's sample of more than 1,500 respondents belonged to the managerial, professional, political, and academic elites in 17 Western and Southern European countries plus Turkey and the United States. They were alumni of the Salzburg Seminar, a high-level international study center in Austria. This chapter (a) summarizes the results of a direct comparison of country scores on four dimensions between Hoppe's and Hofstede's studies, using the 1994 revised formulas of Hofstede's Values Survey Module; (b) explores similarities and differences in results between the two studies, particularly for the Masculinity/Femininity scale, and (c) discusses the significance of the Masculinity/Femininity dimension for cross-cultural leadership.

INTRODUCTION

Hofstede's original research on *Culture's Consequences* (1980) greatly shaped the discussion of cross-cultural management theory and practice during the 1980s and 1990s. More than a thousand entries in the Social Sciences Citation Index (SSCI) since the publication of Hofstede's book bear witness to this fact.

Because Hofstede's original country-level dimensions were derived from answers by IBM employees only, it is a valid question whether the same dimensions are found if other matched samples of respondents are used. In addition, Hofstede derived his four dimensions mainly from answers by *employees* ("followers"). Would the four dimensions equally well discriminate among countries for respondents in *leadership* positions? A positive answer to this latter question would (a) enhance the construct validity of the four-dimensional (4-D) model and (b) help explain the values of the men and women who shape and perpetuate a society's norms and policies through the institutions they direct or influence (Berger & Luckmann, 1967).

The Salzburg Seminar Alumni Study (SSAS), the main results of which will be reported below, provides answers to the above questions. In fact, it was the first and "most extensive replication carried out to date" (Hofstede, 1991, p. 257), designed to test the construct validity of Hofstede's four dimensions with a markedly different sample of respondents from a wide range of employers and occupations. It included 18 of his original 40 countries, plus Malta.

This chapter first provides an overview of the SSAS. It then presents selected results, discusses in some detail the similarities and differences between the SSAS and Hofstede's original study with regard to the Masculinity/Femininity dimension, and concludes with a brief exploration of the dimension's implications for cross-cultural leadership.

THE SALZBURG SEMINAR
ALUMNI STUDY (SSAS)

The respondents for the country comparison in Hofstede's original study were nonmanagerial professionals, technical and clerical employees of marketing and service divisions, and first-line and middle-level managers in national IBM subsidiaries around the world. As IBM employees, they represented a well-matched, but rather narrow, segment of each of the 40 countries and, simultaneously, a strong *corporate* culture.

In contrast, the respondents in the SSAS belonged to the elites of their respective societies. They were highly educated and came from a wide range of educational, occupational, and organizational backgrounds. They worked in high-level positions in academia, government, business and industry, not-for-profit organizations, the media, and supra/transnational organizations. They included CEOs of large corporations, chancellors of universities, judges, professors, journalists, high-level civil servants, administrators of international organizations, and independent lawyers.

The Salzburg Seminar, located in Leopoldskron Castle, Salzburg, Austria, describes itself as a "unique forum for multicultural, interdisciplinary dialogue . . . [where] eminent conceptual thinkers and practitioners meet with mid-career professionals . . . thus fostering the qualities of leadership required by the challenges of our increasingly interdependent and interactive world" (Salzburg Seminar, 1990). Responses in the SSAS were supplied by 1,544 alumni from 17 Western European countries, Turkey, and the United States who had attended one or more of the seminar's sessions between 1964 and 1983. They were surveyed between late 1983 and mid-1984; the "Intercultural Questionnaire" (Hoppe, 1990, pp. 214-217) used included all 47 items of the 1982 version of Hofstede's Values Survey Module (VSM 82; see Hofstede, 1982a, 1982b).

Valid returns ranged from 30 for Malta to 183 for Great Britain, with an almost 60% return rate. Participants from Eastern European countries were excluded from the study at the request of the seminar's leadership at the time, based on political considerations related to East-West realities. Other countries did not have enough alumni to warrant sufficiently large country samples for statistical analysis.

For the 18 overlapping countries, the respondents of SSAS were different from those in Hofstede's IBM study in the following ways: 19% women against 8% for IBM, mean age 43 against 30 in IBM, 5 more years of formal education, one third making their living as college/university faculty members, and only about one fifth from the private sector. More than two thirds of the SSAS respondents held doctorates or master's level degrees. Almost half graduated in either law or economics. About 60% worked in a public service-type environment of either municipal, national, and international governments; academia; or not-for-profit or semigovernmental organizations such as the British Broadcasting Corporation (BBC). About 11% were self-employed.

Country scores for each of Hofstede's four dimensions were calculated using formulas suggested in the VSM 82 manual. They have been reported elsewhere (Hoppe, 1990, 1993). This chapter will use revised country scores based on the 1994 Values Survey Module (VSM 94; see Hofstede, 1994). The latter was developed to integrate the findings of a multitude of replication studies during the 1980s and 1990s, including Hoppe's (1990) original research.

RESULTS

The *new* country scores and ranks for SSAS, together with those reported for the SSAS countries in *Culture's Consequences* (Hofstede, 1980, abbreviated as CC), are summarized in Table 2.1. Despite changes in overall country scores and some noticeable shifts in relative position of some countries (e.g., Austria on PD, France and Italy on IDV, and France on MAS), the rank order correlations between CC and SSAS country scores are highly significant for all four dimensions (see Table 2.2). In addition, the ranges and standard deviations are very similar for the two studies, with the exception of a slightly narrower range for Uncertainty Avoidance in SSAS. In short, the results of the SSAS significantly support the validity of Hofstede's four dimensions for distinguishing among countries.

At the same time, the overall country means for the two studies differ noticeably, reflecting the differences between the IBM and SSAS populations. The same held true—except for IDV, which was almost identical for CC and SSAS—for the overall country means that were produced by the original formulas (Hoppe, 1990, p. 120).

TABLE 2.1 Country Dimension Scores and Ranks for 18 Countries in CC[a] and 19 Countries in SSAS[b]

Country	Power Distance (PD)		Uncertainty Avoidance (UA)		Individualism (IDV)		Masculinity (MAS)	
	CC	SSAS	CC	SSAS	CC	SSAS	CC	SSAS
Austria (AUT)	11 (18)	10 (8)	70 (8)	37 (8)	55 (14)	100 (9)	79 (1)	18 (5)
Belgium (BEL)	65 (3)	23 (5)	94 (3)	53 (5)	75 (5)	102 (7)	54 (9)	–1 (11)
Denmark (DEN)	18 (17)	–12 (17)	23 (18)	12 (16)	74 (6)	101 (8)	16 (15)	–38 (18)
Finland (FIN)	33 (13)	–16 (18)	59 (10)	25 (11)	63 (13)	100 (9)	26 (14)	–6 (12)
France (FRA)	68 (1)	27 (2)	86 (4)	49 (6)	71 (7)	92 (15)	43 (11)	19 (4)
Germany, Federal Republic (GER)	35 (10)	4 (9)	65 (9)	21 (12)	67 (12)	97 (12)	66 (5)	14 (7)
Great Britain (GBR)	35 (10)	–5 (14)	35 (15)	9 (17)	89 (2)	117 (3)	66 (5)	7 (8)
Greece (GRE)	60 (5)	37 (1)	112 (1)	69 (1)	35 (17)	79 (16)	57 (8)	17 (6)
Ireland (IRE)	28 (16)	–2 (13)	35 (15)	21 (12)	70 (9)	99 (11)	68 (4)	5 (9)
Italy (ITA)	50 (7)	15 (7)	75 (7)	57 (3)	76 (4)	97 (12)	70 (2)	32 (2)
Netherlands (NET)	38 (9)	–6 (15)	53 (12)	17 (14)	80 (3)	111 (4)	14 (16)	–25 (16)
Norway (NOR)	31 (14)	–10 (16)	50 (13)	17 (14)	69 (10)	108 (6)	8 (17)	–29 (17)
Portugal (POR)	63 (4)	23 (4)	104 (2)	60 (2)	27 (18)	78 (17)	31 (13)	–24 (15)
Spain (SPA)	57 (6)	17 (6)	86 (4)	49 (6)	51 (15)	96 (14)	42 (12)	–19 (14)
Sweden (SWE)	31 (14)	1 (11)	29 (17)	–4 (18)	71 (7)	118 (2)	5 (18)	–15 (13)
Switzerland (SWI)	34 (12)	–1 (12)	58 (11)	26 (9)	68 (11)	110 (5)	70 (2)	43 (1)
Turkey (TUR)	66 (2)	27 (2)	85 (6)	54 (4)	37 (16)	66 (18)	45 (10)	2 (10)
United States (USA)	40 (8)	2 (10)	46 (14)	26 (9)	91 (1)	130 (1)	62 (7)	21 (3)
Malta (MAT)	—	35 —	—	55 —	—	95 —	—	3 —
Mean	42	9	65	34	65	100	46	1
Standard deviation	17	16	26	21	18	15	24	22
Range	11 -68	–16 -37	23 -112	–4 -69	2 -91	66 -130	5 -79	–38 -43

NOTE: SSAS country scores are based on new formulae (VSM 94; see Hofstede, 1994). Numbers in parentheses are ranks, with 1 = highest.
a. CC = *Culture's Consequences* (Hofstede, 1980).
b. SSAS = Salzburg Seminar Alumni Study.

CONSTRUCT VALIDITY OF
THE MAS/FEM DIMENSION

Hofstede originally operationalized the dimension on the basis of factor scores in his factor analysis of a 40 (country) × 14 (work goal) matrix. This same procedure could not be followed in the SSAS, because not all work goal items from Hofstede's original study were included (only those from the VSM 82). For this version of the questionnaire,

TABLE 2.2   Correlations Between CC[a] and SSAS[b] Country Dimension Scores

	SSASPDI	SSASUAI	SSASIDV	SSASMAS
PDI	**.76***** (.67**)	.70**	−.47	.18
UAI		**.90***** (.64**)	−.72***	.21
IDV			**.72***** (.69**)	.11
MAS				**.83***** (.36)

NOTE: Excludes Malta. Correlations in bold are Spearman rank order correlations based on SSAS country scores computed with new formulae (VSM 94; see Hofstede, 1994). Correlations in parentheses are product-moment coefficients based on original (VSM 82; see Hofstede, 1982) formulae. They were reported in Hoppe (1990, 1993).
a. CC = *Culture's Consequences* (Hofstede, 1980).
b. SSAS = Salzburg Seminar Alumni Study.
**p < .01. ***p < .001.

Hofstede had developed a simplified, approximating formula.[1] When the SSAS country scores on Masculinity were calculated with the VSM 82 formula, they correlated only weakly (.36) with the CC scores (Table 2.2). The VSM 82 formula used the unstandardized means of the following four work goals: "earnings" and "advancement" (masculine) as opposed to "security" and "cooperation" (feminine).

The weak replication of Masculinity (MAS) scores in SSAS can be understood by comparing the factor structure of the 14 work goal questions in *Culture's Consequences* (Table 1.1 in Chapter 1) with the result of a factor analysis of the 19 (countries) × 18 (work goals) matrix produced by SSAS (Table 2.3).[2] SSAS Factor 1 suggests an Individualism construct; its country factor scores correlate highly significantly with the Individualism (IDV) scores in CC ($r = .76***$).[3] SSAS Factor 2 conceptually resembles Masculinity but does not significantly correlate with MAS or with any other dimension in CC. It seems to reflect a side of Masculinity specific to the SSAS population.

"Advancement" and "cooperation" in Table 2.3 load opposite to each other, as they did in CC; however, "earnings" and "security" both show only marginal loadings. In a comparison of factor analyses of CC and SSAS scores, limited to the 12 goals used in both studies,[4] in CC "advancement" and "earnings" together formed one pole of the dimension, but

TABLE 2.3   SSAS[a] 2-Factor Solution for 19 (Country) × 18 (Work Goal) Matrix

Factor 1		Factor 2	
Variety[b]	.86	Prestige	.69
Consulted[b]	.84	Challenge	.62
Earnings	.77	Contribute	.61
Desirable area	.66	Advancement	.61
Personal time	.46[c]	Earnings[d]	.07
Serve country[b]	−.63	Personal time	−.66
Freedom	−.55	Cooperation	−.62
Little stress[b]	−.45[c]	Little stress[b]	−.49
Well-defined work[b]	−.45	Helping others[b]	−.47
Manager	−.44	Security[d]	−.24

NOTE: Eighteen work goals standardized by country. Of the total variance, 28% was explained by Factor 1 and 16% by Factor 2. See Hofstede (1982) or "Intercultural Questionnaire" (Hoppe, 1990, pp. 215-217) for complete wording of items. Answer format: 1 = *of utmost importance* to 5 = *of very little or no importance.*
a. SSAS = Salzburg Seminar Alumni Study.
b. Not part of the study in Hofstede (1980).
c. Second loading.
d. Items included for illustration only.

in SSAS they opposed each other.[5] Similarly, "cooperation" and "security," highly correlated in CC and together used to operationalize the Femininity pole, also opposed each other for SSAS, but on a second factor. In the VSM 82 formula for MAS, the country means for the four work goals in SSAS therefore appear to have canceled each other out two by two, producing tenuous scores.

Obviously, the emotional meanings of these four work goals within the IBM corporate culture around 1970 differed from those across Salzburg Seminar alumni in the 1980s. In fact, each population will have its own best items to capture the meaning of Mas/Fem, as well as of the other dimensions. The new version of the VSM (94) has been based on the experience of a number of replications to find the items that on average best maintain the original emotional meanings of the dimensions across different populations and over time. The new formula for Mas/Fem, used to compute the SSAS scores in Table 2.1, has retained the two work goals "advancement" (masculine) and "cooperation" (feminine) but replaced the other two goals by two belief items, "when people have failed in life it is often their own fault, agree/disagree" (masculine) and "most people can be trusted, agree/disagree" (feminine). Both these items had been included in SSAS. The country scores computed with these items produced the highly significant correlation between MAS scores in CC and SSAS reported in Table 2.2 (Spearman rank correlation coefficient rho = .83***).

The comparison between the two studies remains subject to the influence of sampling differences from country to country. One of the weaknesses of the study in *Culture's Consequences*—the use of a single private sector company—is also one of its greatest strengths. Its country samples are very well matched in regard to age, occupational levels, educational background, and so forth. Country samples in SSAS varied much more in their demographic makeup. For example, the proportion of women ranged from 7% in the Belgian sample to 40% for Greece. Mean ages of respondents varied from 37.5 in Malta to 45.9 in France. Switzerland had 6% of respondents working in academia, Turkey 60%. Of the Spanish respondents, 24% described themselves to be in some type of leadership or managerial role as compared to 52% for Finland. In general, differences in country scores on the Mas/Fem and other dimensions were influenced by differences in demographics. In fact, the original SSAS study showed a significant interaction effect between Masculinity and occupation (Hoppe, 1990, p. 153). Notwithstanding this, SSAS results were very similar (for all four dimensions) when country samples were stratified to control for occupation effects; this result, in turn, informed the decision to retain unstratified country means throughout (Hoppe, 1990, p. 124ff). Thus, most SSAS country samples can be seen as reasonably well matched for meaningful country comparisons to be made.

SSAS SCORES AND GENDER

Men and women differ in the ways in which they acquire knowledge (Gilligan, 1982), communicate with others (Tannen, 1990), and lead (Helgesen, 1995). Hofstede in Chapter 1 cites consistent differences in the importance of work goals between women and men.

A separate analysis of the SSAS work goal importance for women and men shows that they order the 18 work goals significantly the same (rho = .96***). Noticeable differences exist for two items only, with men ranking "contribute" (to organization) 3rd out of 18 goals and women 7th, while women rank "well-defined job" 15th and men rank it last of all (18th). The top four goals are nearly identical for both genders: "challenge" (1st for both), "freedom" (2nd for both), (relation with) "manager" (3rd for women, 4th for men), and "cooperation" (4th for women, 5th for men). The least important work goals are "little stress," "prestige," "serve country," and "well-defined work." An equally significant correlation (rho = .95***) is found for the ranking of the degree to which men and women in SSAS agree or disagree with 24 belief items, such as the ones mentioned above: "most people can be trusted" and "when people have failed in life it is often their own fault."

The similar ranking of goals and beliefs by women and men does not preclude gender differences in the *overall level* of Masculinity (and the other dimensions). In fact, the overall means for MAS across the eight countries with sufficient female respondents for a separate analysis (>17; i.e., France, Germany, Great Britain, Greece, Italy, Portugal, Turkey, and the United States) were 17 for men and 1 for women. This is in line with the very conceptualization of the dimension in values and beliefs surrounding traditional gender roles based on biological differences between men and women. A more operational explanation comes from the observation that in particular, women from the eight countries valued "advancement" less than men and disagreed more than men with the item of "when people have failed in life it is often their own fault." The women, however, agreed *less* than the men with the belief that "most people can be trusted."

DIFFERENCES IN THE OVERALL
COUNTRY MEANS OF MAS/FEM

Overall, MAS scores between CC and SSAS as a whole differ by more than 40 points, whether computed with the old formula or the new (Table 2.1). Differences in computational procedures (factor scores in CC, formula scores in SSAS) can only lead to random shifts. More pertinent explanations should be found in the effects of demographic variables, such as gender mix (see previous section), level of education, occupation, age, type of employer, and possibly the moment in time of the survey.

The SSAS population contained 11% more women. In addition, scores on the Masculinity dimension tend to decrease with age (Hofstede, 1991, p. 105 and Chapter 5 of this volume), and the SSAS population was an average of 13 years older. Furthermore, the occupations and corporate culture of the IBM population very likely were conducive to masculine values: Earnings, advancement, and career motives played a particularly important role. In contrast, the SSAS population consisted mainly of highly educated professionals, about 60% of whom worked in public service-type environments of national and international governments, academia, and not-for-profit organizations where advancement (and high earnings) might be considered less of an issue. All these differences between the two populations work in the direction of a less masculine orientation among SSAS than among CC respondents. This last observation was borne out by a direct comparison of work goal importance between SSAS and CC, as shown in Table 2.4.

Overall, the separate analysis of 12 work goals, common to 15 SSAS and CC countries, shows SSAS and CC respondents to rank the work goals significantly the same (rho = .74*). At the same time, there are noticeable differences. Four goals were significantly more important to IBM employees. Three of them were masculine: "advancement," "earnings," and "prestige." The fourth, "security," was counted as feminine in the VSM 82 but was dropped in the VSM 94. Table 2.4 shows the considerable difference in importance between the two populations in the importance of "earnings": 5th in IBM, 11th in SSAS. Remember that this item did not function well in an MAS formula for SSAS.

In spite of the above, the overall level on the Masculinity dimension is of secondary interest only. Although it provides some insights into the degree of flexibility that respondents as a whole (independent of country) may have acquired around the values and beliefs associated with traditional gender roles, it does not change the results of comparative research's primary interest—the *differences* among countries. Slightly overstated, Masculinity's "absolute value has no meaning" (Hofstede, 1991, p. 255).

TABLE 2.4 Work Goal Importance for CC[a] and SSAS[b] Respondents (15 countries × 12 work goals)

Item	CC			SSAS		
	X̄	Rank	SD	X̄	Rank	SD
Personal time	2.08	9	.15	2.06	6	.12
Challenge	1.70	1	.14	1.62	1	.14
Physical conditions	2.43	11	.22	2.46	9	.17
Manager	1.91	2	.18	1.89	3	.16
Security	2.06***	8	.27	2.52	10	.23
Freedom	1.91*	2	.13	1.70	2	.11
Cooperation	1.91	2	.19	1.98	4	.10
Contribute	2.02	7	.28	2.00	5	.17
Earnings	1.95***	5	.19	2.65	11	.17
Desirable area	2.17	10	.32	2.22	7	.14
Advancement	1.97***	6	.24	2.41	8	.26
Prestige	2.57***	12	.33	2.92	12	.30

NOTE: Includes all SSAS countries except Malta, the Netherlands, Portugal, and the United States. See Hofstede (1982) or "Intercultural Questionnaire" (Hoppe, 1990, pp. 215-217) for complete wording of items. Spearman rank order correlation rho = .74, $p < .05$ (without "earnings"; rho = .85, $p < .01$). Answer format: 1 = *of utmost importance* to 5 = *of very little or no importance*.
a. CC = *Culture's Consequences* (Hofstede, 1980).
b. SSAS = Salzburg Seminar Alumni Study.

CONCLUSIONS

In total, the results of the SSAS significantly support the construct validity of the Mas/Fem dimension, as well as those of the other three. They illustrate its usefulness as a *cultural* dimension for distinguishing among countries. This, of course, is the finding of primary interest in cross-cultural research.

Implicit in these results is the second major conclusion that the values and beliefs of the men and women in leadership roles parallel those who find themselves at societally or organizationally lower levels of responsibility. To use a colloquial expression, "a country's leaders and followers sing from the same hymn book" of societal norms. In the process, they reinforce each other's expectations and behaviors and create the organizations and institutions that help perpetuate these very norms.

Thus, given their locations on the Masculinity/Femininity dimension, countries such as Denmark, Norway, and the Netherlands, as compared to Switzerland, Italy, or the United States, will continue to develop different responses to issues of organizational life, career, or international relations—in spite of the increasing impact of technology and its companion, the "global" market.

At the same time, this chapter has illustrated a few of the methodological complexities that have to be understood to make cross-cultural comparisons meaningful. The most important is the need for well-matched country samples, or at least the possibility of some statistical control for demographic differences.

IMPLICATIONS FOR
CROSS-CULTURAL LEADERSHIP

The SSAS has practical implications for cross-cultural leadership because of the link between the values and beliefs of "leaders" and "followers" that the study established. Cross-cultural leadership is increasingly important in an interdependent world.

Leadership is a complex construct in its own right, as it compresses all the cultural issues present in Hofstede's dimensions—the issue of authority (Power Distance), the challenge of dealing with an unpredictable, ambiguous environment (Uncertainty Avoidance), the issue of identity and relationship to others (Individualism), the definition of success and/or purpose in life (Masculinity), and the orientation toward the long or the short term (Hofstede & Bond, 1988). As a consequence, it is impossible for one single notion of leadership (or followership, for that matter) to suit everybody.

Similarly, no one cultural dimension can fully explain the dynamics in a cross-cultural situation. The dimensions' effects interact in complex ways (Wilson, Hoppe, & Sayles, 1996), so the discussion can only illustrate the likely impact of differences in Mas/Fem on people working together, not establish ultimate causal relationships. For didactic purposes, it will somewhat overstate the intensity and direction of the differences. Moreover, Hofstede's dimensions together explain only about 50% of the country differences in his data, leaving plenty of room for alternative explanations that have to do with country-specific idiosyncrasies.

Last but not least, it is important to remember what the men and women in SSAS, independent of their country of origin, have in common. This will not only provide the backdrop against which country differences and/or similarities in Mas/Fem will be discussed but also will simultaneously convey a summary description of the most and least cherished values and beliefs held by the managerial, professional, and academic elite from the 19 SSAS countries.

As a group, SSAS respondents most value challenging work, freedom in their job, a good working relationship with their superior, working with others who cooperate well, and making a real contribution to their organization. Having an element of variety and adventure on the job as well as time for self or the family are also highly desired. In addition, the respondents believe that conflicts are best resolved by compromise, children are best raised toward independence, and that it is all right for management authority to be questioned and teachers to be criticized.

Equally, they agree that conflict in organizations need *not* be eliminated, that rules may be broken (at times) if employees think that it would be in the best interest of the organization, and that spouses may entertain different opinions on major political or religious issues. In contrast, they disagree with the statement that "the individual who pursues his or her own interests makes the best possible contribution to society as a whole." Their work goals of least importance are having little tension and stress on the job, working in a well-defined job situation, serving their country, and belonging to a prestigious organization.

On the whole, this summary description of SSAS respondents expresses more concretely the overall levels of Individualism, Masculinity, Power Distance, and Uncertainty Avoidance, as shown in their means for each of the dimensions in Table 2.1. They are self-directed individuals who thrive on challenging and varied work, and who recognize that it can best be done by working with others through the inevitable ambiguities and conflicts of their professional and personal lives. In short, the description offers a not surprising overall picture of individuals in organizational or professional leadership roles.

Against this backdrop, then, country differences along the Mas/Fem scale and their expression in organizational life become subtle at times, unless they occur between individuals from countries that occupy opposite ranks in Table 2.1. That applies to Switzerland, Italy, Austria, and the United States, toward the more masculine end of the dimension, and Denmark, Norway, the Netherlands, and Sweden, toward the more feminine. For them, therefore, the following distinctions may be particularly descriptive.

Expressions of Masculinity in organizational life include the following:

1. Job-centeredness: centrality of work and career, emphasis on visible achievements, and desire for tangible expressions of success;
2. Performance-centeredness: challenge, excellence, "going the extra mile," and competition; and
3. Results orientation: initiative, decisiveness, and efficiency.

Expressions of Femininity in organizational life include the following:

1. Employee-centeredness: centrality of personal and family life, emphasis on mutual help and social interaction, and desire for personal fulfillment and belonging;
2. Relationship-centeredness: quality of human relationships and work environment/location, competence ("being a sound contributor"), and collaboration; and
3. People orientation: solidarity, empathy, and consensus.

The core of the differences can be summed up in the juxtaposition of the two slogans "live in order to work" and "work in order to live." In more masculine societies, work tends to be seen as an end in itself. Good working relationships, solidarity among employees, or the quality of the workplace are frequently considered mere means toward that end. In more feminine countries, good working relationships, solidarity among employees, and the quality of the workplace are instead viewed as ends in their own right. What is most apparent to this author, who worked extensively in Germany, the United States, Greece, Austria, and the Netherlands, is the staying power of the assumptions that fuel the Mas/Fem dimension. In general, it makes a big difference whether organizational life is largely guided by notions of performance, competition, and results or mainly by notions of quality of work life, cooperation, and solidarity. The greatest promise in the long run, of course, is marrying the two.

NOTES

1. Hofstede found a product-moment correlation between original and approximated MAS scores of .93 (significant at the .001 level); the mean error of the approximated country scores was six points below or above the original score, with a maximum observed error of 17 points (Hofstede, 1982a, 1982b).

2. The SSAS did not use the work goal items "training," "use of skills," "benefits," and "recognition" but instead included items for "little stress" (have little tension and stress on the job), "consulted" (be consulted by your direct superior in his or her decisions), "contribute" (make a real contribution to the success of your company or organization), "serve (your) country," "variety" (have an element of variety and adventure in the job), "prestige" (work in a prestigious, successful organization), "helping others" (have an opportunity for helping other people) and "well-defined work" (work in a well-defined job situation where the requirements are clear).

3. Throughout this chapter, as elsewhere in the book, * stands for $p < .05$, ** for $p < .01$, and *** for $p < .001$. This chapter uses two-tailed tests.

4. The comparison was based on two matched 15 (country) × 12 (work goal) matrices, for which complete data were available. The factor structure for CC across these 15 countries hardly differed from what was found across 40 countries; the country factor scores based on 15 and on 40 countries correlated .98***.

5. Hofstede, Kolman, Nicolescu, and Pajumaa (1996) found the same in a study of students from eight countries.

3

FEMININITY AND SUBJECTIVE WELL-BEING

Willem A. Arrindell

Data from 36 countries were used to test the influence of the Masculinity/Femininity (Mas/Fem) dimension of national culture on Subjective Well-Being (SWB). Other Hofstede dimensions (Individualism/Collectivism, Power Distance, and Uncertainty Avoidance) were held constant, as were National Wealth (Purchasing Power), Civil Rights, and Income Social Comparison. Contrary to expectations, a feminine national cognitive set alone did not predict high national levels in SWB. Masculinity and National Wealth, however, interacted significantly in predicting national SWB levels: In the poorer countries, Masculinity correlated positively with SWB, but in the richer countries negatively. Wealthy feminine countries reported the highest SWB levels.

NATIONAL CULTURE,
SUBJECTIVE WELL-BEING,
AND NATIONAL WEALTH

Although it is possible to study the somatic and psychological health of individuals in relation to, for example, personality, demographic, or sociocultural variables, it also is feasible to examine the health of countries. At the latter level of analysis, one can acquire an understanding of how broad environmental, demographic, epidemiological, and unalterable, constitutional factors affect the health of large populations. Studies of this kind fall within the so-called holocultural tradition (Rohner, 1986, p. 38), in which cultures or nations are treated as units and culture/national scores on the variables of interest are correlated with one another (e.g., Bond, 1991; Diener & Diener, 1995; Matsumoto & Fletcher, 1996; Waldron et al., 1982).

It has been suggested that the ways in which people around the globe think, feel, and act in response to relevant issues are structured. Hofstede (1991, p. 5) has defined culture as "the collective programming of the mind which distinguishes the members of one group or category of people from another," with the range of cultures reflecting varying solutions to universal basic problems. The sources of different mental programs lie within the social environments (family, school, workplace, living community, etc.) in which one grows up and acquires one's life experiences. These programs affect the functioning of societies, of groups within those societies, and of individual members of such groups (Inkeles & Levinson, 1969).

As described by Hofstede in the first chapter of this book, Masculinity/Femininity represents one of the four major dimensions that describe basic problems of humanity with which every society has to cope. In Hofstede's view, masculine and feminine societies differ in the social roles that are associated with the biological fact of the existence of two sexes, and in particular in the social roles that are attributed to males.

Hofstede's dimensional system originated in the domain of industrial-organizational psychology, but the four dimensions are also potentially relevant to the area of clinical psychology. For example, the Mas/Fem dimension may relate to and predict national levels of subjective well-being (SWB).

If dimensions of national culture can be shown to predict national mental health, this means that there is a functional relationship between cultural characteristics and psychological functioning. Such a relationship could then predict manifestations of normal or abnormal behavior from cultural characteristics, and infer cultural characteristics from manifestations of normal or abnormal behavior (Draguns, 1990, p. 269).

Veenhoven (1984, p. 22) has defined SWB as the degree to which an individual judges the overall quality of her or his life as a whole in a favorable way. SWB has two components: satisfaction and happiness. "Satisfaction implies a judgmental or cognitive experience while happiness suggests an experience of feeling or affect" (Campbell, Converse, & Rodgers, 1976, p. 8; see also Diener, 1984, 1994; Myers & Diener, 1995). Satisfaction has been defined as "the perceived discrepancy between aspiration and achievement, ranging from the perception of fulfillment to that of deprivation" (Campbell et al., 1976, p. 8). Happiness is the "hedonic level," the pleasantness experienced in feelings, emotions, and moods (Diener, 1994, p. 106).

Hofstede did not predict any relationship between Mas/Fem and SWB. On the basis of inferences made from survey data and correlations between MAS and country-level characteristics, however, Hofstede (1980, 1986, 1991) provided a number of key descriptors of masculine and feminine cultures that led the present author to expect an association of femininity with SWB (Arrindell et al., 1997). Following Diener, Diener, and Diener (1995), the guiding framework utilized was that predictor variables would influence SWB if they would affect people's ability to achieve their personal goals (see Emmons, 1986).

Hofstede pointed out that cultures labeled as masculine strive for maximal distinction between how men and women are expected to behave and to fulfill their lives: Masculine cultures

> expect men to be assertive, ambitious and competitive, to strive for material success, and to respect whatever is big, strong, and fast. [Masculine cultures] expect women to serve and to care for the non-material quality of life, for children and for the weak. Feminine cultures, on the other hand, define relatively overlapping social roles for the sexes, in which, in particular, men need not be ambitious or competitive but may go for a different quality of life than material success; men may respect whatever is small, weak, and slow. (Hofstede, 1986, p. 308).

Thus, in masculine cultures (e.g., Japan, Venezuela, the United States), political/organizational values emphasize material success and assertiveness, whereas in feminine cultures (e.g., Sweden, Norway, the Netherlands), they accentuate other types of quality of life (e.g., a welfare rather than a performance society), interpersonal relationships, and sympathy and concern for the weak.

Hofstede's IBM surveys contained a question about "overall satisfaction in the company" and one about job stress ("being nervous or tense at work"). He found both to be most strongly associated with Uncertainty Avoidance, but there were also indications of a relationship with Masculinity, in the sense of lower satisfaction and higher job stress in more masculine countries (Hofstede, 1980, pp. 288, 299). Job stress and job dissatisfaction have been shown to be important correlates and determinants of satisfaction with life as a whole (e.g., Diener, 1984; Near & Rechner, 1993). Subjective job stress was linked with depression and with decrements in interpersonal and cognitive/motivational aspects of job performance (e.g., Motowidlo, Packard, & Manning, 1986), which in turn relate to overall work dissatisfaction (e.g., Motowidlo, 1984). We therefore expected masculine nations to produce significantly lower average scores on SWB than their feminine counterparts.

Hofstede's descriptions of feminine versus masculine societal norms and their consequences for societies also led us to argue that more masculine societies should manifest lower levels of SWB than more feminine ones. Hofstede described feminine and masculine countries as respectively characterized by the following societal norms:

- Sex roles in society should be fluid versus sex roles in society should be clearly differentiated.
- Differences in sex roles should not imply differences in power between the sexes versus men should dominate in all settings.
- Unisex and androgyny as ideal versus machismo (ostentatious manliness) as model.
- Both father and mother are used as models by boys and girls versus father is used as model by boys and mother by girls.
- Quality of life and of environment are important versus performance and growth are crucial (Hofstede, 1980, pp. 294-295).

In addition to these norms, Hofstede (1980, pp. 296-297) pointed to some consequences for society at large. For more feminine countries:

- Less occupational segregation (e.g., male nurses)
- Men and women can both be breadwinners and follow the same types of higher education
- Belief in equality of the sexes
- Stronger position of the mother in the family.

For more masculine countries:

- Some occupations are considered typically male, others essentially female
- Men are breadwinners, women are cakewinners
- Men and women follow different types of higher education
- Belief in inequality of the sexes
- Weaker position of the mother in the family.

Thus, compared to the masculine countries, the more feminine ones would offer both sexes, especially women, greater opportunities for the fulfillment of multiple social roles (employment, marriage, parenthood) that are associated with good self-rated health status, low morbidity, fewer restrictions on activities, infrequent use of medical care, and low drug use for both men and women, and that also have additive positive health effects for both sexes (Barnett & Baruch, 1987; Barnett & Rivers, 1996; Cleary, 1987). These benefits obviously should influence overall subjective well-being positively (Diener, 1984).

An exploration of our data led us to realize that *national wealth* will play a moderating role in the relationship between Femininity and SWB. National wealth and Mas/Fem are independent: There are both rich and poor feminine and masculine countries. The practical impact of a feminine mentality, however, is more easily achieved if a country is wealthy than if it is poor (Hofstede, 1980, p. 295): Only in the former case has it the financial resources for construing a welfare society. Also and not surprisingly, greater wealth predicts higher national levels of SWB (cf. Diener et al., 1995), so some form of interaction between Mas/Fem, national wealth, and SWB is predictable.

Using data that were available for 36 nations, we have studied the correlation between Mas/Fem and SWB, taking into account a possible influence of national wealth.

METHOD

Database

Arrindell and colleagues (1997) compiled data on SWB and dimensional measures of national culture for 36 nations[1] by combining the "happiness" and "life satisfaction" survey materials collected by Michalos (1991) and Veenhoven, Ehrhardt, Sie Dhian Ho, and De Vries (1993) with Hofstede's (1980, 1991) dimensional index data.

Predictor Variables

The predictive capability of the Masculinity Index (MAS) in relation to SWB forms the central theme of this chapter. To counteract spurious relationships (Baron & Kenny, 1986), we included Hofstede's indices for Individualism/Collectivism (IDV), Power Distance (PDI), and Uncertainty Avoidance (UAI), plus some interactions among these (PDI × UAI, PDI × IDV, and MAS × UAI). As argued above, we included a measure of national wealth, but we also added available measures of civil rights and income social comparison as additional potential predictors of SWB (for theoretical and/or empirical arguments for their selection, see Arrindell et al., 1997). Thus, the question actually addressed was whether MAS would still correlate with and predict national SWB levels after controlling for the joint effects of other predictors.

National wealth was operationalized as the per capita income of nations in terms of the purchasing power of individuals (World Bank, 1994, Table 30). Purchasing power was computed at the World Bank by taking a standard basket of market goods and determining how much of this could be purchased with the mean per capita income in each nation. Measures for civil rights and income social comparison were derived from Diener and colleagues (1995). The civil rights score was based on the number of different human rights (out of a total of 40) considered guaranteed in a country (e.g., no searches without warrant, independent courts, innocent until proven guilty, no secret trials, freedom to teach ideas, no arbitrary seizure of property). Income social comparison was measured by comparing a country's average per capita income to that of neighboring nations, the idea being that if a country

TABLE 3.1   Regressions of Hofstede's Dimensions of National Culture,
Wealth, Civil Rights, and Income Social Comparison on
National Levels of Subjective Well-Being (SWB)

Predictor	r^a	Partial r	β^b	$t(\beta)^c$
Masculinity (MAS)	−.12	−.02	−.02	< 1
Individualism (IDV)	.58***	−.00	−.00	< 1
Power Distance (PDI)	−.52***	−.19	−.20	< 1
Uncertainty Avoidance (UAI)	−.56***	−.28*	−.34	−1.4*
Wealth	.60***	.16	.23	< 1
Civil Rights	−.43**	−.02	−.02	< 1
Income Social Comparison	.57***	.19	.25	< 1
PDI × UAI	—	—	−.04	< 1
PDI × IDV	—	—	−.14	< 1
MAS × UAI	—	—	−.04	< 1

NOTE: n = 33-36.
a. r = product-moment correlation coefficient.
b. β = adjusted partial slopes of criterion variable against predictor variable.
c. $t(\beta)$ = Student's t distribution value of this β.
*$p \leq .10$. **$p \leq .01$. ***$p \leq .001$. All tests are one-tailed, except for t values pertaining to interaction terms, which are two-tailed.

is surrounded by nations that are much poorer or much richer, this would serve as a basis for comparison for the inhabitants of the target nation and therefore influence their SWB.

RESULTS

Table 3.1 summarizes the results of a standard multiple correlation and regression analysis that incorporated the four Hofstede dimensions; their three interaction terms; and wealth, civil rights, and income social comparison as predictors and SWB as the criterion measure. Contrary to our expectations, MAS did not significantly correlate with or predict SWB. The only significant predictor of SWB was the Uncertainty Avoidance Index (UAI): High UAI marginally predicted low national levels of SWB ($\beta = -.34$, $t = -1.38$, $p < .10$, one-tailed). After controlling for the effects of nine other independent variables, UAI still

TABLE 3.2   Regressions of Wealth, MAS, and Wealth × MAS on National
Levels of Subjective Well-Being (SWB)

Predictor	Multiple R	R^2	F_{change}	β	$t(β)$
Wealth	.60	.36	17.8***	.64	4.8***
MAS	.61	.37	9.2***	.10	< 1
Wealth × MAS	.69	.47	8.9***	−.39	−2.4**

NOTE: Hierarchical multiple regression analysis with interaction term. n = 33-36.
**$p ≤ .01$. ***$p ≤ .001$. All tests are one-tailed for t values and two-tailed for F values.

correlated somewhat with SWB (partial $r = -.28$, $p < .10$). Significant
zero-order correlations of SWB with IDV and PDI dropped to nonsignificant levels when the other independent variables were held constant. For IDV, .58***[2] became −.00; for PDI, −.52*** became −.19. The
significant negative zero-order correlation between UAI and SWB (−.56***)
is a replication of previous studies showing UAI to be negatively
associated with SWB, health ratings, and work satisfaction (see Hofstede,
1991, pp. 116, 126).

Although neither MAS nor wealth made a significant independent
contribution to predicting SWB, the effect on SWB of a MAS × Wealth
interaction term had not yet been addressed. Applying hierarchical
regression analysis (Cohen & Cohen, 1983) for this specific problem
entailed entering Wealth and MAS first (in this order), in a stepwise
incremental fashion, as the two main effects, followed by their interaction.[3] The outcome is summarized in Table 3.2, where, among other
things, it can be seen that R^2, the share of variance explained, increased
significantly (with 10%) from step 2 (MAS) to step 3 (Wealth × MAS), to
47%. In addition, as hypothesized, with β = −.39** (one-tailed), the
interaction term emerged as an independent predictor of national SWB
levels.

Plotting the regression lines as in Figure 3.1, we observe that in the
poorer countries (those with purchasing power scores below the median; $n = 17$), MAS correlated marginally *positively* with SWB ($r = .32$,
$p = .10$), whereas in the richer countries (purchasing power scores above
the median, $n = 17$[4]), MAS correlated *negatively* with SWB ($r = -.51*$). In
terms of effect size (Cohen, 1992), low MAS (or high Femininity) corre-

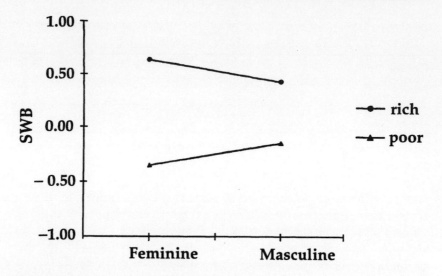

Figure 3.1. The Interaction Between MAS and Wealth in Relation to National Levels of Subjective Well-Being (SWB).

lated more strongly with high SWB in the richer countries (large effect size) than high MAS did with high SWB in the poorer countries (medium effect size). When nations were categorized on the basis of their combined median scores on MAS (51) and wealth (as above), namely "masculine and rich," "masculine and poor," "feminine and rich," and "feminine and poor," the respective mean SWB scores were as follows: .44 (SD = .63, n = 11), −.14 (SD = .78, n = 6), .64 (SD = .52, n = 6), and −.35 (SD = .63, n = 11).[5] Thus, as was foreseen, countries that were both feminine and rich had the highest average levels of SWB.

DISCUSSION

The present findings demonstrate the power of two of Hofstede's dimensions of national culture, Uncertainty Avoidance on the one hand and Masculinity in relation to national wealth on the other, as *independent* predictors of cross-national differences in subjective well-being. Arrindell and colleagues (1997) also demonstrated that these predictive capabilities were independent of cross-national differences in the major dimensions of personality (Lynn & Martin, 1995). This opens the way for predicting cross-national differences that are of psychopathological interest. In addition, specific characteristics of nations on the relevant dimensions may be inferred from national differences in how SWB is manifested (Draguns, 1990).

Controlling across nations for variables other than measures of national culture (national wealth, civil rights, and income social comparison), we found that only low Uncertainty Avoidance on its own remained significantly associated with high national levels of SWB. Thus, a feminine national cognitive set *alone* neither correlated with nor predicted high national SWB levels.[6]

The significant negative interaction between MAS and national wealth in relation to SWB implied that the highest levels of SWB were found in feminine, rich countries. Relative wealth is an essential condition for a nation to live up to the societal norms and political priorities dictated by a feminine mentality (see Hofstede, 1991, pp. 96-101). Relative wealth also is a condition for feminine values to affect the abilities of both males and females to achieve their personal goals (Emmons, 1986). Relative wealth therefore is a necessary condition for femininity to influence overall subjective well-being (Diener, 1984). In feminine countries such as Sweden and the Netherlands, a welfare society provides a minimum quality of life for each and every inhabitant, collecting the necessary funds from those who have the means. The interaction between Mas/Fem and national wealth surely provides further support for the view that a feminine mentality is more easily maintained if a country is wealthy than if it is poor (Hofstede, 1980, p. 295).

NOTES

1. Australia, Austria, Belgium, Brazil, Canada, Chile, Colombia, Denmark, Finland, France, Germany, Great Britain, Greece, India, Ireland, Israel, Italy, Japan, Korea (South), Malaysia, Mexico, Netherlands, New Zealand, Norway, Panama, Philippines, Portugal, Singapore, South Africa, Spain, Sweden, Switzerland, Thailand, Turkey, United States, and Yugoslavia.

2. As in other chapters, * stands for $p \leq .05$, ** for $p \leq .01$, and *** for $p \leq .001$ (except in Table 3.1, where * is $p \leq .10$.).

3. In this kind of analysis, raw scores on the variables pertaining to the main effects have to be *centered* prior to multiplication.

4. Purchasing Power data were available for 34 countries only—data for South Africa and Yugoslavia were missing.

5. ANOVA, overall $F = 4.58^{**}$, $df = 3$.

6. On the basis of an explorative analysis, Hofstede (1980, p. 299) had observed that on his one-item measure of overall work satisfaction, respondents in masculine countries scored significantly less satisfied than their equivalents in feminine countries. We did not replicate this finding, but we used a broader operationalization for SWB than satisfaction with work alone (Arrindell et al., 1997).

4

MASCULINITY/FEMININITY AND CONSUMER BEHAVIOR

Marieke de Mooij

Consumer behavior varies with culture. Data from 16 European countries collected in three large consumer surveys were compared to these countries' scores on Hofstede's dimensions of national culture. The data refer to product use and attitudes. Products covered are dresses, clothes and fashion, watches and jewelry, cosmetics and personal care products, the home, and the car. Other data refer to the buying decision-making process and the media. A number of significant correlations with culture dimensions were found. The Masculinity/Femininity (Mas/Fem) dimension in particular explains cross-national differences in consumer behavior that otherwise would have remained obscure. The concept of "self" used in marketing theory is not the cultural universal it often is assumed to be; it varies along the dimensions of Individualism/Collectivism (Ind/Col) and Mas/Fem.

CONSUMER BEHAVIOR
IS CULTURE-BOUND

People's decisions to buy certain products and services are influenced by a number of factors. Although income or spending power is a precondition, in the developed world consumption behavior is not based on rational economic choice between alternatives. Other factors influencing consumer behavior are of social and psychological origin. One important factor is the concept of "self" and how product ownership and use are supposed to influence the self. Products may serve a social purpose of self-projection and status communication. In different cultures, people have different concepts of self and varying needs for status.

Marketing involves influencing consumers to buy certain products and to prefer certain brands over others. Understanding consumer behavior is a prerequisite for controlling this process, and to this end, marketing borrows from economics, sociology, and psychology. Examples of concepts borrowed from sociology and psychology are the influence of the group, consumer needs, and motivation. Like management theory, marketing theory was in large part developed in the United States and thus includes U.S.-centered concepts related to the above-mentioned three disciplines.

These concepts, combined with a universalistic attitude among American marketing management, have led to marketing practice based on the principle that companies, products, and brands should be differentiated from the competition and positioned as strong personalities. They should "stand out in a crowd of other brands" to be competitive. Common metaphors used are "corporate identity" and "brand personality." This type of marketing practice reflects the typical configuration of individualism and masculinity within U.S. culture.

Academics worldwide have adopted the consumer behavior theories developed by their U.S. colleagues without realizing that these are not necessarily valid for other parts of the world. What motivates people to buy and use certain products is largely a matter of culture. Culture influences how people relate to each other in the buying process, whether decisions are made by individuals or groups, and what motivates someone to buy specific products.

Many consumer behavior data will be shown in this chapter to correlate with Hofstede's dimensions of national culture (Hofstede, 1980, 1991). The Masculinity/Femininity (Mas/Fem) dimension is especially important; it explains differences in the need for success as a component of status, resulting in varying appeal of status products across countries. It also explains the roles of males and females in buying and in family decision making. The dimension cannot be viewed in isolation: Often, the configuration with other dimensions provides the full picture.

The kinds of consumer behavior to be discussed in this chapter are those relating to consumption behavior and to communication. Consumption behavior includes needs and motives for consumption, choice behavior and consumer decision making, product use, and attitudes toward products and brands. Communication behavior includes media use such as readership and viewership patterns, and reactions to advertising. The purpose of advertising is to influence consumption behavior; therefore, advertising appeals tend to include motives for buying products or preferring one brand over another. Most advertising adds value to products and thus is an important means of creating and positioning brands. Consequently, to develop effective advertising across cultures, companies have to understand the differences in values, needs, and motives across cultures (De Mooij, 1994).

DATA SOURCES

Consumer behavior data in this chapter are taken from three large surveys: the Reader's Digest Eurodata 1991 (*Reader's Digest*, 1991), the European Media and Marketing Survey 1995 (Inter/View, 1995), and Euromonitor's Consumer Europe 1997 (Euromonitor, 1997). The Reader's Digest Eurodata survey was a study of the lifestyles, consumer spending habits, and attitudes of people in 17 European countries: Austria, Belgium, Denmark, Finland, France, Germany (West), Great Britain, Greece, Ireland, Italy, Luxembourg, Netherlands, Norway, Portugal, Spain, Sweden, and Switzerland. The study was based on parallel sample surveys conducted in the early summer (May/June) of 1990. Approximately 22,500 personal interviews were involved. The study was commissioned by the Reader's Digest Association, Inc., in cooperation with its editions and offices in Europe. Except in Sweden, it was conducted by the Gallup affiliated companies and institutes in Europe; it was coordinated by Gallup, London.

The European Media and Marketing Survey (EMS) is a research survey of print media readership and television audience levels within the upscale consumer group in Europe (European Union [EU], Switzerland, and Norway). It was initiated by the Inter/View market research agency with the long-term support of *Time* magazine. Other guarantors are *Reader's Digest* magazine, NBC Super Channel, CNN International, EBN (European Business News), Eurosport, Newsweek International, Philips, ABN-Amrobank, and Bozell 20/20 Media. EMS is a continuous survey, reported twice annually on a rolling base (minimum annual sample $N = 18,000$). Data collection is carried out by the combination of computer-aided telephone interviewing and a self-completion questionnaire for additional target group information.[1]

Consumer Europe 1997 (Euromonitor, 1997) is a compendium of market information on consumer trends in all the major countries of Western Europe, the scope being all the major retail items purchased for use in European households. These data were compiled from many hundreds of different sources, desk research, and telephone interviews.

For the present chapter, relevant data from these consumer surveys were correlated with Hofstede's index values across the 16 overlapping countries (all but Luxembourg, for which Hofstede has no data). Rank correlations (Spearman) were used, which reduces the impact of single outlying scores.

NEEDS, MOTIVES, PRODUCT USE,
AND ATTITUDES

Consumption decisions can be driven by functional or social needs. Clothes satisfy a functional need, whereas fashion satisfies a social need. Some personal care products serve functional needs, but others serve social needs. A house serves a functional need and a home, a social need. Culture influences the type of house in which people live, how they relate to their homes, and how they tend to their homes. A car may satisfy a functional need, but the type of car for most people satisfies a social need. Social needs are culture-bound, as will be demonstrated below.

Clothes, Fashion, and Watches

The degree to which people pay attention to their appearance varies by culture. At face value, one would expect a relationship between Mas/Fem and fashion, but a range of needs are connected with fashion: Dressing fashionably can be done to satisfy a need to be well groomed, a need for status, or a need to be different. Other dimensions than masculinity and femininity therefore also relate to fashion.

Members of small Power Distance and weak Uncertainty Avoidance cultures are generally not well groomed as compared with members of large Power Distance and strong Uncertainty Avoidance cultures. Particularly in strong Uncertainty Avoidance cultures, people pay attention to the way they dress. It is one way of facing a threatening world. Observant travelers in Europe may have noticed the difference between the careful way of dressing of the Belgians, French, and Italians as opposed to the carefree (sometimes sloppy) way of dressing of the British, Danes, and Dutch. Interestingly, this relationship between Uncertainty Avoidance and the need to be well groomed cannot be extended to the use of cosmetics, as will be demonstrated in the next section.

Making one's own clothes as a hobby also is influenced by culture. In feminine cultures, people like making their own dresses more than in masculine ones; this follows from a negative correlation between the Masculinity Index (MAS) and the share of households in the Eurodata survey with a member who does dressmaking or knitting (−.73***[2]), as illustrated in Figure 4.1.

If fashion is perceived as "foreign," status can be derived from its foreignness. In masculine cultures, foreign goods appear more attractive: Agreement with a statement "foreign goods are more attractive than our own" correlated positively with the Masculinity Index MAS (.52*).[3]

Status is acquired by expressing either one's success or one's power and position in society, and therefore can be expected to be related to Masculinity and/or to Power Distance. Two correlations with product use demonstrate the two relationships. EMS 95 (Inter/View, 1995) in-

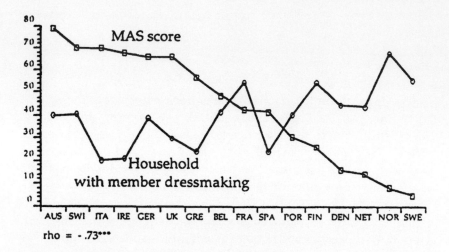

MAS score

Household
with member dressmaking

AUS SWI ITA IRE GER UK GRE BEL FRA SPA POR FIN DEN NET NOR SWE

rho = - .73***

Figure 4.1. Correlation of MAS With Member Dressmaking.

SOURCE: Data are from Reader's Digest Eurodata (*Reader's Digest*, 1991), a consumer survey of 17 European countries sponsored by the Reader's Digest Association, Inc.

cluded questions about watches, asking for the number and value of watches people own or intend to buy. Owning a main watch costing less than £100 correlated negatively with MAS (−.51*): Members of feminine cultures tend to buy cheap watches. Wearing very expensive watches, however, appears to appeal to another status need, that of demonstrating one's position in society. The answer "over £1,000" to the question about the amount respondents are willing to spend on their watch correlated with the Power Distance Index, PDI (.62**).

Data reported in *Consumer Europe 1997* (Euromonitor, 1997) show a significant correlation (.66**) between value per capita of (real) jewelry sold and MAS. There is no significant correlation (.23) between sales of real jewelry and level of purchasing power (World Bank, 1994, Table 30).

Cosmetics

At face value, one would expect that the degree of masculinity of a culture would influence females' needs to look nice, so as to be more attractive to males, and that cosmetics would be used for that purpose. Cosmetics, however, primarily satisfy two other needs: the need to differentiate oneself from others and the need to look young. The use

		lip stick/ gloss	eye cos- metics	face clean- sers	face pow- der	hair gel, mousse	nail var- nish	deo- do- rants
United Kingdom		79	60	57	46	47	48	81
Austria		61	48	43	29	38	49	53
Belgium		57	51	45	34	27	50	61
Denmark		78	58	62	36	38	58	89
Finland		69	54	56	40	51	51	81
France		60	46	59	14	23	51	66
Germany		59	43	50	24	43	53	70
Greece		48	44	35	21	18	41	35
Ireland		74	45	61	30	36	43	72
Italy		59	46	47	27	19	50	60
Netherlands		68	59	50	29	37	50	76
Norway		65	44	48	21	42	50	85
Portugal		39	24	33	10	11	33	52
Spain		63	50	36	23	62	46	66
Sweden		78	65	54	28	62	63	86
Switzerland		62	45	56	15	50	52	74
Spearman rank correlation with:	PDI	-.64**	-.22	-.41	-.44*	-.47*	.29	-.56*
	IDV*)	.58*	.67**	.63**	.53*	.12	.41	.58*
	MAS	-.32	-.32	-.06	.0	-.33	-.26	-.54*
	UAI	-.90***	-.49*	-.74***	-.51*	-.52*	-.48*	-.89***
*) 15 countries								

Figure 4.2. Cosmetics and Personal Care: Percentages From "All Women Using These Days . . ."

SOURCE: Data are reproduced from Reader's Digest Eurodata (*Reader's Digest*, 1991), a consumer survey of 17 European countries sponsored by the Reader's Digest Association, Inc.

of cosmetics thus correlated positively with Individualism and negatively with Power Distance. In small Power Distance cultures, people want to look younger. The use of cosmetics and body products, however, basically goes against nature or is a potential harm to the skin. Most of these products, therefore, are less easily adopted by members of strong Uncertainty Avoidance cultures who are concerned with purity. This concern with purity can be found in the use of and attitudes toward other products (such as in the importance of "Reinheit" for Germans); there is a .64** correlation between the use of bottled mineral water and Uncertainty Avoidance (Euromonitor, 1997).

The Eurodata Survey asked questions about the use of a variety of cosmetics. On the basis of "all women using these days,"[4] there are correlations with Individualism (IDV),[5] Power Distance (PDI), and Uncertainty Avoidance (UAI), but not with MAS (see Figure 4.2). Examples of significant correlations are lipstick or lip gloss with IDV (.58*),

PDI (–.64**), and UAI (–.90***); eye pencil/mascara/eye cosmetics with IDV (.67**) and UAI (–.49*); related to this, face cleansers/cream/lotion with IDV (.63**) and UAI (–.74***); and face powder with IDV (.53*), PDI (–.44*), and UAI (–.51**). Use of hair gel, setting lotion, or mousse, and use of nail varnish appear not to be linked with needs to differentiate oneself. The use of hair gel, setting lotion, or mousse correlated with PDI (–.47*) and UAI (–.52*). The use of nail varnish correlated only with UAI (–.48*).

Personal care products are things like body milk, creams, and deodorants. Contrary to what was found for cosmetics, use of these products does relate to Mas/Fem. The wording "personal care" already stresses the care element of these products, which suggests they will be more used in more caring—that is, less masculine—cultures. Their use also correlates with the dimensions found of importance for cosmetics. The use of deodorants correlated negatively with MAS (–.54*) and with PDI (–.56*), and positively with IDV (.58*). An important need satisfied by deodorants is the need for privacy. In individualistic cultures, people do not want to smell other people, whereas in collectivistic cultures, they do not mind so much. As with other personal care products, there is a negative correlation with UAI (–.89***). Figure 4.2 presents the data and correlations.

The Home

The home and what it means for people obviously is a central issue in any culture. In individualistic cultures, people prefer their own separate house, however small, whereas members of collectivistic cultures prefer to live in apartment buildings. The Eurodata survey included a question about the type of house: "accommodation comprising whole house" answers correlated positively with IDV (.62**), whereas "accommodation in apartment/flat" correlated negatively with IDV (–.61**). Much of social life in collectivistic cultures takes place outside the home, in public places. Consequently, members of such cultures are less interested in having a private garden. Data on "possession of private garden" correlated strongly with IDV (.83***). At face value, possession of a private garden may be viewed as a luxury and thus may be expected to correlate with wealth, but this is not the case: There was no correlation between possession of a private garden and World Bank data on purchasing power (.06).[6]

The type of products one uses in the home, how one tends to the home, and the activities one does in the home are also culture-bound. The languages of the feminine cultures in the north of Europe, Sweden, Norway, Denmark, and the Netherlands contain special words to express the typical relationship that members of these cultures have to the home. There are no linguistic equivalents in English for the words *gezellig* (Dutch), *mysigt* (Swedish), and *hyggelig* (Danish). They express a very intimate type of coziness or togetherness. Related to this is a typical, intensive use of coffee all morning in the home and during gatherings, meetings, and discussions at work. Words in the languages of these countries associate coffee with togetherness, for example *kafferep* (coffee party) in Swedish. This behavior influences the way people make coffee: A fast espresso does not fit in this culture. Electric filter coffee makers serve the purpose. Ownership of electric filter coffee makers correlated negatively with MAS (–.44*).

The feeling of connectedness with the home also influences the way people organize their vacations; it is reflected in the ownership of caravans ("trailers" in American English). Members of feminine cultures feel the need to take a sort of home with them when they go on vacation. Across these European countries, ownership of caravans correlated negatively with MAS (–.57**).

How one tends to the home and the amount of do-it-yourself work in the home are related to Individualism, Masculinity, and Uncertainty Avoidance. The percentage of "household members doing carpentry" correlated negatively with MAS (–.56**). Doing carpentry means interior decorating, giving special care, and refining the home, all feminine values. Whether one also paints walls and woodwork as an amateur or leaves it to the expert depends on one's tolerance for uncertainty, so there is a negative correlation with UAI (–.67**).

Cars

When somebody buys a car, the main influence on the choice between a new or a secondhand car generally is assumed to be income. The choice also appears to be influenced by culture. The respondents to the EMS 95 survey, who are of a relatively high income class, report culture-bound behavior with respect to buying new or secondhand automobiles. This influence of culture is confirmed by the Reader's Digest Eurodata Survey (*Reader's Digest*, 1991). There appears to be a strong correlation between buying new cars and Uncertainty Avoidance. Eurodata shows a strong negative correlation between UAI and percentage of both first and second car bought used (–.87***). EMS 95 shows a negative correlation between UAI and percentage of answers "main car acquired secondhand" (–.84***). The respondents of Eurodata reflect the whole population, whereas the respondents of EMS 95 reflect business people of higher income levels. This confirms that in this case, culture overrides income as a decision influence: Particularly for this high-level target group, income is not the decisive factor.

Other culture-related factors are the preferred body type of a car, design, and engine. The percentage of answers of "strongly agree" to "I like cars with individualistic styling" correlated with Power Distance (.47*). From content analysis of advertising for cars in a number of European countries, I had already found that design and style of a car were the most frequently used sales argument in large Power Distance cultures; these cater to the need for status. The importance of the engine size of a car is not the same across cultures. In feminine cultures, people are not even interested in the engine size, as demonstrated in both surveys. The Eurodata survey data show a negative correlation between *knowledge* of engine size and MAS (percentage of "no answer" about size of their car's engine correlated with MAS –.60**). In EMS 95, with more highly educated respondents and a larger percentage of males, the percentage of answers of "don't know" still correlated negatively with MAS (–.52*).

Certain body types of car appear to be more appealing to some cultures than to others. The Eurodata survey shows that in 1990, the feminine cultures in Europe preferred the coupé type of car. The "most used car type is coupé type" answers correlated negatively with MAS (–.67**). In 1996, coupé type cars were not popular anymore, and there appears to be another type of car correlating with the Mas/Fem dimension: the hatchback. In EMS 95, for the second car in the family, the percentage of answers "hatchback" correlated positively with MAS (.57**). In EMS, the second car is a better measure, because a large number of first cars in certain countries are company cars to which other selection criteria apply. Figure 4.3 lists data and correlations related to

	Eurodata: Engine size main car % no answer	EMS: Engine size main car % 'don't know'	EMS: Car type second car = hatchback
United Kingdom	4	2.4	29.6
Austria	10	8.2	19.0
Belgium	10	4.9	19.8
Denmark	9	10.2	4.7
Finland	14	7.7	18.5
France	35	20.6	13.4
Germany	3	9.7	22.8
Greece	3	1.0	10.9
Ireland	8	5.8	18.2
Italy	1	1.9	33.4
Netherlands	14	8.7	16.3
Norway	10	10.9	11.6
Portugal	11	4.1	20.9
Spain	33	11.6	8.3
Sweden	25	33.6	9.7
Switzerland	5	8.5	17.8
Spearman rank correlation with MAS	-.60**	-.52*	.57**

Figure 4.3. Masculinity/Femininity and Automobiles.

SOURCE: Data are reproduced from Reader's Digest Eurodata (*Reader's Digest*, 1991), a consumer survey of 17 European countries sponsored by the Reader's Digest Association, Inc., and the European Media and Marketing Survey (Inter/View, 1995). ©Copyright 1995 by Inter/View. Reprinted with permission.

MAS and automobiles. It is evident that preferences for specific car types are related to the Mas/Fem dimension, even if the reasons why are obscure. Cars are extensions of the self, and the type of car plays a strong role in showing what kind of person one is or is not.

THE DECISION-MAKING PROCESS

Decisions on consumption behavior are rarely purely individual. There are a number of influences. The role of the group, its reference function, and the individual's place in the group vary by culture. The degree of Uncertainty Avoidance will play a role in the type of reference group—professional or formal rather than informal. In collectivistic cultures, individual decisions will be made in consensus with the group;

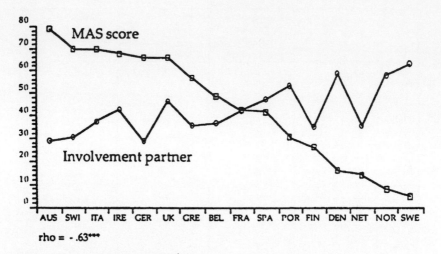

rho = - .63***

Figure 4.4. Correlation of MAS and Involvement of Partner in the Choice of Make and Model of Main Car.

SOURCE: Data are from the European Media and Marketing Survey 1995 (Inter/View, 1995).

there are no purely individual decisions. In feminine cultures, basic decisions are shared between partners: Data from EMS 95 show a negative correlation (–.63**) between MAS and involvement of the partner in the choice of make and model of the main car (Figure 4.4).

This chart shows how people from geographically close countries may show very different behavior, with important consequences for advertising. Denmark and Germany, although sharing a geographical border, are far apart in this chart. So are Belgium and the Netherlands. The Dutch generally manifest little role differentiation between marriage partners, although in this particular chart the Dutch show a dip. This is because the Dutch respondents in the EMS survey have a particularly high percentage of company cars, for which the company is the main decision partner.

An example of how strongly decision-making differences can affect advertising is a 1996 television commercial for the Renault Mégane automobile. It depicts a man who wants to surprise his wife with the new Renault Mégane, at the same time demonstrating the short brake path. He stops in front of what he thinks is his house, shouting "Darling, I have bought the Renault Mégane," but it appears he has entered his similar neighbor's house because he was not used to the short brake path. The text of this Belgian commercial had to be changed radically for the Netherlands, although half of Belgium and the Netherlands share the same Dutch language. Whereas in Belgium, apparently, the husband can buy a car without consulting his wife, this is not done in the Netherlands.

In collectivistic cultures, members of the inner and outer circle play different roles. Whereas in individualistic cultures, few other people will influence decision making, which is an individual activity, Japanese housewives refer to an average group of eight other housewives who influence their decisions. This explains the importance of network marketing in collectivistic cultures. The success of Yakult in Japan was the result of door-to-door sales and network marketing, whereas in Europe the mass media had to be used.

Culture influences buying behavior. Elders, such as grandparents, play a more important role in large Power Distance and collectivistic cultures than they do in small Power Distance and individualistic cultures. In masculine cultures, with strong role differentiation, housewives will not share their chores with their husbands to the degree that they do in feminine cultures. Whether the women or the men do the food shopping in Europe correlates with MAS: In masculine cultures men are less involved in the shopping chores than in feminine cultures. For the 16 European countries of the Eurodata Survey 1991, the correlation between "women main food shoppers" and MAS was .68**. When the more traditional, less affluent Southern countries—Greece, Portugal, and Spain—were excluded, the correlation for the remaining 13 countries became .91***. It seems that cultural values influencing role behavior that are latent in the more traditional countries become manifest when countries modernize.

Related to role differentiation are culturally defined attitudes with respect to roles of women. Eurodata 91 included a number of questions on attitudes toward social phenomena. The answers demonstrated that attitudes related to women's liberation issues often can be better explained by dimensions other than by Mas/Fem. Strong agreement with the statement "a woman's place is in the home" correlated with Power Distance (.66**) and Uncertainty Avoidance (.81***). Strong agreement with the opposite statement "women should have more freedom to do what they want" correlated negatively with PDI (−.42*) and UAI (−.44*).

Cultures with large PDI and strong UAI manifest a wish to conserve the status quo and feel threatened by change. In cultures of the opposite configuration, small PDI and weak UAI, women wish more freedom, and this wish is tolerated and even supported by men. The Eurodata Survey produced demographics that lend substance to this difference: The percentages "men are chief income earners" also correlated with PDI (.63**) and UAI (.55*). Cultural differences thus affect the agenda of women's liberation movements in different countries.

THE CONCEPT OF SELF

A core element of Western marketing is the focus on product/brand attributes, benefits and values that are to distinguish the user's self from others. The self is said to have an "I" component (the personal, private, individual I) and a "Me" component, (the socially acceptable Me), with internalized, learned, and accepted norms and values. In Western theories, another distinction is between the *actual self* and the *ideal self*. People will buy products that are compatible with their self-concept, or rather that enhance their "ideal self" image. Often mentioned drives related to the ideal self are self-esteem, self-actualization, and the need for achievement. Implicit in the concept of personality is the individualistic notion that people should distinguish themselves from others, as opposed to the conformity to the group that is the norm in collectivistic cultures.

The self-concept, as used in consumer psychology, is based on a psychoanalytic theory of the self and personality that was mainly developed in the United States. According to the mental health model prevalent in the United States, a young person has to develop an identity that enables him or her to function independently in a variety of social settings, apart from the family. Failing to do so can cause an identity crisis. The mental health models of collectivistic cultures are different. Indian and Japanese models, for example, stress encouragement of dependency needs in the earlier phases of childhood, and negotiated adaptation to the complex familial hierarchical relationships (Roland, 1988, p. 314). The mental health model of masculine cultures is based on the need for success. Success must be shown; the successful must "shine." This is opposed to the mental health model of feminine cultures, in which people must be liked. In this case, "modesty" is an essential virtue, and those who shine too much are disliked.

Contrary to what is suggested in much of the consumer psychology literature used to explain consumer behavior and marketing models, there is no single concept of "self" applicable across all cultures. All of Hofstede's dimensions potentially play a role in the concept of self, but the most important are Ind/Col and Mas/Fem. Differentiating oneself from others is a basic aspect of individualistic cultures, as demonstrated above by the correlations of IDV with the use of cosmetics. Masculinity adds to that in the sense that people want to distinguish themselves. EMS asked about agreement to a statement "I like to stand out in a crowd." The percentage of answers of "strongly agree" correlated with MAS (.49*) and with UAI (.51*), with a multiple correlation coefficient $R = .63**$. Wishing to stand out in a crowd is not part of the psyche of members of feminine cultures, to whom modesty is a core value. It is a typical value of masculine cultures, and in combination with Uncertainty Avoidance it leads to an overt display of oneself as a successful person.

MEDIA BEHAVIOR

Media behavior is related to cultural communication styles. Individualistic cultures are more verbally oriented, with low context communication behavior; collectivistic cultures are more visually oriented, with high context communication behavior. The verbal orientation of individualistic cultures is demonstrated by the correlation between the use of "teletext services used personally" and IDV (.51*). More verbally oriented cultures tend to read more. In individualistic cultures, there are more national and regional daily newspapers. There is a .75*** correlation across 35 countries around the world between the existence of daily newspapers and IDV.[7] The Reader's Digest Eurodata Survey includes a question about how many books respondents read. The answer "12 or more books read in the past year" correlated strongly with IDV (.90***).

What people read—whether they prefer fiction or nonfiction—correlates with masculinity. Members of feminine cultures read more fiction, and members of masculine cultures more nonfiction. Members of masculine cultures are more concerned with data and facts and prefer nonfiction, whereas members of feminine cultures are more interested in the story behind the facts, thus preferring fiction. In the Eurodata survey, a number of answers about buying fiction or nonfiction correlated with masculinity. There was a negative correlation between MAS and the percentage answering "bought mostly fiction" of all adults who in the past year bought at least one book (−.53*) and of all adults who in the past year bought 10 or more books (−.49*).

Members of small Power Distance cultures are heavy readers of newspapers, but they do not have as much confidence in the press as members of large Power Distance cultures. The small Power Distance cultures are democracies with more citizen involvement in government. This involvement implies that people have to be informed. This does not necessarily mean they trust their sources; thus, they have to consult a number of different ones. Two relevant measures correlate negatively with PDI: seven days a week reading of newspapers as reported in Eurodata 91 (−.69**) and number of daily newspapers bought per capita as reported by Consumer Europe (−.75***). The percentage answering "a great deal/quite a lot of confidence in the press" correlated positively with PDI (.55*) and with UAI (.51*). Members of the configuration of large Power Distance/strong Uncertainty Avoidance obviously view the press as an authority. Members of individualistic cultures use newspapers as their "main source of information" (correlation with IDV .59**).

HOW PEOPLE RELATE
TO ADVERTISING

The degree to which people like or dislike, or approve or disapprove of, advertising in general also is related to their culture. Notoriously, the Dutch and the Scandinavians have a critical attitude toward advertising, whereas Americans, the British, and especially the Japanese have made it a part of their daily lives. In the Reader's Digest Eurodata Survey (*Reader's Digest*, 1991) across 16 European countries, a significant correlation was found between confidence in the advertising industry and both the Masculinity and the Uncertainty Avoidance dimensions. The multiple correlation between confidence in the advertising industry,

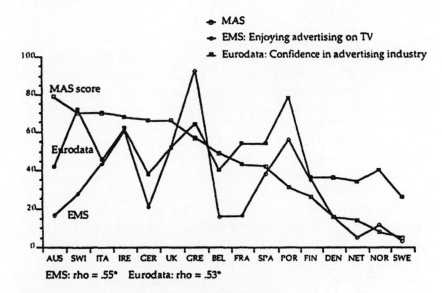

Figure 4.5. Correlation of MAS and Advertising.

SOURCE: Data are reproduced from Reader's Digest Eurodata (*Reader's Digest*, 1991), a consumer survey of 17 European countries sponsored by the Reader's Digest Association, Inc., and the European Media and Marketing Survey 1995 (Inter/View, 1995).

MAS, and UAI is even more significant ($R = 0.66^{**}$). A similar significant multiple correlation ($R = 0.61^{**}$) was found in EMS 95, in the "strongly agree" answers to the statement "I often enjoy advertising on TV." The correlation with MAS in both surveys is illustrated in Figure 4.5.

What does this multiple correlation mean? First, a characteristic of cultures of weak Uncertainty Avoidance combined with Femininity is skepticism and dislike of "hype." Advertising in general does exaggerate, which may be the cause of skepticism. Added to that, most feminine cultures of the 16 countries studied represent relatively small markets that may have been relatively swamped by advertising reflecting U.S. masculine values. Advertising thus was not made for the local culture and was not liked. This masculine orientation of import advertising from the United States is a lesser problem for other masculine markets, such as the United Kingdom and Germany, which also happen to have more indigenous advertising. The cultural factors making people in general more or less receptive to advertising as a phenomenon must be taken into account when comparing advertising effectiveness across borders.

CONCLUSION

Cultural differences as measured by the Hofstede dimensions provide important explanations for variances in consumer behavior. They influence decision making regarding purchases, product use, needs, motives, and media behavior. The Mas/Fem dimension plays a crucial role and explains differences not covered by the other dimensions.

Academic research in marketing and advertising issues has only recently discovered the importance of cross-cultural value differences for international marketing and advertising. Two comparative studies conducted by U.S. academics used Hofstede's dimensions (Zandpour et al., 1994; Zandpour & Harich, 1996). Their objective was to develop a model for discriminating between advertising that is culturally fit from that which is not. Unfortunately, the authors excluded the Mas/Fem dimension. No reason was given; I assume the exclusion was based on considerations of what was deemed "politically correct" within the United States. This happened while the countries covered varied considerably in their Mas/Fem scores. The culture fit of advertising includes criteria such as the use of argument, hard sell, and celebrity testimonial. These are conceptually linked to the Mas/Fem dimension. There is no rational excuse for excluding this dimension from research. It seems paradoxical that academics operating within a culture accustomed to focusing on facts, data, and truth can be so biased in their research approach.

The purpose of this chapter was to demonstrate the potential of cross-cultural analysis of consumer behavior. In particular, country differences along the Mas/Fem dimension have amazingly relevant implications. In the globalization debate in marketing and advertising, a common expectation is that consumer needs worldwide will homogenize. The surveys I consulted show little sign of such homogenization; cultural differences in consumer behavior are alive and well.

NOTES

1. From 1997 onward, the Values Survey Module 1994 (VSM 94) published by IRIC (the Institute for Research on Intercultural Cooperation, founded by Geert Hofstede) is included in the EMS questionnaire. A first tryout on a small sample (430 respondents) in seven countries found scores for four of the five dimensions correlating with

the Hofstede data (IDV = .69, MAS = .78*, UAI = .79*, and LTO = .80). Only Power Distance did not correlate as predicted, probably because of differences in education levels between the samples used.

2. As elsewhere in this book, significance levels are indicated as *$p < .05$, **$p < .01$, and ***$p < .001$. Tests are one-tailed.

3. In fact, the answer "strongly disagree" to this question correlates *negatively* with MAS.

4. The questions about usage of women's toiletries were asked only to women. The question was "Which products are you using these days?" In the Eurodata report, answers are reported for all respondents ("all women") and by life stage, social group, age group, family stage, and working/not working. I used only answers by all women, reported as "all women using these days."

5. The correlations with Individualism are for 15 countries. Italy is not included. There is contradictory information about the level of individualism or collectivism in Italy, probably because Italy is bicultural: The North is individualistic but the rest of the country is collectivistic. Hofstede's IBM data were mainly collected in the North, and he found strong individualism. Consumption and media behavior data are based on a country average; where these relate to individualism or collectivism, Italy tends to score similar to Spain, that is, much more collectivistic.

6. See World Bank (1992). Income per capita is for 1990, the year in which the data of the Reader's Digest Eurodata report were collected.

7. Data are from Benn's Media Directory 1992, cited in De Mooij (1994). Data are used for the following countries: Argentina, Austria, Belgium, Brazil, Chile, Colombia, Costa Rica, Denmark, Ecuador, El Salvador, Finland, France, Germany, Great Britain, Guatemala, Hong Kong, India, Indonesia, Italy, Japan, Malaysia, Netherlands, Norway, Philippines, Portugal, Spain, Sweden, Switzerland, Turkey, Singapore, South Korea, Taiwan, Thailand, Peru, and Venezuela.

PART II

CULTURE
AND GENDER

5

THE CULTURAL CONSTRUCTION OF GENDER

Geert Hofstede

This chapter shows evidence of gender role variation across countries, in particular when related to the Masculinity/Femininity (Mas/Fem) dimension of national cultures. It discusses how children are socialized by the father-mother and the parents-children relationships within the family, which differ across cultures. It argues how this socialization affects the larger society, opposing the value of modesty in feminine cultures to assertiveness and ego boosting in masculine ones. Men's values differ more from women's values in masculine than in feminine cultures, and more for younger than for older persons. The position of a country on the Mas/Fem dimension impacts the trade-off between career and family interests. In feminine countries, women present gender stereotypes that differ more from men's than in masculine cultures; the same is true for their self-concepts. In feminine countries, women more often see their gender group as "responsible." Characteristics for choosing a marriage partner vary mainly with Individualism and/or

national wealth, but the difference between men's and women's emphasis on "chastity" and "industriousness" of the partner was larger in
masculine countries. Criteria for the choice of a husband versus a
boyfriend differ more in masculine countries. Family sizes are more
adapted to the available resources in feminine countries.

WHAT DOES A HERO LOOK LIKE?

Lucas, a 14-year-old boy, is unlike other kids. He's slight, inquisitive, and
something of a loner, more interested in science and symphonies than in
football and parties. But when he meets Maggie, a lovely 16-year-old girl
who has just moved to town, things change. They become friends—but for
Lucas it is more than friendship.

During the summer they seem to have the same idea: football players and
cheerleaders are superficial; but when school begins, Maggie shows an
increasing interest in this side of school life, leaving Lucas out in the cold.
He watches from the sidelines as Maggie becomes a cheerleader and starts
dating Cappie Roew, the captain of the football team.

Suddenly, Lucas wants to "belong," and in his attempt to win back
Maggie, risks life and limb in the game of football . . . (From a description of
the in-flight U.S. motion picture *Lucas*, shown on a KLM transatlantic flight)

Mainstream motion pictures are modern myths: They create hero models according to the dominant culture of the society in which they are
made. Both Lucas and Maggie in this movie go through a *rite de passage*
toward their rightful roles in a society where men fight while playing
football and girls stand adoringly and adorably by the sidelines as
cheerleaders. This is a model of a masculine society, but it is not the only
one possible.

NATIONAL DIFFERENCES IN
GENDER ROLE DIFFERENTIATION

"Gender" is the modern term for "sex" where it does not mean
"sexuality" but refers only to the distinction between women and men.
This book follows this code. "Gender" literature usually focuses on
women. Italian sociologist Silvia Gherardi (1995, p. 187) writes, "I too
have inherited a tradition which only recently has become aware that

half of the history of gender is missing if the social construction of masculinity is not considered." In this chapter, I will try to do justice to both halves, and to the links between them.

If the Mas/Fem dimension of national cultures has any implications at all, it must be for the division of gender roles in a country. There are universals that apply across countries, and there are differences that set countries apart.[1] In Chapter 1, I argued that studies of work goals by gender in different societies reveal a universal trend of men stressing ego goals and women stressing social goals; one can call this the dominant difference in their "gender cultures" (Hofstede, 1989). I referred to Tannen (1990), who studied female and male discourse in the United States and found a predominance of "report talk" for the men— transferring factual information—versus "rapport talk" for the women— using the conversation to exchange feelings and establish a relationship.

Weinreich-Haste (1979) studied stereotypes of academic disciplines in the United Kingdom and found science to be seen as masculine (except for biology) and arts as feminine (except for philosophy). Kelly (1978, p. 41) compared performances of 14-year-old girls and boys in schools across 14 countries and found boys doing significantly better on science subjects in all countries; gender differences were smallest in biology. The association of science with masculinity seems to be universal; however, as we saw in Chapter 1, there is less gender segregation in higher education in feminine than in masculine countries, especially if they are affluent. The implications of such a trend therefore differ along the Mas/Fem dimension.

In *Culture's Consequences* (Hofstede, 1980, p. 74), I showed that Europe-wide and worldwide IBM survey results produced basically the same gender differences in work goals as earlier studies in the United States. From the 14 goals listed in Chapter 1, Table 1.1, the following were nearly always more important to one gender than the other. For men, advancement, earnings, and training were more important than they were for women; for women, physical conditions, manager, and cooperation were more important than for men.

Although these differences seem to be universal, their degree as well as other differences associated with gender vary across societies. Cross-cultural comparative studies do show differences in gender-related values across cultures, not only among adults but also among young children (Best & Williams, 1993). Gender role programming evidently starts immediately after birth, in the differential ways in which adults treat girl and boy babies (Meyer, 1994), and in the different behaviors the children perceive in female and male adults. It is confirmed and extended in schools, at universities, and in the societies at large. Families, schools, universities, and societies are products of culture, and their socialization processes are culturally constructed.

GENDER DIFFERENCES
IN THE FAMILY

The typical family, where most people receive their first cultural programming, contains two unequal but complementary role pairs: parent-child and husband-wife. Different degrees of inequality in the parent-child relationship correspond to differences on the dimension of Power Distance (Hofstede, 1980, 1991). The prevailing role distribution between husband and wife reflects that society's position on the Mas/Fem scale.

In Figure 5.1, Power Distance Index (PDI) scores for 50 countries and three regions are plotted against country Masculinity Index (MAS) scores; abbreviations used are listed in Table 5.1. In the right half of the diagram, where PDI values are high, inequality between parents and children is a societal norm. Children are supposed to be controlled by obedience. In the left half, children are rather controlled by the examples set by parents. In the lower half of the diagram, where MAS scores are high, inequality between fathers' and mothers' roles (father tough, mother less tough) is a societal norm. Men are supposed to deal with facts, women with feelings. In the upper half, both men and women are allowed to deal with facts and with the soft things in life.

The lower right-hand quadrant (unequal and tough) therefore shows the model of a dominant, tough father and a submissive mother who, although also fairly tough, is at the same time the refuge for consolation and tender feelings. In the Latin American countries in this quadrant, the internationally current term *machismo* has been coined for the attitude expected of men. Less known is the corresponding term *marianismo* for women, a combination of near-saintliness, submissiveness, and sexual frigidity (Stevens, 1973).

The upper right-hand quadrant (unequal and tender) represents a societal norm of two dominant parents, sharing the same concern for

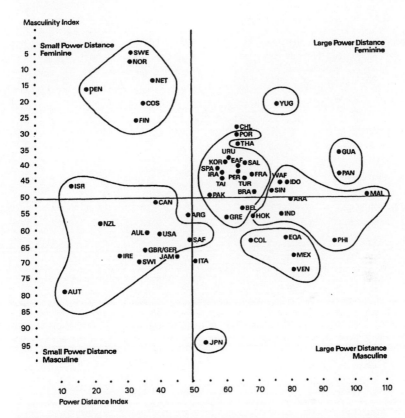

Masculinity Index

Small Power Distance
Feminine

Large Power Distance
Feminine

Small Power Distance
Masculine

Large Power Distance
Masculine

Power Distance Index

Figure 5.1. Power Distance Versus Masculinity Index Scores for 50 Countries and Three Regions.

SOURCE: From Hofstede (1991, p. 87).
NOTE: For country name abbreviations, see Table 5.1.

the quality of life and for relationships, both providing at times authority *and* tenderness.

In the countries in the lower left-hand quadrant (equal and tough) the norm is for nondominant parents to set an example in which the father is tough and deals with facts and the mother is somewhat less tough and deals with feelings. The resulting role model is that boys should assert themselves and girls should please and be pleased. Boys do not cry and should fight back when attacked; girls may cry and do not fight.

TABLE 5.1   Abbreviations for the Countries and Regions Studied

ARA	Arab-speaking countries (Egypt, Iraq, Kuwait, Lebanon, Libya, Saudi Arabia, United Arab Emirates)	ITA	Italy
		JAM	Jamaica
		JPN	Japan
		KOR	South Korea
ARG	Argentina	MAL	Malaysia
AUL	Australia	MEX	Mexico
AUT	Austria	NET	Netherlands
BEL	Belgium	NOR	Norway
BRA	Brazil	NZL	New Zealand
CAN	Canada	PAK	Pakistan
CHL	Chile	PAN	Panama
COL	Colombia	PER	Peru
COS	Costa Rica	PHI	Philippines
DEN	Denmark	POR	Portugal
EAF	East Africa (Ethiopia, Kenya, Tanzania, Zambia)	SAF	South Africa
		SAL	El Salvador
EQA	Ecuador	SIN	Singapore
FIN	Finland	SPA	Spain
FRA	France	SWE	Sweden
GBR	Great Britain	SWI	Switzerland
GER	Germany F.R.	TAI	Taiwan
GRE	Greece	THA	Thailand
GUA	Guatemala	TUR	Turkey
HOK	Hong Kong	URU	Uruguay
IDO	Indonesia	USA	United States
IND	India	VEN	Venezuela
IRA	Iran	WAF	West Africa (Ghana, Nigeria, Sierra Leone)
IRE	Ireland		
ISR	Israel	YUG	Yugoslavia

Finally, in the upper left-hand quadrant (equal and tender), the norm is for mothers and fathers not to dominate and both to be concerned with relationships, with the quality of life, and with facts *and* feelings, setting an example of a relative equality of gender roles in the family context.[2]

The interaction between Mas/Fem and Power Distance pictured in Figure 5.1 explains why effects of Mas/Fem differences are frequently mixed with Power Distance differences: They call for a simultaneous analysis on both dimensions (see the section in Chapter 1 on Mas/Fem differences as a secondary influence).

The division of countries into four quadrants in Figure 5.1 represents a typology, and all typologies have their limitations: Real-life situations are nearly always somewhere in between. Also, what is the "family" context depends strongly on the country's position on the dimension Individualism/Collectivism (Ind/Col). In a collectivist society, the "family" is the extended family, and the center of dominant authority could very well be the grandfather as long as he is still alive, with the father as a model of obedience. Ultra-individualist societies contain many one-parent families in which role models are incomplete, or in which outsiders provide the missing roles. Mas/Fem differences will sometimes be mixed with Ind/Col differences.

Whereas gender roles in the family strongly affect the values concerning appropriate behavior for boys and for girls, they do not determine the forms of gender differentiation in the wider society. Studies of traditional societies show these to vary considerably (Hendrix, 1994), but men, being on average taller, stronger, and free to get out, have traditionally dominated in professional and social life outside the home in virtually all societies. Only exceptional women, usually belonging to the upper classes, had the means to delegate their child-rearing activities to others and to step into public roles.

The much greater liberty of choice among social roles, beyond those of wife, mother, and housekeeper, that women in many industrialized societies nowadays enjoy is a recent phenomenon. Its impact on the distribution of gender roles outside the home is not yet fully felt; therefore, a country's position on the Mas/Fem scale need not be closely related to women's activities outside the family sphere. Economic possibilities and necessities play a bigger role in this respect than values. This explains why the effects of Mas/Fem differences on societal issues frequently appear only for countries that have reached a certain level of economic development (see Chapter 1). Religious traditions also play an important role, especially in Muslim countries, but this does not at all mean that Muslim countries necessarily have masculine cultures. They vary in this respect, and within the Muslim home, mothers may be quite powerful (Bank & Vinnicombe, 1995).

ASSERTIVENESS
VERSUS MODESTY

In the Scandinavian countries, people often refer to "the Law of Jante" (*Janteloven*). Jante is a pseudonym for a Danish town; the Law of Jante was codified by the Danish/Norwegian author Aksel Sandemose, and in an English translation it runs as follows:

> *You should not believe that*
> *you are anything*
> *you are just much as us*
> *you are wiser than us*
> *you are better than us*
> *you know more than we do*
> *you are more than we are*
> *or that you are good at anything*
> *You should not laugh at us*
> *You should not think*
> *that anybody likes you*
> *or that you can teach us anything.*[3]

The Law of Jante expresses an obsessive concern with modesty in these feminine cultures; in fact, Sandemose poking fun at it is a way of being modest even about this need for modesty. Many Danes, Norwegians, and even Swedes enjoy invoking the Law of Jante in explaining their own and others' behavior.

The need for modesty in feminine cultures contrasts with a need for assertiveness in masculine ones, as in the motion picture script about Lucas and Maggie. Within all national cultures I know of, modesty belongs more to women and assertiveness to men; however, the Mas/Fem dimension implies that a national culture as a whole takes a position on the assertiveness contra modesty continuum. In a more masculine cultures, everybody is socialized toward assertiveness—not only the boys but also, to some extent, the girls. In masculine countries, both boys and girls learn to be ambitious and competitive, although the ambition of the girls may be directed toward the achievements of their brothers and later of their husbands and sons. They become "cheerleaders" like Maggie in the case that opened this chapter. In feminine countries, both boys and girls learn to be nonambitious and modest. Assertive behavior and attempts at excelling that are appreciated in masculine cultures are easily ridiculed in feminine ones. Excellence is something one keeps to oneself.

More in general, both men *and* women hold tougher values in masculine countries, and both hold more tender values in feminine ones. The relationship between a society's level of masculinity or femininity and the Mas/Fem values of men versus women is outlined in Figure 5.2.[4]

Figure 5.2 illustrates that the gender gap in values is larger in masculine than in feminine cultures. In a masculine culture like the United States, women who want to move ahead in a male world are offered "assertiveness training." This kind of training is unlikely to become popular in feminine cultures. Another way of describing the value contrast between feminine and masculine cultures is that in the first, the stress in socialization is more on *who* you are and in the second, on *what* you are (Hofstede, 1980, p. 266).

Assertiveness means ego boosting. I found a remarkable confirmation of differences in ego-boosting behavior related to MAS in a seven-country study on literacy (Organisation for Economic Cooperation and Development [OECD], 1995). In 1994, representative samples of between 2,000 and more than 4,000 adults, aged 16-65, in each of seven countries were given equivalent tests to measure their literacy for three skills: reading, writing, and numeracy. Each of these skills was scored on three scales: a prose scale, a document scale, and a quantitative scale. In this way, each respondent received $3 \times 3 = 9$ ratings. I looked at the subset in each country who received the highest ratings (literacy levels 4 and 5 out of 5): They were the ones who objectively had been found to be quite literate. All respondents were also asked to *subjectively* rate their reading, writing, and numeracy skills in their daily life. Table 5.2 lists for each country the percentage of those objectively literate respondents who subjectively rated their skills "excellent" rather than "good," "moderate," or "poor." Data for Switzerland are separated into German speaking and French speaking.

Average percentages of "excellent" self-ratings were lowest in the Netherlands (31.4) and highest in the United States (78.7). The rank correlation with MAS across the seven cases for which MAS scores are available (excluding Poland) is a significant .71*.[5] Respondents in masculine

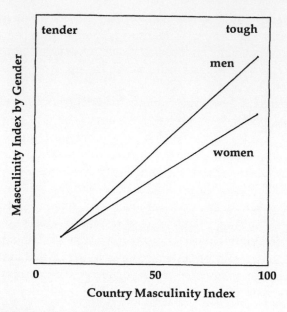

Figure 5.2. MAS Index Scores and Gender.
SOURCE: From Hofstede (1991, p. 83).

countries more often rated themselves as "excellent" than equally skilled respondents in feminine ones.

Verhulst, Achenbach, Ferdinand, and Kasius (1993) report on a surprising difference between matched groups of U.S. and Dutch adolescents (aged 11-18, more than 800 per country) who completed Youth Self-Reports (YSRs) about their personal problems and competencies. Americans reported many more problems *and* competencies than the Dutch, although earlier studies had shown no difference in the frequencies of adolescents' problem behavior as perceived by parents and teachers. U.S. parents rated their children's competencies higher than Dutch parents did. Some of the YSR items on which Americans scored higher were "argues a lot," "can do things better than most kids," "stores up unneeded things," and "acts without thinking." The only item on which the Dutch scored higher was "takes life easy." The differences can be explained from the ego-boosting norm in U.S. society, which socializes young people to take both their problems and their competencies more seriously than the ego-effacing norm in the Nether-

TABLE 5.2 Percentages of Respondents With High Literacy Who Rated Their Skills in Daily Life as Excellent

Countries in Order of MAS	*Skills/Scales*[a]									
	1	*2*	*3*	*4*	*5*	*6*	*7*	*8*	*9*	*Mean*
Switzerland (German)[b]	87	82	77	79	74	69	81	73	78	77.8
Germany	73	72	66	69	66	62	59	56	56	64.3
United States	79	79	78	79	79	78	79	79	78	78.7
Switzerland (French)[b]	75	69	67	60	53	50	64	59	58	61.7
Canada	84	82	85	72	68	72	60	64	67	72.6
Poland[c]	50	36	35	34	25	24	43	39	38	36.0
Netherlands	38	32	36	31	25	28	30	29	34	31.4
Sweden	66	63	61	57	54	52	61	63	63	60.0

SOURCE: Data are from Organisation for Economic Cooperation and Development (1995, pp. 191-199).
NOTE: Respondents had objectively tested literacy levels 4 and 5 (highest). Percentages given are those who rated their reading, writing, and numeracy skills in their daily life "excellent" rather than "good," "moderate," or "poor."
a. Skills/scales are as follow: 1 = reading, prose scale; 2 = reading, document scale; 3 = reading, quantitative scale; 4 = writing, prose scale; 5 = writing, document scale; 6 = writing, quantitative scale; 7 = numeracy, prose scale; 8 = numeracy, document scale; and 9 = numeracy, quantitative scale.
b. MAS scores for Switzerland: German, 72; French, 58 (Hofstede, 1980, p. 337).
c. No MAS score for Poland.
Spearman rank correlation with MAS across 7 cases = .71, significant at $p < .05$.

lands. A Dutch comment I overheard is "Americans always talk about themselves." An earlier comparison of YSRs between the United States and Germany had shown considerable similarity. Germans are more like Americans in this respect; their culture is equally masculine.

Assertiveness is not the same as competitiveness. In Chapter 7, Van de Vliert looks at self-rated *competitiveness* by country and gender. He finds that levels of overall competitiveness in countries are unrelated to MAS, but that the gender gap in self-rated competitiveness does relate to MAS: In some feminine countries, women even score themselves as *more* competitive than men do.

Besides varying by gender, values related to the Mas/Fem dimension also vary by age category. When people grow older, they tend to become more socially and less ego oriented. The value gap between women and men closes in middle age, as shown in Figure 5.3. This is at the time their differential roles in procreation are usually finished.

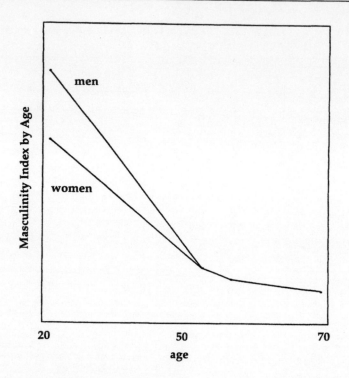

Figure 5.3. MAS Index Scores and Age.
SOURCE: From Hofstede (1991, p. 83).

In traditional societies, if women occupy respected positions in society along with men, this is mostly after age 45, when their status changes from mother into grandmother and when they are, or could have been, mothers of men. Unmarried women were and are still rare in traditional societies and are often ostracized.

WOMEN IN LEADING POSITIONS

As I argued in Chapter 1, the access of women to jobs depends primarily on the level of economic development of a country. Lower-class women have nearly everywhere entered work organizations in low-status, low-paid jobs, not for self-fulfillment but out of necessity

(Harris, 1981, p. 87). Statistics show no relationship between a country's percentage of women working outside the home per se and its degree of Femininity.

Only recently in history, and mainly in developed countries, have women in any numbers been sufficiently freed from other constraints to enter the worlds of work and politics as men's equals. In Chapter 1, I showed that there is more participation of women in technical and professional jobs in countries with smaller Power Distances (which tend to be the wealthy ones); there is even more if the country's culture is also feminine. Admitting women into these jobs previously taken by men means a sharing of power, which comes more easily in small PD countries;[6] it also means a redefinition of men's roles that comes more easily in feminine countries.

There is a very good case for the potential benefits to organizations of placing more women in management jobs. Kanter (1983, p. 281) has put it as follows:

> Clearly, decision makers, via their patterns of attention and inattention, intervene between a company and its environment. And this, of course, means that a company with a diverse group in the "dominant coalition" at the top . . . is more likely to pick up more external cues.

Etymologically, the root of the word "manage" is linked both with the French *manège* (place where horses are drilled) and *ménage* (household). *Manège* is the masculine element and *ménage* the feminine element in the management process. Classical American studies distinguish two dimensions in individual leadership: "initiating structure" and "consideration" (Fleishman, Harris, & Burtt, 1955) or concern for work and concern for people (Blake & Mouton, 1964); again, a masculine and a feminine element exist. Both are equally necessary for the success of an enterprise. Statham (1987), in an in-depth interview study of 22 female and 18 matched male U.S. managers and their secretaries, found that the women predominantly saw job and people orientation as interdependent, whereas the men opposed them.

Historically, management is an Anglo-Saxon concept, developed in masculine British and American cultures. In Britain, Mant (1979) and Roper (1994) have explicitly described the masculine bias in management that women have to overcome and that rewards those who most

TABLE 5.3   Percentage of Women in Management of National Subsidiaries
of Unilever, 1985

Countries in Order of MAS	Women as Percentage of All Managers
Austria	7
Italy	3
Switzerland	3
Ireland	4
Great Britain	5
Germany	3
Greece	10
Belgium	8
France	8
Spain	4
Portugal	8
Finland	15
Denmark	11
Netherlands	2
Sweden	13

SOURCE: Data are from Ford (1985, p. 16).
NOTE: Spearman rank correlation with PDI = −.09 and with MAS = .45*; without
Netherlands = −.74***.
*$p < .05$. ***$p < .001$.

behave like men. In the United States, a longitudinal survey study
published in the *Harvard Business Review* (Sutton & Moore, 1985) showed
that between 1965 and 1985, executive women had become an accepted
phenomenon, but the women who entered still saw resistance to their
progress and were, in fact, paid less than men in similar positions.
Jacobs (1992), on the basis of U.S. census data for 1969 and 1987,
concluded that over this period the gender gap in earnings among
managers had narrowed but that it still exceeded the gender gap in
earnings of the labor force as a whole. A gender gap in authority that
he was able to demonstrate, however, had remained constant. The
question is to what extent disadvantages for women in power also exist
in other countries with less masculine national cultures.

The large Dutch/British multinational Unilever published figures on
the percentage of women in the management ranks of its 15 European
subsidiaries (Ford, 1985, and Table 5.3). The percentages were nowhere

very high: The highest figure was 15%, in Finland; Sweden and Denmark came next.[7] Across these developed countries, the percentages of female managers did not correlate with PDI, nor with GNP per capita. The only significant correlation was with MAS (Spearman rho = −.45*).

The Netherlands, one of Unilever's two parent countries, in Table 5.3 scores exceptionally low, with only 2% female managers, whereas its low score on MAS would make one expect a high percentage (without the Netherlands, the correlation jumps to .74***). Other Dutch business companies at that time also had few women in management positions (Schieman, 1985). The extreme situation of the Netherlands was a temporary phenomenon caused by a unique demographic development. In other European countries, poverty forced women to enter paid employment in large numbers around 1915. Birthrates in these countries dropped drastically around this time. Mainly through its colonial trade, the Netherlands was more prosperous than other countries; it also traditionally had an effective welfare system for the poor. Most women, therefore, did not need to go out working, and birthrates remained high. Only around 1965 did the country follow the demographic drop of its European neighbors.[8] After that time, Dutch women did appear on the labor market in larger numbers, particularly looking for the more qualified jobs. In 1991, the labor force participation of women in the Netherlands in the age group 35-44 years already had climbed to 92%; only Denmark, Britain, Germany, and France scored higher (Eurobarometer, 1991, p. 41).

The aftereffect of the late arrival of women on the Dutch labor market is most noticeable in business, where promotion to the higher levels is a slow process, determined by the retirement of old men. Female managers have become more common in public organizations, where staffing policies react faster to changes in society.[9] The participation of women as students in higher education is around 50%, but they are still rare among the faculty. Women in the Netherlands are best represented in elected political offices: Elections in democracies are one of the most sensitive indicators of the mood of society. Table 5.4 shows that in its percentage of female parliamentarians and of government ministers, the Netherlands in 1995 came close to the equally feminine Nordic countries.

Across the 22 countries in Table 5.4, the percentages of both parliamentarians and ministers are primarily negatively correlated with the Uncertainty Avoidance Index (UAI). Uncertainty Avoidance stands for

TABLE 5.4   Percentage of Women in Parliaments and Governments of
Developed Countries, 1995

Countries in Order of MAS	Percentage of Women in Parliament	Percentage of Female Ministers
Japan	6.7	6.7
Austria	23.2	21.1
Italy	13.0	3.4
Switzerland	16.7	16.7
Ireland	12.8	18.2
Great Britain	7.8	9.1
Germany	25.5	16.0
United States	10.4	21.1
Australia	13.5	13.3
New Zealand	21.2	7.4
Greece	6.0	0.0
Canada	18.0	19.2
Belgium	15.4	10.5
Israel	9.2	13.0
France	5.9	6.5
Spain	14.6	15.0
Portugal	8.7	9.1
Finland	33.5	35.0
Denmark	33.0	30.4
Netherlands	28.4	26.3
Norway	39.4	40.9
Sweden	40.4	47.8

SOURCE: Data are from United Nations Development Project (1996, Tables 3 and 35).
NOTE: Spearman rank correlation with UAI = $-.48^*$ for percentage of women in parliament and
$-.62^{***}$ for percentage of female ministers. Spearman rank correlation with MAS = $-.44^*$ for
percentage of women in parliament and $-.45^*$ for percentage of female ministers. Multiple
correlation with UAI and MAS = $.61^{***}$ for percentage of women in parliament and $-.72^{***}$ for
percentage of female ministers.
$^*p < .05.$ $^{***}p < .001.$

"what is different, is dangerous," and from a traditional point of view,
women in politics are different. The second correlate is MAS, and MAS
and UAI together explain a considerable share of the differences in both
columns (37% of variance for parliament, 52% for ministers). Low
Uncertainty Avoidance, feminine countries are most likely to have a
strong representation of women in their government. As shown in
Chapter 1, the combination of low UAI and low MAS also differentiates

TABLE 5.5 Answers by Representative Samples From 15 Countries on Two Questions About Equal Opportunities

Countries in Order of MAS	Percentage Answering "Yes" to Question 1[a]	Percentage Answering "Yes" to Question 2[b]
Developed Countries		
Japan	23	79
Great Britain	28	93
Germany	18	94
United States	34	91
Canada	41	93
Taiwan	49	86
France	35	97
Spain	32	94
Less Developed Countries		
Mexico	71	98
Colombia	54	98
India	65	88
Panama	67	97
El Salvador	76	96
Thailand	80	91
Chile	34	96
Spearman rank correlations		
With GNP per capita	−.87***	−.29
With MAS (developed)	−.62[c]	−.01
With MAS (less developed)	−.02	.57

SOURCE: Data are from Burkholder, Moore, and Saad (1996, Tables 15 and 16).
a. Question 1: Do you think that women in this country have equal job opportunities with men, or not?
b. Question 2: Do you think that women in this country should have equal job opportunities with men, or not?
c. Significant at $p < .10$.
***$p < .001$.

Protestant from Catholic Christian countries. Catholic and Orthodox Christianity maintain a strong gender segregation in church leadership, but the data in Table 5.4 imply that there is also a strong negative relationship between these forms of Christianity and the admission of women into secular politics. I will come back to this in Chapter 12.

In 1996, the Gallup organization (public opinion research) published a report on gender issues, based on representative samples (at least 1,000 per country) of the adult population (aged 18 and over) of 22 countries around the world (Burkholder, Moore, & Saad, 1996). Fifteen countries overlapped with my IBM set. Two of the Gallup questions dealt with equal job opportunities for women and men; see Table 5.5.

In the table, I divided the countries into economically developed (1994 GNP per capita > $5,000) and less developed. Answers on Question 1, concerning actual equal job opportunities, are strongly determined by the level of economic development, and inversely from what one might expect: Poorer countries (all but Chile) rate job opportunities for women more equal. It is evident that in these countries, "job opportunities" are taken to refer to simple manual jobs. There is no overall correlation with MAS, but for the developed countries only, job opportunities are rated less unequal in feminine than in masculine countries. The correlation is only marginally significant, but data for the countries at the feminine end of the MAS scale (the Nordic countries and the Netherlands) were not available. On Question 2, whether job opportunities *should* be equal, answers are universally positive, and there is no significant relationship with wealth or MAS. In the case of gender-related job opportunities, practices differ more than ideologies.

These data confirm again that gender roles should always be seen in the context of economic development. Development limits the demand for women in low-paid labor, limits women's home tasks, and opens their educational possibilities. In Chapter 6, Best and Williams show that the affective meanings of gender stereotypes (measured on three dimensions of Osgood's Semantic Differential) presented a wider gender gap in poorer and less literate countries, and in those where fewer women attended university, than in more developed ones. The same was true for the affective meaning of men's and women's self-concepts. In the latter case, the gender gap was also correlated with the Power Distance Index (.78*** across 12 countries). In more developed countries and in those with smaller Power Distances, the burden of being a woman is rated lighter.

CAREERS AND FAMILIES

In Table 1.3, and also in Hoppe's discussion in Chapter 2, the Mas/Fem dimension was associated with, among other things, the contrast between "live in order to work" (masculine) and "work in order to live" (feminine). This contrast becomes operational, for example, in the pri-

TABLE 5.6 Answers by Business Executives From 10 European Countries to Two Questions About Career and Family Life

Countries in Order of MAS	Percentage Answering "Yes" to Question 1[a]	Percentage Answering "Yes" to Question 2[b]
Italy	72.1	55.4
Switzerland	43.4	49.0
Great Britain	66.2	56.0
Germany	44.2	53.2
Belgium	64.0	48.4
France	56.1	51.8
Spain	54.1	50.0
Denmark	44.1	28.0
Netherlands	36.9	43.8
Sweden	42.0	38.0
Spearman rank correlation with MAS	.60*	.73*
Spearman rank correlation with PDI	.53	.41
Multiple correlation with MAS and PDI	.74*	.79**

SOURCE: = Data are from Arbose (1980).
a. Question 1: Do you aspire to be the chief executive of a company? (base: respondents who are not yet chief executives, $n = 571$).
b. Question 2: To further your career, would you uproot your family now to move to a new location for a higher paying and more responsible job? (base: all respondents, $n = 930$).
*$p < .05$. **$p < .01$.

ority given to careers versus families. A survey study by the magazine *International Management* (Arbose, 1980), which I had overlooked earlier, asked questions about relationships between career and family to more than 900 male[10] business executives in 10 Western and Southern European countries. Table 5.6 shows the answer percentages by country on two questions.

Both the percentages of those indicating that they aspire to become chief executive and of those indicating preparedness to uproot their family on behalf of their career are significantly correlated with MAS. Adding the Power Distance Index (PDI) in both cases reinforces the correlation: It is the masculine, large Power Distance countries in which the power of being chief executive appeals most, and in which family considerations count least.

COUNTRY-LEVEL
GENDER STEREOTYPES

One aspect of the role division between women and men is gender stereotypes, that is, the characteristics believed to belong to one gender rather than the other. Another is self-descriptions according to these characteristics. Both will be dealt with by Best and Williams in Chapter 6. The relationship between gender stereotypes and national cultures is complex. In their first cross-national study, Williams and Best (1982) collected gender stereotypes among university students in 25 countries (50 men, 50 women per country), using the 300-item ACL (Gough and Heilbrun Adjective Checklist; Gough & Heilbrun, 1980). In Williams and Best (1990a), five more countries were added. Across 21 countries that participated in both studies,[11] Williams and Best found two variables correlating with my MAS scores beyond the .01 significance limit. One, referred to in Chapter 6, Table 6.3, is the *differentiation in the characteristics associated with the two sexes within each country*, which is significantly larger in feminine than in masculine countries ($r = -.56**$). This means that in countries scoring feminine in my studies, a larger share of the respondents associated adjectives from the Williams and Best list with one sex only than in countries scoring masculine. I have interpreted this as follows: In feminine countries, respondents do not feel inhibited in classifying an adjective as associated with men or with women, because this does not imply a positive or negative value judgment; women are as good or bad as men (Hofstede & Vunderink, 1994, p. 331).

This is confirmed in the second study to which Best and Williams refer in Chapter 6, published in Williams and Best (1990b). In this case, they collected actual and ideal self-descriptions of female and male students in 14 countries, using the same list of 300 adjectives as in the gender stereotypes project. These actual and ideal self-descriptions were then given a country Masculinity score by referring to the gender stereotypes for the given country found in the earlier Williams and Best studies; thus, each country was measured by its own standards for masculinity. Across 12 overlapping countries, Best and Williams found *the difference between the actual self-concepts of men and women* on their masculinity measures to be correlated $-.67**$ with MAS (Table 6.3). This means that in countries with higher MAS scores, female respondents scored their self-concepts more like men. In masculine societies, women used more masculine terms to describe themselves. In feminine societies, women again were differentiating their terms more from men's. There was no significant correlation with MAS for the differences in *ideal* self-concepts.

From a culturally masculine point of view, the fact that men and women use the same terms for their self-concepts is positive: It creates equality between the genders. From a culturally feminine point of view, the imposition of masculine terms for female self-concepts represents a violation of the freedom of women to be themselves. If the facts of life are that women and men experience their selves differently, then this should be acknowledged. The same cultural difference can be found in the dispute between two kinds of feminism already referred to in Chapter 1. In culturally masculine cultures, a "competitive" feminism prevails that wants to open to women all possibilities open to men. An example is Scarr (1996), who is opposed to pregnancy leave because it damages women's careers. This cultural environment also leads to an emphasis on "politically correct" language use with regard to gender. In culturally feminine cultures, a "complementary" feminism prevails that stresses the interdependence between male and female roles, and the contributions to society that women can make precisely because they are different from men.[12]

The other variable in Williams and Best (1990a) that relates to the Mas/Fem dimension (not referred to in Chapter 6) is the *typicality of the gender stereotypes when compared across countries*, calculated as a pooled index from three scores that measure the extent to which the stereotypes in a country differ from the average across all countries studied. It correlates .52** with MAS across 21 countries. The stereotypes recognized in the feminine countries are those associated with the male or female role worldwide, that is, those rooted in the basic human facts of life dictated by nature, such as women bearing children and men begetting them. The stereotypes recognized in the masculine countries are more country specific, that is, more arbitrary from a universal point of view.

Fioravanti, Gough, and Frère (1981) reported on a small study in which they gave the 300-item ACL in translation to 18 French, 51 Italian, and 28 U.S. male and female raters, and asked them to judge the desirability of the items for men and for women. In their article, they

TABLE 5.7   Social Desirability of Adjectives for a Man or for a Woman in
                 Three Countries/Languages

Social Desirability Score[a]	Country/Language		
	Italy (MAS = 70)	United States (MAS = 62)	France (MAS = 43)
Feminine			
For a man	1.6	2.9	3.2
For a woman	5.3	5.8	5.4
Weak			
For a man	2.1	2.0	2.3
For a woman	2.6	2.2	2.7
Gentle			
For a man	5.3	5.7	5.8
For a woman	6.0	6.4	6.2
Forceful			
For a man	5.5	5.2	5.2
For a woman	4.8	4.7	4.1

SOURCE: From Fioravanti, Gough, and Frère (1981).
NOTE: Raters: Italy, 25 men and 26 women; United States, 14 men and 14 women; France, 8 men and 10 women.
a. Social desirability rated on a scale from 1 = *very undesirable* to 7 = *very desirable*.

report the scores by country for four adjectives (out of 45 that showed significant gender differences). See Table 5.7, which is meant as a qualitative illustration rather than as statistical proof.

In France, the more feminine culture, "feminine" and "weak" for a man are less undesirable and "gentle" for a man is more desirable than for the other two countries. In the United States, it is more desirable for a woman to be "feminine" and "gentle" than in the other countries, but less desirable for her to be "weak." In Italy, to be "forceful" is more desirable for both genders than in the other countries.

In a journal article (Hofstede, 1996), I analyzed gender stereotypes among young women in eight Asian capital cities, using data collected by the Japanese market research agency Wacoal. Stereotypes found were very similar to those identified by Williams and Best, but they also differed between masculine and feminine cultures. The extent to which *sense of responsibility* was seen as a characteristic of men only rank correlated almost perfectly with MAS.[13] In the more masculine countries, *decisiveness, liveliness*, and *ambitiousness* were also more often seen as masculine, *caring* and *gentleness* more often as feminine. In the more feminine cultures, all these terms were seen as applying to both men and women.

The Gallup study on gender issues across 22 countries referred to earlier (Burkholder et al., 1996) also asked about gender stereotypes. There was more consensus across countries about the female than about the male stereotypes. In all countries, women were perceived as more *emotional, affectionate,* and *talkative* than men, both by women and by men. Women were rated as more *patient,* except by men in Thailand and by women in Panama and El Salvador. Men were seen as more *aggressive,* except by women in Thailand and by both genders in Iceland. Men were also seen as more *ambitious,* except by both genders in Spain and by women in Hungary. Men, finally, were rated more *courageous,* except by women in Chile, France, and Colombia. The exceptional stereotypes are mostly from women in countries scoring feminine on MAS,[14] supporting Williams and Best's finding of more differentiation in feminine countries.[15]

One of the practical consequences of gender stereotypes is that they determine what is considered healthy by mental health professionals. Broverman, Vogel, Broverman, Clarkson, and Rosenkrantz (1972, p. 71) argued that in the United States, the mental health profession maintains a double standard of health for men and women.

PREFERRED PARTNERS

Buss (1989, 1994) reports on a study of criteria for selecting a potential marriage partner, as scored by samples of young women and men (average age 23) in 37 countries. He found some characteristics to be universally desired: mutual love, kindness, emotional stability, intelligence, and health. Some others varied strongly across countries: chastity (no previous sexual experience), preferred age difference, wealth, industriousness, and good looks. Correlations of Buss's (1989) scores with my indices across 28 overlapping countries show a strong relationship with Ind/Col. In collectivist countries, bridegrooms prefer age differences at marriage to be larger, and they put more stress on the bride being industrious, wealthy, and chaste. Brides in collectivist countries also want their husband to be the right age and wealthy; his industriousness plays a smaller role and his chastity none at all. There were no relationships between either grooms' or brides' preferences and Mas/Fem.

The differences between grooms' and brides' desires, however, produced two significant correlations with MAS: for *chastity* and for *industriousness*. For chastity, the grooms-brides difference correlated significantly with both the Uncertainty Avoidance Index (rho = .49**) and with MAS (rho = .39*); the multiple correlation coefficient on UAI and MAS was $R = .61$***. The influence of Uncertainty Avoidance can be explained by the following quotation from Buss:

> We expected that men worldwide would value chastity, and would value it more than women. This is because of the differences between men and women in the certainty of their parenthood. Women are 100 percent certain that they are the mothers of their children. But men can never be exactly sure that they are the fathers. . . . Valuing chastity might have been one way that men could be "confident" that they were the fathers. We found that not all men feel that way. (Buss, 1994, p. 198)

In fact, the data show that this certainty is more highly valued in strongly uncertainty avoiding cultures. The fact that the difference is also larger in more masculine countries follows from the fact that roles and values of men and women differ more in masculine than in feminine societies.

The difference between industriousness of the partner as desired by grooms versus brides was only significantly correlated with MAS (rho = −.50***). The negative correlation means that in masculine countries, industriousness is deemed more important for women than for men; in feminine countries, it is equally important or unimportant for both.

My study of gender stereotypes among young women in eight Asian cities (Hofstede, 1996) also analyzed data about partner preferences. Preferences were asked for characteristics of husbands and also of steady boyfriends. There was an almost perfect rank correlation for the extent to which *personality* was looked for in a boyfriend rather than in a husband.[16] In the more masculine cultures, husbands also should be more *healthy, wealthy,* and *understanding*; boyfriends should not only have more personality but also show more *affection, intelligence,* and *sense of humor.* In the more feminine cultures, there was hardly any difference between the preferred characteristics of husbands and of boyfriends. If we see the boyfriend as the symbol of love and the husband as the symbol of family life, this means that in the masculine countries, love and family life are more often seen as separated, whereas in the feminine countries, they are expected to coincide. In the feminine countries, the husband is the boyfriend.

FAMILY SIZE

In *Culture's Consequences*, I showed that the relationship between MAS and population growth was *negative* for the wealthier countries and *positive* for the poorer ones. The feminine end of the scale is associated with slower population growth in poorer countries and faster population growth in wealthier countries. Population growth depends strongly on the average family size (and, of course, on the level of medical care); thus, femininity means smaller families in poorer countries and larger families in wealthier countries. This is precisely what we would expect in those cultures in which the woman has a say in the number of children she bears: She will adapt the family size to the available resources. Where male choice prevails in matters of family size, we find (too) large families in poor countries and small families in wealthy countries (Hofstede, 1980, p. 292; Hofstede, 1991, p. 105). Family planning programs falter on the attitudes of men (Adebayo, 1988). The United Nations fund for children, UNICEF, has published a graph (based on a study by Ken Hill of Johns Hopkins University) showing that if in all countries women could choose their number of children, they would have an average of 1.41 fewer children, which amounts to 1.3 billion fewer people in the world in 35 years' time (UNICEF, 1995, p. 29).

Mas/Fem differences may or may not contribute to what has become a dramatic problem for mainly Asian countries: the prevention or suppression of female births. In all of Asia, there are an estimated 100 million fewer births of females than would have been produced by normal birthrates (Emerson, 1995). The reason is the desire of parents to have sons rather than daughters, which can be achieved through availability of ultrasound scanning of the sex of a fetus followed by selective abortion, as well as the old practice of female infanticide. The female/male ratio in the population is higher in feminine cultures like

Thailand and Indonesia than in masculine cultures like India, Hong Kong, and China.[17] It is also high, however, in masculine Japan (which has a low birthrate for girls *and* boys) and low in Taiwan and South Korea, which scored below the mean on MAS. Specific historical factors that play a role are the Confucian obligation of carrying on the (male) family line, which is mitigated in Japan by the possibility of passing through a son-in-law, and the Indian dowry system, which makes daughters costly.

A SUMMARY TABLE

Table 5.8 summarizes the differences in gender-related norms and behaviors associated with feminine versus masculine national cultures.

OTHER CONTRIBUTIONS IN PART II

Two chapters in this part deal with macro studies across large numbers of countries; the other two deal with two-country in-depth comparisons.

In Chapter 6, Best and Williams summarize their two landmark cross-national studies in the areas of gender stereotypes and gender-related self-descriptions. They found no convergent validity between what was considered masculine or feminine and my Mas/Fem dimension of national cultures. There are relationships between their results and mine, but they are more complex. Best and Williams's attitude toward the usefulness of the Mas/Fem dimension in general is rather skeptical, although they admit that their studies and mine used different measures and described different phenomena.

Chapter 7 is Van de Vliert's study of competitiveness, self-rated by male and female students in 42 countries, to which I referred earlier in this chapter. He shows that overall levels of competitiveness do not directly relate to MAS. Competitiveness, therefore, is not the same as assertiveness. In the second part of Chapter 7, Van de Vliert goes on to test a hypothesized relationship between masculinity, temperature, and

TABLE 5.8 Differences in Gender-Related Values Associated With the
Masculinity/Femininity Dimension of National Cultures

Feminine Cultures	*Masculine Cultures*
Modesty norm	Assertiveness norm
Tender values	Tough values
Stress on who you are	Stress on what you are
Ego-effacing norm	Ego-boosting norm
Smaller gaps between the norms and values for women and men	Wider gaps between the norms and values for women and men
In developed countries, more women in management positions	In developed countries, fewer women in management positions
In developed countries, more women elected in parliaments	In developed countries, fewer women elected in parliaments
In developed countries, more female ministers in government	In developed countries, fewer female ministers in government
In developed countries, job opportunities for both genders rated as more equal	In developed countries, job opportunities for both genders rated as less equal
In developed countries, family affects career	In developed countries, career takes precedence over family
National gender stereotypes similar to universal gender stereotypes	National gender stereotypes specific to the country
More adjectives associated specifically with either women or men	Few adjectives associated specifically with either women or men
Women describe themselves in different terms from men	Women describe themselves in the same terms as men do
Senses of responsibility, decisiveness, liveliness, and ambition are also for women	Senses of responsibility, decisiveness, liveliness, and ambition are only for men
Caring and gentleness are also for men	Caring and gentleness are only for women
Women use the same criteria for husbands and boyfriends	Women want boyfriends who have personality, affection, intelligence, and sense of humor; and husbands who are healthy, wealthy, and understanding
Industriousness as important or unimportant for grooms as for brides	Men prefer industrious brides; women do not prefer industrious bridegrooms
Chastity as unimportant or important for both genders	Men prefer chaste brides; women do not prefer chaste bridegrooms
Woman has a say in the number of children she bears	Male choice prevails in matters of family size

violence, across 53 countries. He finds that both masculinity and violence are higher in moderately warm than in cold and very warm countries, which he explains by the competitiveness of fathers.

Van Rossum, in Chapter 8, gives evidence that the goals that 10-year-old children pursue in the games they play differ less between boys and girls in the Netherlands than in the United States, illustrating that the gender differentiation in child socialization is less in the first country than in the second.

Vunderink and Hofstede, in Chapter 9, show to what extent male and female students in their early twenties from the United States and from the Netherlands differed in their goals for an ideal future job. On the basis of in-depth interviews, they describe what kind of culture shock the Americans experienced when they went to study in the Netherlands for a semester.

NOTES

1. Authors on gender-related issues are often strongly ideologically and polemically motivated, and they often assume their own and their country's problems and solutions to be the world norm. An example is a contribution to a reader by Mills (1989, p. 42). Mills quotes part of a sentence from the 1984 abridged edition of *Culture's Consequences*, and, by truncating it, reverses its meaning. On the basis of this misquotation, he classifies me as one of those who "excludes gender from the dynamics of organizational experience and from the construction of organizational culture and human identities." He might have read the chapter from which he quotes.

2. Odom (1989) has published a theory that successful men and women worldwide were socialized by dominant mothers, rather than fathers. He developed a 2×2 typology of dominant/nondominant husband $\times$ dominant/nondominant wife that superficially resembles Figure 5.1. His analysis, however, in the American tradition is entirely at the level of individual personality (as well as highly speculative).

3. In the Danish version: *Du skal ikke tro . . . du er noget -du er ligeså meget som os—du er klogere end os—du er bedre end os—ved mere end os—er mere end os—at du du'r til noget. Du skal ikke le ad os. Du skal ikke tro . . . nogen bryder sig om dig—at du kan lære os noget.* From Aksel Sandemose (1933/1938). This translation is by the author, with thanks to Marieke de Mooij and Denise Daval Ohayv.

4. Based on an analysis across 10 countries; see Hofstede (1980, pp. 282-283; in the 1984 abridged edition, pp. 192-193).

5. As elsewhere in this book, significance levels are indicated as $*p < .05$, $**p < .01$, and $***p < .001$. One-tailed tests are used.

6. Kanter (1977, p. 266) has argued that "the problem of equality for women cannot be solved without structures that potentially benefit all organization members more broadly."

7. Even in the Nordic countries, the access of women to higher positions in companies meets with many traditional barriers (Billing & Alvesson, 1989).

8. I have labeled this the "Heine effect." German poet Heinrich Heine wrote in the early 19th century that when the world would come to an end, he would go to the Netherlands, because there everything happens 50 years later.

9. According to the Dutch newspaper *NRC/Handelsblad* (March 6, 1993), the number of female managers in Dutch public and not-for-profit organizations from 1987 to 1991 increased by 51%, in agriculture by 42%, and in service businesses by 26%, but in industry it remained constant. Because the service sector as a whole is growing at the expense of agriculture and industry, this further improves the opportunities for female managers in the Netherlands.

10. The survey report does not mention the gender distribution of the respondents; gender was not asked in the survey questionnaire. I assume the questionnaire has only been sent to male executives (this was 1980!).

11. From the 40 countries in *Culture's Consequences*, 25 overlapped with Williams and Best's 30 (Williams & Best, 1982, pp. 341-345). Their correlation calculations overlooked the scores in *Culture's Consequences* for Chile, South Africa, Taiwan, and Thailand.

12. In the 1960s, David McClelland pleaded for a new self-image for American women that came close to what I call "feminine feminism": avoiding thinking in categories defined by men (McClelland, 1965, p. 174). He reflects a minority opinion. See also McClelland's analysis of the Quaker culture with which he had come into contact as a young man (Hofstede, 1980, p. 266). The Quakers are a culturally feminine minority in the United States (see Chapter 12).

13. Spearman rank correlation .96*** across seven overlapping countries.

14. Panama, El Salvador, Thailand, Spain, Chile, and France. Only Colombia scored masculine; in Thailand and Spain, both genders agreed. MAS scores are not available for Iceland and Hungary.

15. Unfortunately, the term *responsible* (sense of responsibility), which differentiated most strongly between masculine and feminine cultures in the Wacoal study, was not included by Gallup.

16. Spearman rank correlation .94*** across seven countries.

17. The MAS score for China has been estimated at 66 (Hofstede, 1996, p. 543).

6

MASCULINITY AND FEMININITY IN THE SELF AND IDEAL SELF DESCRIPTIONS OF UNIVERSITY STUDENTS IN 14 COUNTRIES[1]

Deborah L. Best
John E. Williams

This chapter summarizes two large international research projects, one dealing with gender stereotypes across 25 countries and the second with masculinity and femininity in the self and ideal self descriptions of individuals across 14 countries. Both gender stereotypes and self/ideal self descriptions show similarities across countries as well as differences. In both studies, the cultural nature of the differences becomes evident only when the country results are scored for their affective meaning, on the dimensions of favorability, strength, and activity. Affective meaning differences tend to be larger in socioeconomically less developed countries; they were also positively correlated with Hofstede's Power Distance measure. Differences in gender stereotypes and in self-descriptions were unrelated to Hofstede's MAS scores, except that in countries high on MAS, both gender stereotypes and men's and women's self-descriptions were less differentiated than in countries lower on MAS.

INTRODUCTION

The twin concepts of masculinity and femininity appear in most, if not all, cultures. Moreover, a concern for what is manlike and woman-like in an individual seems an intrinsic component of the folk psychology of human societies. Such widespread popular use of the concepts of masculinity and femininity, and the social importance ascribed to them, have led psychologists to consider these concepts worthy of systematic study.

An examination of the popular conception of masculinity and femininity (M/F) suggests that it is predicated on two general propositions. First, certain attributes or characteristics are, or are believed to be, found more frequently in one gender or the other. These characteristics may be referred to as gender stereotypes. The second idea underlying the conception of masculinity and femininity is based on the observation that within each gender group there is substantial variation in attributes among individual persons. That is, all women are not alike, and neither are all men. The conception of M/F is thus based first on the establishment of what is manlike and womanlike and second on the assessment of the individual person's various attributes with regard to this classification.

To put this more formally, the scientific study of M/F as a characteristic of individuals requires (a) a method for the empirical definition of gender stereotypes, the characteristics believed to be differentially distributed among women and men; (b) a procedure for assessing the attributes of the individual person; and (c) a system for comparing the individual's attributes to the gender stereotypes. Using this approach, gender stereotypes serve as the criterion, or "yardstick," against which the masculinity or femininity of the individual person is assessed.

In the research we will present, we have taken this approach to the definition and assessment of masculinity and femininity. First, to determine what characteristics compose the gender stereotypes of men and women, we asked young adults to serve as "cultural reporters" and to identify traits that are differentially ascribed to men and women. Next, to assess the attributes of individuals, we asked young men and women to provide self and ideal self descriptions with the stereotype traits included among the traits that they could endorse. Third, we compared each self and ideal self description to the gender stereotypes identified earlier. Given this framework, each of the three steps in the process of studying masculinity and femininity will be described in more detail.

GENDER STEREOTYPE
DEFINITION STUDY

First, let us describe the gender stereotype study (Williams & Best, 1982, 1990a) that serves as the basis for the study of M/F. In this study, university students in different countries were presented with a list of 300 adjectives and were asked to indicate whether, in their culture, each adjective was more frequently associated with men, more frequently associated with women, or not differentially associated by gender. The adjectives employed were the item pool of the Gough and Heilbrun Adjective Checklist (ACL, Gough & Heilbrun, 1980), which included adjectives such as absent-minded, active, adaptable, adventurous, affected, affectionate, aggressive, alert, aloof, and ambitious. Subjects were approximately 100 university students evenly divided by gender in each of 25 countries. The items were presented in English when appropriate and in 1 of 12 other languages when necessary.

In each country, the data were tallied separately for male and female subjects to determine the frequency with which each adjective was associated with men and with women. Having determined that the responses of men and women subjects were highly similar, we pooled the data in each country for all subjects to determine the number of subjects associating each adjective with women and the number associating each with men. These frequencies were then converted to an M%

score, equal to %Mas/(%Mas + %Fem), in which %Mas is the percentage of respondents in a country associating this adjective with men and %Fem the percentage of respondents associating it with women. High M% values (over 67) therefore indicated items that were mainly associated with men, and low values (under 33) indicated items that were mainly associated with women. Scores in the mid-range (around 50) indicated items that were associated equally with men and women. In this manner, an array of 300 M% scores was obtained in each country.

The M% data were first analyzed for similarity between countries. We computed a correlation coefficient between each pair of the 25 countries across all 300 items. The resulting coefficients were all positive in sign, ranging from .35 for Pakistan versus Venezuela to .94 for Australia versus England. Thus, across all comparisons this analysis indicated varying degrees of similarity in the gender stereotypes in the different pairs of countries. When the correlation coefficients were squared to obtain an index of common variance (r^2), the mean common variance across all 25 countries was 42%, indicating a substantial degree of agreement concerning the psychological characteristics differentially associated with men and women.

The correlation and variance analyses just presented are quantitative measures and provide no sense of the varying *qualities* that are differentially associated with the male and female gender stereotypes. To address this, we identified in each country all items with M%s of 67 and higher and all items with M%s of 33 and lower, which were referred to, respectively, as the *focused male stereotype* items and the *focused female stereotype* items. These item sets were then compared using an affective meaning scoring system (Best, Williams, & Briggs, 1980; Williams & Best, 1977). This system, patterned after Osgood's three factors of affective meaning (Osgood, Suci, & Tannenbaum, 1957), scores adjective sets with regard to their mean favorability, strength, and activity. What we found is that, in all countries, the male stereotype items were more active and stronger, whereas the female stereotype items were more passive and weaker. It is interesting that there was no pancultural effect for favorability: The male stereotype was more favorable in certain countries (e.g., Japan, South Africa, Nigeria) and the female stereotype in others (e.g., Italy, Peru, Australia), with approximately equal numbers of countries in each group.

Although the general differences between the male and female stereotypes just discussed were clearly present in the data from all countries, there were variations between countries in terms of the *degree* to which a particular effect was observed. Some of these variations could be explained by relating them to variables from other sources indicating cultural differences.

It is a basic rule in cross-cultural research that observed differences between different cultural groups are not necessarily cultural in origin; they may also reflect error variance, such as inaccuracies in translation and differences in subject sampling. In keeping with this principle, our observed differences between countries in male and female stereotypes should not be considered cultural unless the observed differences correlate with significant cultural comparison variables. Consequently, our gender stereotype scores across the 25 countries were correlated with a variety of other indices, including economic-social development, religion (for example, percentage Christian and percentage Muslim), status of women (for example, percentage of women employed outside the home and percentage of women in the university), and general demographics (for example, percentage urban and geographic latitude).

No significant correlations were found between M% scores and these comparison variables, but when affective meaning scores were examined, several significant relationships emerged. For example, the magnitude of both the strength and activity differences between the male and female stereotypes was greater in socioeconomically less developed countries than in more developed countries. Strength and activity differences also tended to be greater in countries where literacy was low and the percentage of women attending university was low. These findings suggest that economic and educational advancement are accompanied by a reduction in the general tendency to view men as stronger and more active than women. We noticed, however, that the effect was merely reduced, not eliminated.

In sum, in the area of gender stereotypes the evidence for pancultural similarities greatly outweighs the evidence of cultural differences, but there is some variation in the gender stereotypes from country to country that can be attributed to cultural variables. This variation makes it necessary to define masculinity/femininity on a culture-specific basis.

MASCULINITY/FEMININITY STUDY

Having defined the male and female stereotypes in our first study, in our second study we focused on our next two tasks: assessing attributes of individuals and comparing them with the culturally defined gender stereotypes. In this study (Williams & Best, 1990b), we obtained descriptions of actual self and ideal self from young women and men in each of 14 countries. In each country, we scored the self descriptions for M/F by using the gender stereotype data that had been obtained in our earlier study in that country (Williams & Best, 1982, 1990a). This enabled us to use culture-specific or emic definitions of M/F, an approach that, to our knowledge, had never been used in a study involving this many countries.

Most previous cross-cultural studies of M/F had taken a scale developed in one country, often the United States, administered it to persons from one or more other countries, if necessary after translation, and compared the scores obtained by women and men. Such an imposed etic approach ignores the likely possibility that the definition of M/F differs by country and, thus, whatever scores are obtained cannot be considered a valid reflection of the masculinity or femininity of persons in those countries.

Data for the new study were collected in 14 countries: five Asian—India, Japan, Malaysia, Pakistan, and Singapore; five European—England, Finland, Germany, Italy, and the Netherlands; two North American—Canada and the United States; one African—Nigeria; and one South American—Venezuela. The number of subjects in each country ranged from a low of 70 in Pakistan to a high of 285 in Japan, with 100 subjects being typical in most countries; they were evenly divided between men and women.

In each country, the subjects were presented with the 300 items of the ACL, or their translated equivalents. For self-descriptions, subjects were asked "to describe yourself by selecting adjectives which you consider to be descriptive of yourself as you really are, not as you would like to be." After the subjects had completed this task, they were asked to describe their ideal self by "selecting adjectives that you consider to be descriptive of the person you would like to be, not the person you really are."

A total of eight different language versions of the ACL were employed in the study. In each case, the language version employed to obtain the self and ideal self descriptions was the same as that used in the earlier gender stereotype study in that country.

In each country, men's and women's self and ideal self concepts were scored for masculinity and femininity by employing the M% scores obtained for each of the 300 ACL items in that country in the earlier gender stereotype study. A mean M% was computed for the items that the subject checked as being descriptive of self and of ideal self. Higher mean M% scores would be indicative of relatively masculine self-concepts, and lower mean M% scores would be indicative of relatively feminine self-concepts, with mean M% scores around 50 indicative of self-concepts that are relatively balanced between masculinity and femininity.

An overview of the mean M% scores obtained for the self and ideal self concepts of the men and women can be seen by examining the *ranges* of M% scores obtained in the 14 countries. M% scores for the men's self-concepts ranged from a low of 48.3 to a high of 61.0, and women's self-concepts ranged from 43.8 to 57.6. For the ideal self, men's scores ranged from 51.4 to 64.9 and women's scores ranged from 48.9 to 61.3. All the scores cluster around the midpoint of the scale, indicating that there were no countries in which the self and ideal self concepts were extremely masculine or extremely feminine. For both self and ideal self, there is substantial overlap in the distributions of M/F scores of men's and women's self, indicating that the self-concepts of the two gender groups are not highly differentiated in this regard.

As expected, the men's self-concepts were generally more masculine than the women's self-concepts. More important, for both gender groups the ideal self was relatively more masculine than the actual self. It appears, therefore, that there is a general tendency for both men and women to wish to be more "masculine" than they are.

The self and ideal self concept M% scores for men and women in the different countries are presented in Table 6.1. The means are arranged from highest to lowest, that is, from the relatively most masculine to the relatively most feminine.

Examination of the distributions for the men's and women's self-descriptions, in columns 1 and 2 of the table, indicates that the mean M% scores were highest in Italy and lowest in Canada. The scores in

TABLE 6.1 Mean M% Scores: Group Means for Men (M) and Women (W) Arranged in Rank Order From Highest to Lowest

Self						Ideal Self					
M		*W*		*M – W*		*M*		*W*		*M – W*	
1		2		3		4		5		6	
ITA	61.0	ITA	57.6	NET	8.9	JPN	64.9	JPN	61.3	NIG	4.3
IND	55.7	IND	53.6	MAL	7.1	ITA	63.7	ITA	61.2	NET	4.3
NET	54.9	VEN	51.5	NIG	4.7	NET	58.4	IND	57.0	JPN	3.6
VEN	53.5	PAK	50.2	USA	4.7	IND	57.8	SIN	56.0	USA	3.4
MAL	53.3	ENG	49.5	CAN	4.5	SIN	57.5	MAL	55.2	FIN	2.7
PAK	52.7	SIN	48.9	FIN	3.5	MAL	57.3	NET	54.1	CAN	2.5
USA	52.7	GER	48.7	ITA	3.4	NIG	56.7	GER	53.6	ITA	2.5
SIN	52.1	FIN	48.3	SIN	3.2	GER	55.2	VEN	53.3	MAL	2.1
ENG	51.9	USA	48.0	GER	2.9	PAK	55.0	ENG	53.2	PAK	1.9
FIN	51.8	JPN	47.9	JPN	2.5	ENG	54.9	PAK	53.1	ENG	1.7
GER	51.6	NIG	46.6	PAK	2.5	VEN	54.3	NIG	52.4	GER	1.5
NIG	51.3	MAL	46.2	ENG	2.4	USA	53.9	FIN	50.9	SIN	1.5
JPN	50.4	NET	46.0	IND	2.1	FIN	53.6	USA	50.6	VEN	1.0
CAN	48.3	CAN	43.8	VEN	2.0	CAN	51.4	CAN	48.9	IND	0.8

columns 4 and 5 indicate that the ideal self of both men and women was highest in Japan and again lowest in Canada. Taken at face value, the four distributions indicate considerable cross-country variation in the relative masculinity or femininity of both the self and the ideal self concepts.

The men *minus* women difference scores in each country are presented in columns 3 and 6. All difference scores are positive in sign, reflecting, for both self and ideal self, our earlier observation of greater masculinity for men than for women. It is also interesting to note that there appears to be less average difference between the men and women for ideal self (column 6, mean = 2.41) than for the self (column 3, mean = 3.89); that is, the ideal selves of men and women appear somewhat more similar in terms of M/F than do their perceived selves.

A comparison of the rank orders of the countries seen in columns 1, 2, 4, and 5 indicates considerable similarity in the four arrays. This was confirmed by computing correlations between columns, shown in Table 6.2. These correlations indicate that in countries where men's self-concepts were relatively masculine, the women's also were, with a comparable finding for ideal self. In countries where the women's self-descriptions were relatively masculine, their ideal self descriptions also tended to be masculine, with a similar finding for men. In other words, men's and women's self-concepts were more likely to match, both being more

TABLE 6.2   Correlations Between Men's and Women's Self and Ideal Self
                M% Scores

Group Means of M% Scores	Columns	Correlation
Men's Self-Concept × Women's Self-Concept	1-2	.81**
Men's Ideal Self-Concept × Women's Ideal Self-Concept	4-5	.95**
Men's Self-Concept × Men's Ideal Self-Concept	1-4	.51
Women's Self-Concept × Women's Ideal Self-Concept	2-5	.59*

*$p < .05$. **$p < .01$.

masculine or both more feminine, rather than to be complementary,
such that if men's self-concepts were more masculine, women's would
be more feminine.

Using many of the same measures as in our gender stereotype study,
we examined the relationship between our M/F scores and other cultural
variables, such as measures of economic-social development and the
status of women. Similar to the findings with gender stereotypes, we
found no significant relationships between our M/F scores and these
cultural comparison variables. This does not mean, however, that there
was no cultural variation in the self-concepts of men and women
generally. When we scored the men's and women's self and ideal self
descriptions according to the affective meaning scoring system used in
the stereotype study, we did find significant correlations with cultural
variables.

Self-concepts were again evaluated in terms of their relative favorability, strength, and activity. Because of the pattern of differences
found in the stereotype study, we relied on the difference scores obtained between the men's and women's self-concepts on each of the
three affective meaning factors in this analysis. After considering the
degree to which the men's and women's self-concepts differed on each
of the three affective meaning factors considered separately, we developed a composite index of the degree to which the men's and women's
self-concepts in each country differed in terms of total affective meaning. This overall affective meaning difference score was found to be
related to a large number of cultural variables. Men's and women's
self-concepts tended to be less differentiated in terms of affective meaning in countries that are high in social-economic development, high in

the percentage of the population with a Christian religious preference, high in the percentage of women employed outside the home and in the percentage of women in the university population, and from the higher northern latitudes. Using Hofstede's (1980) work-related values as cultural comparison variables, a highly significant correlation of .78***[2] was found between Power Distance (PDI) scores and affective meaning difference scores, indicating that in large Power Distance countries the self-concepts of men and women tended to be more highly differentiated than in small Power Distance countries. The correlation between Hofstede's Masculinity (MAS) scores and the affective meaning difference scores was only .34, which was not statistically significant.

On the basis of the foregoing analyses, we concluded that when the self-concepts of men and women are evaluated in terms of the affective meaning scoring system, substantial evidence is found for genuine cultural variation. This contrasts with our observation that when the self-concepts of men and women are evaluated in terms of culture-specific definitions of masculinity and femininity, no evidence of true cultural variation was observed.

RELATIONSHIPS BETWEEN
M% AND MAS SCORES

We explored possible relationships between Hofstede's MAS scores and our measures of gender stereotyping and of M/F. Hofstede's MAS scores were available for 20 of the 25 countries in our gender stereotype study and for 12 of the 14 countries in our M/F study.[3] The intercorrelation coefficients are presented in Table 6.3. Nonsignificant correlations were obtained between the MAS scores and gender stereotypes, and between MAS scores and the M% of the self and ideal self concepts of men and women. The only noteworthy finding in Table 6.3 is that both gender stereotypes (variance of M%) and men's and women's actual self-concepts (M – W difference scores) are less differentiated on M/F in high MAS countries. Beyond this, the observed differences in gender stereotypes and in M/F in our studies were unrelated to Hofstede's MAS variable.

Two general conclusions can be offered from our research. First, no evidence was seen of convergent validity between our culturally spe-

TABLE 6.3   Correlations Between Hofstede's MAS Scores and Williams and
Best's M% Scores

	M% vs. MAS Scores
Gender stereotypes (across 20 countries)	
Total subjects	.09
M% variance	−.56**
Actual self-concept (across 12 countries)	
Men (M)	−.32
Women (W)	.28
M − W	−.67**
Ideal self-concept (across 12 countries)	
Men (M)	.35
Women (W)	.45
M − W	−.27

**p < .01.

cific definition of M/F and Hofstede's definition of masculinity. We
suspect that this may be related to the way the measures were derived
and the different phenomena being described. Research conducted by
other researchers in the United States has reached similar conclusions
concerning the lack of definitional clarity of the concepts of masculinity
and femininity (Marsh & Myers, 1986; Myers & Gonda, 1982; Spence,
1991). Our second conclusion is that the use of the concepts of masculinity and femininity in the study of men's and women's self-concepts
is not a particularly useful one. Men and women do differ in their
self-perceptions, but these differences are best approached by concepts
other than the overworked and often poorly defined concepts of masculinity and femininity.

NOTES

1. This is a slightly edited version of Best and Williams (1994). Reprinted with
permission of Swets & Zeitlinger, Publishers.

2. As in the other chapters, * stands for $p < .05$, ** for $p < .01$, and *** for $p < .001$.

3. Editor's note: My count is 21 overlapping countries for the gender stereotype
study and 13 for the M/F study—14 if Nigeria is equated with my West Africa. This
difference does not affect the conclusions. The correlation between actual self-concept
M − W and MAS across 14 countries is −.62**.

7

GENDER ROLE GAPS, COMPETITIVENESS, AND TEMPERATURE

Evert Van de Vliert

This chapter consists of two parts. The first part relates Hofstede's Masculinity/Femininity (Mas/Fem) dimension to Lynn's data on competitiveness, self-rated by women and men in 42 countries. It turns out that the dimension is significantly related to the ratio between men's and women's competitiveness scores.

The second part shows a curvilinear relationship between ambient temperature and Mas/Fem. Masculinity mediates the curvilinear relationship between ambient temperature and domestic political violence; this can be explained by the Paternal Investment Theory.

PART I: GENDER GAP,
COMPETITIVENESS, AND MASCULINITY

The Dual Nature of the Mas/Fem Dimension

Hofstede (1980, 1991) based his Mas/Fem construct on the following two closely knit empirical observations. First, systematic variation exists in the gap between the work goals of men and women in different countries. In the countries labeled "masculine," gaps tend to be wider, and this is because gender roles in these countries are more distinct: Males are supposed to fulfill "ego" roles and females to fulfill "social" roles; in "feminine" countries, male and female roles show more overlap. Second, the combined responses of men and women across countries reflect a dimension opposing competitiveness to cooperativeness. In "masculine" countries, male and female inhabitants are more competitive, assertive, and ambitious; in "feminine" countries, male and female inhabitants are more cooperative, modest, and nurturing. As a consequence of this dual origin, masculinity constitutes a rather complicated conceptual domain that allows differences in emphasis (see Figure 5.2 for a graphical illustration).

Gaps Between Gender Roles

Hofstede has shown in his books, as well as in Chapter 5, that a country's position on the Mas/Fem dimension is reflected in the roles of women and of men in society, but only after a certain level of economic development has been reached. Sullivan (1991, p. 290) published a Gender Gap Index (GGI) based on 20 indicators of male-female inequality in the areas of political and economic discrimination, marriage status, level of education, and employment situation. Across 53 countries, Sullivan's index is correlated with economic development, but not with Hofstede's Masculinity Index MAS.[1] Across the 27 wealthier countries (1988 GNP per capita > US$2,470), however, the correlation between GGI and MAS becomes a significant .38*.[2]

Lynn (see below) collected data on the preferences of male and female students for a number of occupations, among them "company director" and "small business owner" (predominantly chosen by males) and "social worker" (predominantly chosen by females). Across 32 countries, male/female gaps in these preferences are not correlated with MAS, neither for relatively wealthy nor for relatively poor countries.[3]

Overall Competitiveness

Hofstede did not have an explicit measure of competitiveness. One "general belief" item in his IBM database is "competition between employees usually does more harm than good," but this was related to Uncertainty Avoidance, not to MAS (Hofstede, 1980, p. 412). Lynn (1991) published an international study on values possibly related to economic development. His respondents were university students, at least 150 males and 150 females in each of 42 countries. Lynn's questionnaire included an existing American "competitiveness" scale (Spence & Helmreich, 1983). It consists of the following five items: "I enjoy working in situations involving competition with others," "It is important to me to perform better than others on a task," "I feel that winning is important in both work and games," "It annoys me when other people perform better than I do," and "I try harder when I'm in competition with other people." This scale is not ideal for a cross-cultural instrument: It was developed inside the United States for comparisons at the individual level and expresses a U.S. emic conception of competitiveness, it is based on self-descriptions, and all five items are scored in the same direction, which makes it sensitive to response set. It did, however, produce a large database.

We transformed the country mean scores of male and female students on Spence and Helmreich's competitiveness scale into two aggregate scores with the help of a recently developed procedure.[4] For each nation separately, the means for males and females were marked off on the Y-axis and X-axis of a coordinate system, respectively, resulting in a triangle (see Figure 7.1). The length of the hypotenuse of that triangle, calculated by applying the Pythagorean theorem, was then used as an index of overall competitiveness: The national degree of competitiveness is the square root of the sum of squared male and squared female means. The scores range from highest in Arab countries (Egypt, Iraq, Jordan, Syria, United Arab Emirates) and the Indian subcontinent (Bangladesh, India) to lowest in European countries (France, Germany, Norway, Spain, Sweden, Switzerland; see Table 7.1). Across 32 countries,

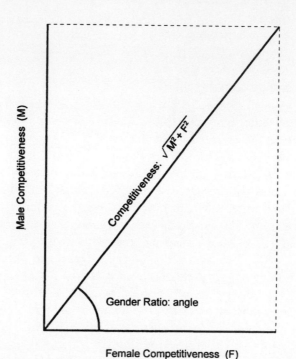

Figure 7.1. National Competitiveness (Hypotenuse) and the Ratio Between Male and Female Competitiveness (Angle).

this competitiveness index is unrelated to MAS but is significantly correlated with Power Distance and Individualism.[5]

Male-Female Ratio of Competitiveness

The gender ratio in competitiveness is represented by the angle in Figure 7.1.[6] An angle of 45° means equal competitiveness for men and women; a smaller angle means more competitiveness for women, and a larger angle means more competitiveness for men. Angles found ranged from 41.0° in Norway (women more competitive) to 51.4° in Germany (see Table 7.1). The overall mean is 46.7°.

Across all 32 overlapping countries, both wealthy and poor, gender ratio angles are significantly correlated with Hofstede's MAS index:

TABLE 7.1   Overall Competitiveness Index (OCI) and Gender Ratio of
Competitiveness Index (GRCI) for 42 Countries

Country	OCI[a]	GRCI[b]
1. Argentina	12.06	48.87
2. Australia	16.15	46.13
3. Bangladesh	20.16	46.25
4. Belgium	15.24	48.83
5. Brazil	15.80	47.13
6. Bulgaria	17.44	43.21
7. Canada	17.09	50.46
8. Chile	16.32	44.95
9. China	17.50	47.57
10. Colombia	18.36	47.30
11. Egypt	22.14	45.90
12. France	14.41	46.43
13. Germany	12.94	51.43
14. Great Britain	15.08	48.95
15. Greece	19.55	45.73
16. Hong Kong	17.88	44.41
17. Iceland	18.42	49.31
18. India	20.49	46.86
19. Iraq	19.86	43.45
20. Ireland	15.57	48.44
21. Israel	16.45	50.11
22. Japan	17.28	47.25
23. Jordan	20.89	46.40
24. Korea	19.31	44.06
25. Mexico	19.55	46.68
26. New Zealand	15.74	46.93
27. Norway	13.61	40.95
28. Poland	16.98	46.86
29. Portugal	16.89	45.29
30. Romania	19.34	44.98
31. Singapore	16.09	45.63
32. South Africa	17.68	47.27
33. Spain	14.79	47.30
34. Sweden	12.80	46.52
35. Switzerland	12.74	48.50
36. Syria	19.84	44.35
37. Taiwan	18.94	47.12
38. Turkey	18.07	45.61
39. United Arab Emirates	20.29	45.30
40. United States	18.08	49.01
41. Venezuela	15.54	45.99
42. Yugoslavia	15.90	47.98

a. OCI = square root of the sum of squared male competitiveness and squared female
competitiveness.
b. GRCI = arctan of the ratio male/female competitiveness multiplied by $180/\pi$ to obtain the
angle in degrees.

$r = .44^{**}$ (23 wealthy countries: $r = .43^*$; 9 poor countries: $r = .70^*$). Gender ratio angles are weakly negatively correlated with the competitiveness index computed from the same data (see above; across 42 countries $r = -.31^*$). It is interesting that certain Asian countries including Bangladesh, India, Iraq, and the United Arab Emirates are characterized by strong overall competitiveness rather than high male/female competitiveness ratios, whereas certain Western countries including Canada, Germany, Iceland, and Ireland are characterized by the opposite combination (see Table 7.1).

Discussion

Our analysis of Sullivan's Gender Gap Index scores has shown that the reduction of gender gaps within societies is mainly a function of economic development. Only for the wealthier countries does the influence of MAS become visible: A wealthy, feminine culture further reduces the gender gap. Competitiveness in societies as measured by the Spence-Helmreich scale does not correlate with MAS but does correlate positively with Power Distance and negatively with Individualism. The gender ratio (male/female self-ratings) for this competitiveness, however, is significantly positively related to MAS, and this applies across all countries studied, both wealthy and poor. In some feminine countries, women score themselves as more competitive than men do.

PART II: TEMPERATURE, VIOLENCE, AND MAS/FEM

Mas/Fem differences evolved and did not appear out of the blue. There are arguments in favor of the assumption that a country's position on the Mas/Fem dimension may well be a hidden function of ambient temperature (see Van de Vliert, Schwartz, Huismans, Hofstede, & Daan, in press). Compared to other potential antecedents of masculinity, ambient temperature is of special interest because the direction of causality is unequivocal: Temperature must be a cause; it cannot be an effect.

Using geographical latitude as a crude measure of climate, Hofstede observed that warmer countries tend to be less individualist, show larger Power Distances, and are somewhat more masculine. The relationship between latitude and masculinity becomes much stronger if one controls for national wealth (considering wealthy and poor countries separately; Hofstede, 1980, pp. 330-331). Hofstede submitted the explanation that "in more moderate climates, survival presupposes the mastery of complex skills by both men and women, which makes extreme inequality between the sexes unlikely" (Hofstede, 1980, p. 292). This intriguing finding has two limitations. First, in this early work, a number of African and South American countries with hot climates were not included because of small respondent samples (Hofstede, 1983). Second, curvilinear relationships were not considered. In particular, warm countries were not contrasted with both cold and hot countries. These empirical restrictions will be remedied after a theoretical introduction.

Theoretical Viewpoints

In line with Hofstede's (1980) perspective and data, some theories (e.g., Anderson & Anderson, 1996; Nisbett & Cohen, 1996; Peterson & Smith, 1997; Van de Vliert & Van Yperen, 1996) also hold that ambient temperature shapes the cultural software of the mind, which in its turn shapes human behavior. Particularly salient in the present context is the Paternal Investment Theory (e.g., Coltrane, 1988; Endicott, 1992; Katz & Konnor, 1981; Kenrick, 1994; Miller, 1994). This theory can be presented in the form of the following three postulates: a trade-off proposition, a climate proposition, and a behavioral proposition.

Trade-off Proposition

From the perspective of evolution and reproductive success, males more than females have a trade-off possibility between investing time and effort in providing for a single family, and investing in fertilizing multiple partners to increase offspring. The choice men make is partly dependent on climatological circumstances.

Climate Proposition

In cooler climates with a prolonged winter, meeting basic needs for food, safety, and security is much more demanding, which promotes intense parental care for the family. Warmer climates that permit easy survival, in contrast, encourage different reproductive behavior by men and women, namely male investment in mate-seeking and leaving many children with multiple wives, versus female investment in provisioning and child rearing. Cross-disciplinary evidence confirms that the optimal balance shifts from monogamy and a more caring and sharing role as a husband and father in cooler climates, toward polygamy and low concern for wives and offspring in warmer climates (Kenrick, 1994; Miller, 1994; Woodburn, 1988). Note that the climate proposition leaves aside extremely hot climates that might, just like cooler climates, be more demanding, evoking relatively high parental investment in the family.

Behavioral Proposition

In cooler climates, parental investment in the family requires sacrifice, delay of gratification, and cooperative or at least nonviolent behavior by both men and women (Bjorklund & Kipp, 1996; Woodburn, 1988). In contrast, male investment in mate seeking in warmer climates allows immediate gratification and requires contentious behavior against male rivals and (initially) resisting females. This supports more "masculine" cultures manifested by male domination versus female submission in warmer regions (Galtung, 1996; Miller, 1994). According to the Paternal Investment Theory, remnants of stronger masculinity in warmer climates can be observed in modern men and women. Scattered support for the connection between ambient temperature and male versus female contentiousness was recently brought together by Galtung (1996) in an attempt to provide a more solid scientific underpinning for the ill-founded relation between male sexuality and male-based violence (see also Mesquida & Wiener, 1996).

In sum, the Paternal Investment Theory explains why, over many generations, warmer climates supported stronger masculinity. The next section confirms, refines, and extends the proposed temperature-masculinity relationship.

Temperature-Violence Studies

Ambient temperature is related not only to masculinity but also to individual and collective aggression (e.g., Anderson, 1989; Anderson &

Anderson, 1996; Goldstein, 1994; Rotton, 1986). A clear manifestation of aggression at the national level of analysis is domestic political violence. In a 51-nation study, Schwartz (1968) found that, from 1948 to 1964, the frequency of coups, assassinations, terrorism, guerrilla wars, and revolts covaried with mean annual temperature in a curvilinear way. Such violent events occurred more frequently in warm countries (mean daytime temperature 24°C, 76°F) than in cold (17°C, 62°F) and hot (30°C, 86°F) countries.

We replicated this study, using as the dependent variable the number of political riots and armed attacks against and by the government in 136 countries between 1948 and 1977 (for a detailed report, see Van de Vliert, et al., in press). Again, temperature showed a curvilinear relationship with violence, with the inflection point at a mean daytime temperature of 24°C (76°F). Political riots and armed attacks occurred more frequently in warm countries than in both cold and hot countries, even after effects of population size and density, and levels of socioeconomic development and democracy, were controlled. Replications of the analysis for each of two 15-year periods (1948-1962; 1963-1977) separately, and for the northern and southern hemispheres separately, yielded basically the same results. Furthermore, after excluding the 36 largest countries, to avoid large within-country variation in ambient temperature, we still obtained the same pattern of findings.

Obvious subsequent questions are the following: How can this curvilinear shape of the robust temperature-violence link be explained? Does cultural masculinity mediate the relationship?

Theoretical Refinement

Some anthropological reports suggest a refinement of the Paternal Investment Theory that connects ambient temperature, reproductive strategy, and cultural masculinity, as discussed above. The linear temperature-masculinity association may actually be curvilinear if human populations from very hot countries are included. Notably, among the extraordinary peaceful Aka pygmies in the Central African Republic, fathers provide more direct infant care than fathers in any other known society, and they keep up extremely cooperative relationships with their wives and children (Hewlett, 1992). The Batek who live in the tropical jungle of Kelantan, Malaysia, are renowned both for their peaceful

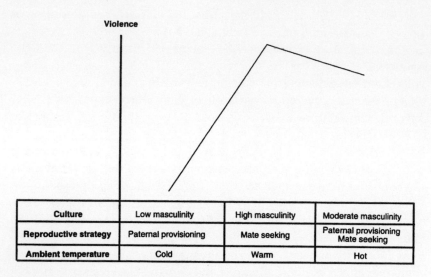

Figure 7.2. Theoretical Links Between Ambient Temperature, Reproductive Strategy, Cultural Masculinity, and Violence.

nature and for the fact that no one has power over others through economic, religious, or social advantage (Endicott, 1992). Like survival in cold climates, offspring survival in very hot climates appears to require paternal care to protect the family against the hardships of nature and to prevent shortages of water and food.

Such data support the assumption that ambient temperature could be related to *both* cultural masculinity *and* violence in the tent-shaped manner represented in Figure 7.2 (the left upward and right downward slopes in the diagram are based on the temperature-violence data from 136 countries). As will be reported next, we found empirical support for this assumption.

Empirical Verification

Hofstede (1980, pp. 150, 328) found four indicators of domestic political violence to be related to Power Distance, but not to masculinity. Recall, however, that his early empirical work did not highlight hot climates. In addition, he did not consider that the levels of masculinity and domestic political violence in hot countries might be related in a curvilinear fashion, such that hot countries might have more in common with cold than with warm countries. This made it especially interesting to test the model in Figure 7.2 (see Van de Vliert, et al., in press).

All 53 countries were included for which MAS scores are available from Hofstede (1991); the scores for Hofstede's regions of Arab countries, West Africa, and East Africa were assigned to Egypt, Nigeria, and Zambia, respectively. The average daytime temperature of each country's capital city (Garver, Payne, & Canby, 1990) was chosen as the indicator of ambient temperature. As in the preceding 136-nation study, the annual numbers of political riots and armed attacks between 1948 and 1977 (Taylor & Jodice, 1983) were additively combined into a reliable indicator of domestic political violence.

Population size and density, plus levels of socioeconomic development and democracy, predicted 53% of the variance in violence. Over and above this set of control variables, temperature accounted for an additional 6% of the variance in violence. As expected, in this subsample of countries, violence occurred more in warm than in cold and hot countries ($\beta = -.25^*$). Power Distance scores showed a linear correlation with temperature of $.65^{***}$, but without a curvilinear component, so it could not play a role in explaining the tent-shaped association between temperature and violence. We next examined whether cultural masculinity mediated the temperature-violence association by analyzing the temperature-MAS, MAS-violence, and temperature-MAS-violence relations, in this order. Temperature predicted 13% of the variance in MAS. In support of our inferences from the Paternal Investment Theory, warm countries, compared with cold and hot ones, tend to have cultures characterized by relatively high MAS ($\beta = -.42^*$). The inflection point of the curvilinear temperature-MAS association occurred at a mean daytime temperature of 23°C (74°F). In turn, MAS added 5% to the prediction of the variance in violence, over and above the control variables ($\beta = .23^*$). When temperature was then entered, it no longer made an independent contribution to the prediction of violence.

Discussion

These findings are compatible with the view, presented above, that cultural masculinity mediates the tent-shaped association between temperature and violence, represented in Figure 7.2. Several alternative explanatory variables that might have rendered this causal path spurious can be dismissed on empirical grounds: Population size and density, levels of socioeconomic development and democracy, and Power Distance did not account for the temperature-masculinity-violence link.

Several arguments provide additional support for the proposition that ambient temperature is not accidentally related to the culturally programmed tendency of a country's male inhabitants to manifest masculinity and to use violence. First, both masculinity and political violence are associated with temperature despite the restriction of range in the temperature dimension. Extremely cold countries such as Mongolia and Iceland (mean daytime temperature 6°C; 43°F), and extremely hot countries such as Sudan, Niger, Chad, Mali, and Upper Volta (36°C; 97°F) could not be included in the subsample because their MAS scores were not available. Second, the complexity of the combination of a curvilinear temperature-masculinity link, a linear masculinity-violence link, and a curvilinear temperature-violence link that disappears if masculinity is controlled, reduces the probability that these findings are attributable to chance. Third, the temperature-masculinity and temperature-violence associations have similar inflection points (23°C and 24°C, respectively). This is unlikely to be a coincidence. All in all, the findings lend plausibility to the reasoning underlying the temperature-masculinity-violence model outlined above and portrayed in Figure 7.2.

CONCLUSION

This chapter enriches our understanding of the Mas/Fem dimension of national culture in at least four regards. First, across all countries studied, MAS reflects more competitiveness of men and less competitiveness of women rather than more general differences in gender roles or in overall competitiveness. Second, there are theoretical and empirical reasons to believe that, over many generations, in countries with warm climates more masculine cultures have evolved than in colder and hotter countries. Third, countries with warm climates have also fostered more violent cultures than colder and hotter countries. Fourth, masculinity appears to account for the fact that domestic political violence occurs more frequently in countries with warm climates than in colder and hotter countries.

Taken together, these four conclusions suggest that temperature-related violence is a function of larger male-female gaps in competitiveness. It makes sense that men in countries with warm climates, compared to men in colder and hotter countries, expect and accept more violence. Women in these societies are socialized toward more submissive and docile behavior. Men try to bend not only women but also other men to their will. Violent actions also serve to impress women and win their sexual favors. In these societies, emancipation of women serves the promotion of peace.

NOTES

1. Unpublished manuscript by Van de Vliert, Nauta, and Huismans (n.d.). The correlation between Sullivan's reversed coded Gender Gap Index (GGI) and wealth (1988 GNP per capita) across 60 countries is highly significant ($r = .56^{***}$), whereas the correlation between GGI and MAS across 51 countries is a nonsignificant $-.11$. It is interesting to also document that GGI across 51 countries is significantly related to PDI ($r = -.54^{***}$) and IDV ($r = .59^{***}$), but not to UAI ($r = -.16$).

2. As in the other chapters, * stands for $p < .05$, ** for $p < .01$, and *** for $p < .001$. Actually, the correlation is $-.38$, but GGI is scored in reverse.

3. Van de Vliert, Kluwer, and Lynn (1998). Across 32 countries, correlations between MAS and male-female differences in occupational preferences are .04 for company director, .00 for small business owner, and $-.10$ for social worker. The correlations are not increased by controlling for wealth.

4. Van de Vliert, Kluwer, and Lynn (1998). The procedure is described in Van der Togt and Van de Vliert (1998).

5. The correlation with PDI is $r = .49^{**}$ and with IDV $r = .41^{*}$.

6. The angle was computed from the arctan of the ratio male/female competitiveness by multiplying it by $180/\pi$.

8

WHY CHILDREN PLAY

American Versus Dutch Boys and Girls[1]

Jacques H. A. Van Rossum

Children spend large amounts of their free time playing games. Girls usually choose different games than boys do. An investigation of the types of goals children pursue in the games they play showed that American girls and boys differed in the importance they attach to performance goals, relationship goals, and avoidance goals. Using a translated questionnaire, such gender differences were not obtained with Dutch children. These results fit with Hofstede's findings about differences in values in the United States and the Netherlands.

INTRODUCTION

School-aged children spend lots of time playing games. Children differ in the amount of time they spend playing, as well as in the games

130

TABLE 8.1 Games Preferences of Dutch Children[a]

	Grade		
	1	3	5
Dressing up	80	63	44
Playing school	75	68	33
Playing doctors and nurses	73	55	29
Playing with dolls	58	52	29
Playing with construction set	13	36	40
Doing handstands	12	52	48
Jumping rope	52	73	64
Climbing	83	78	73

SOURCE: Data are from Van Rossum and Timmer (1985).
NOTE: $n = 249$.
a. Percentage of children who claimed to prefer the activity (results shown separately for each of the grades involved in the study).

they prefer. Interindividual differences in games preferences are often described in terms of gender. Children's games preferences have a long tradition of being used for measuring their masculinity or femininity. Rosenberg and Sutton-Smith (1959) updated the Terman and Miles (1936) attitude interest test for this purpose. This "Play and Game List" (Sutton-Smith & Rosenberg, 1959) has been used in a series of investigations (Rosenberg & Sutton-Smith, 1960, 1964; Rosenberg, Sutton-Smith, & Morgan, 1961; Sutton-Smith & Rosenberg, 1960, 1961; Sutton-Smith, Rosenberg, & Morgan, 1963); it is an easy way to take stock of the games preferences of school-aged children. An adaptation of the original list was compiled for use in the Netherlands (Van Rossum & Timmer, 1985). Some results obtained with the Dutch adaptation of the list are presented in Tables 8.1 and 8.2.

Table 8.1 shows that the attractiveness of games changes with the age of the child (approximately 7 for Grade 1, 9 for Grade 3, and 11 for Grade 5). Most games are equally attractive to girls and boys (Van Rossum & Timmer, 1985). There is a limited category of gender-typed, stable girls' or stable boys' games (Table 8.2).

While such investigations of the games played and preferred by children of different age and/or gender might offer interesting information on, for example, the amount of differentiation between children, it sketches individual differences only at a superficial level. Children

TABLE 8.2   Games Preferences of Dutch Children[a]

Girls	Boys
Ballet dancing	BMX racing
Jumping rope	Shooting with catapult or pop gun
Sewing	Playing with bows and arrows
Knitting	
Embroidery	

SOURCE: Data are from Van Rossum and Timmer (1985).
NOTE: $n = 249$.
a. Gender typed games at grade levels 1, 3, and 5.

might be attracted to games for different reasons, or, in other words, have different goals while playing games. The same game may have different meanings or offer different options to different children. Such goal orientations have been described by Asher and colleagues (Parkhurst & Asher, 1985; Renshaw & Asher, 1983; Taylor & Asher, 1984, 1985) in the context of social interactions between children. It is their assumption that individual differences in social competence are caused by differences in goal orientation (i.e., what children want to obtain from social interactions). Some goals might simply be inappropriate for the social situation at hand. Taylor and Asher (1985) distinguish four different goal orientations for peer interaction:

1. enhancement of one's own outcomes (*performance* goal orientation): "wants to win, to be the best, to be the leader, to beat others";

2. initiation and maintenance of positive interactions and relationships with peers (social *relationship* goal orientation): "wants to play with other children, to get along well, to have fun";

3. avoidance of negative outcomes or negative interactions and relationships with peers (*avoidance* goal orientation): "worries about not being liked, being not good enough, being left out, being teased, being clumsy"; and

4. making sure that the game is played by the rules (*rule* goal orientation): "make sure others don't cheat, play by the rules, play fair."

The four approaches to peer interaction have been operationalized in the Goals Orientation Questionnaire (Taylor & Asher, 1984). Significant gender differences in goals orientations in U.S. children are reported by

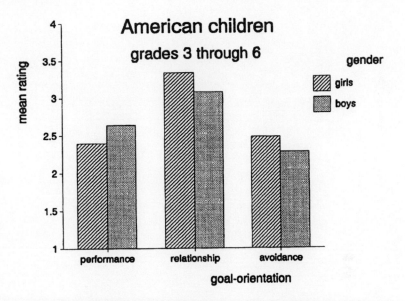

Figure 8.1. Mean Scores of American Primary School Children, Ages 9-12, on Scales of Goals Orientation Questionnaire.

SOURCE: Data are from Taylor and Asher (1985).

Asher and colleagues (e.g., Taylor & Asher, 1985): Boys rate performance goals higher than do girls, and girls obtain higher scores on both the relationship scale and the avoidance scale; no gender differences are reported on the rule scale. Taylor and Asher reported their results in summary fashion for more than 500 American children (see Figure 8.1). All gender differences shown were highly statistically significant.

The questions asked in the present study were the following: Do Dutch children recognize these goals too, and do Dutch boys and girls differ in goals in ways similar to those of American children?

METHOD

Children of Grades 5 and 6 of three primary schools (age 11-12; $n =$ 129, 76 boys and 53 girls) filled in the Dutch version of the Goals Orientation Questionnaire as well as a shortened version of the Dutch

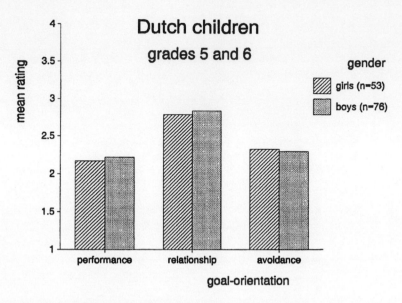

Figure 8.2. Mean Scores of Dutch Primary School Children, Ages 11-12, on Scales of Goals Orientation Questionnaire.

adaptation of the Play and Games List. The Goals Orientation Questionnaire consists of 50 items, in Likert scale format; each item has to be answered on a 4-point scale, ranging from 1 = *not at all important* to 4 = *very important*. As in the original U.S. version, the performance scale consists of 17 items, the relationship scale of 15, the avoidance scale of 13, and the rule scale of 5 items.

The full Dutch adaptation of the Play and Games List consists of 218 items, of which 147 were also part of the original U.S. list of 180. For the present study, only those items have been selected that refer to outdoor games and games in which gross motor skills are needed. Board games (such as Game-of-Goose, Monopoly, and chess), memory and card games (such as Master-Mind and Beggar-My-Neighbor), and fine motor activities (such as Mikado, tiddledywinks, sewing, and embroidery) were excluded. The shortened list consists of 98 items. For each item or activity, three questions have to be answered: Do you know it? (yes/no), Do you play it? (yes/no), and Do you play it nearly every day? (yes/no).

RESULTS

An item analysis performed on the Goals Orientation Questionnaire data showed adequate values of Cronbach's alpha (measuring the reliability of the scale in terms of its internal consistency) for the performance scale (.77), for the relationship scale (.74), and for the avoidance scale (.79), but not for the rules scale. To investigate the effects of grade and gender, analyses of variance (ANOVAs) were performed separately for each of the three remaining scales. On the performance scale, no significant effects were found: No differences were found between grades nor between genders (all $ps > .05$). The same applied to the relationship and avoidance scales. These Dutch boys and girls were highly similar in their rating of goals. Figure 8.2 depicts the mean scores of both genders on each of the three scales.

CONCLUSIONS

The gender differences found in U.S. samples by Asher and colleagues were not replicated in our Dutch samples. Girls and boys in the Netherlands do not appear to value performance, relationship, or avoidance orientation differently. That is, Dutch boys do not appear to attach more importance to winning a game, or to being the best or being the leader, than do Dutch girls. Similarly, Dutch girls do not rate the initiation and maintenance of positive interactions and relationships with peers higher than Dutch boys do, nor do they envisage the avoidance of negative outcomes or negative interactions and relationships with peers to be of more importance. Dutch girls and boys are thus much more alike in their goal orientations than U.S. girls and boys. This finding was essentially replicated in a further study by this author in which 139 Dutch children (56 boys and 83 girls) participated: Again no gender differences were obtained on each of the three scales of the Goals Orientation Questionnaire ($ps > .05$).

Before any interpretation is undertaken in terms of differences between the cultural groups to which the children studied belong (that is, addressing the "external validity"), options regarding the "internal validity" of the investigation should be carefully taken into consideration. Two such options are briefly discussed here: the acquiescence notion and the notion of gender (or psychological) categorization of children. A third option, qualities of the translated questionnaire, does not seem to be of interest, given the results of the item analysis.

Hofstede (1980, p. 77ff) warns against the influence of acquiescence (the tendency to give a positive answer to any question, regardless of its content), which might produce differences between groups in their tendency to rate things. The absolute importance scores of girls and boys should therefore be compared in the present study, to prevent easy, and possibly false, interpretations. The mean importance score over all 45 items (excluding the rule scale) of girls (n = 53) and boys (n = 76) were: 2.44 (SD = .26) and 2.46 (SD = .28); these means are not statistically different (p > .05). The results obtained cannot, therefore, be attributed to a general difference between Dutch girls and boys in rating things as important.

A second option is to check whether, within the present data set, subgroups of children can be selected that are homogeneous on their games preference. In the analysis of the data reported above, boys and girls were distinguished on the basis of their biological sex. It is well known that among the subgroup of biological boys, large differences exist. On one extreme are masculine boys ("real" boys) and on the other are feminine boys ("sissies"). A similar distinction holds for girls. It has been documented (e.g., Sutton-Smith, 1971) that such subgroups are easily identified through their play and games preferences. The Play and Games List has in fact been employed as a measurement tool for masculinity/femininity in psychological and anthropological research (Schwartzman, 1978). The shortened Dutch version of the Play and Games List was used (see the section on method) to obtain individual scores on two sets of activities: those that had been chosen by the children as boys' games and those that had been chosen as girls' games. Those children who preferred nearly all items of one set, while disregarding items of the other set, could be said to compose the subgroup of masculine and feminine children, respectively. These two groups are thus distinguished on a psychological instead of a biological criterion. Within the group of 129, subgroups of 18 masculine children (all boys) and 19 feminine children (18 girls, 1 boy) could be identified.

Separate one-way ANOVAs were performed on the data of the three Goals Orientation scales. Again, no significant differences were found

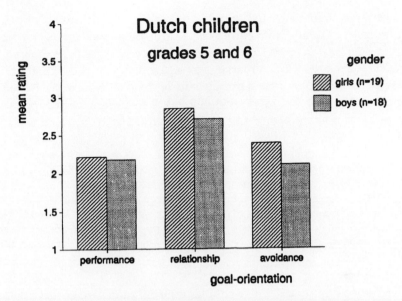

Figure 8.3. Mean Scores of Two Subgroups of the Sample of Dutch Primary School Children, Ages 11-12, on Scales of Goals Orientation Questionnaire.

NOTE: The group of feminine children are indicated as "girls," and the group of masculine children as "boys."

between the two groups (this time, between feminine and masculine children) on the performance scale, on the relationship scale, or on the avoidance scale ($ps > .05$). The mean scores of the two subgroups on each of the scales are presented in Figure 8.3.

The earlier results and those obtained in the further analysis are therefore completely in agreement: No differences exist between Dutch girls and boys in the importance they attach to performance goals, relationship goals, and avoidance goals, even if the biological criterion is exchanged for a more sophisticated psychological one. These findings indicate that Dutch children differ from U.S. children: Dutch children do not show the gender differences in value orientations found in U.S. children.

The interpretation of these findings appears to be a reflection of cultural value differences between the United States and the Netherlands. Hofstede (1980, 1991) has shown that the two countries are similar on the dimensions of Power Distance, Individualism/Collectivism, and

Uncertainty Avoidance, but widely different on the dimension of Masculinity/Femininity. Hofstede's U.S. sample scored well above average on this dimension (rank 15 out of 53 countries and regions; see Table 1.2 in Chapter 1), reflecting a masculine culture, whereas the Netherlands was ranked 51st, near the feminine end of the continuum and close to Sweden, Norway, Denmark, and Finland. This difference is supposed to reflect dominant patterns of socialization ("mental programming") in nations, where

> Masculinity pertains to societies in which social gender roles are clearly distinct (i.e., men are supposed to be assertive, tough, and focused on material success whereas women are supposed to be more modest, tender, and concerned with the quality of life); Femininity pertains to societies in which social gender roles overlap (i.e., both men and women are supposed to be modest, tender, and concerned with the quality of life). (Hofstede, 1991, pp. 82-83).

The findings presented in this chapter are easily interpreted as supportive of the difference on the Masculinity/Femininity dimension between the United States and the Netherlands: Differences in goals orientation found between U.S. girls and boys were not replicated with Dutch girls and boys. It should also be mentioned, however, that in both the U.S. and the Dutch studies (Figures 8.1 and 8.2), children on average scored higher on the relationship scale than on the performance or avoidance scales, suggesting that in both cultures their socialization favored social relationship goals above those of performance or avoidance.

It might not come as a surprise that differences between nations at the level of adults (as found by Hofstede, 1980, 1991) are already present in children. Children's play has been identified by researchers and theorists of children's play "as a vehicle for the learning and practicing of culturally appropriate sex roles" (Schwartzman, 1978, p. 111; see also Roberts & Sutton-Smith, 1971). This chapter has reported findings showing the differences between two nations in this socialization function of play. The child is the father of the man, and the mother of the woman.

NOTE

1. This is an edited version of Van Rossum (1996). Reprinted with permission.

9

FEMININITY SHOCK

American Students in the Netherlands[1]

Mieke Vunderink
Geert Hofstede

Successive groups of students from U.S. universities attended a one-semester program at a university in the Netherlands. In a survey of work goals for an ideal job, these Americans scored "earnings" and "advancement" as relatively important; matched Dutch students scored "freedom" and "being consulted by one's boss" as more important. Within both national groups, "earnings" and "advancement" were considered less important by women than by men. These findings are illustrated with interview quotations collected by the first author during a intensive qualitative study within one particular group of the Americans.

A COMPARISON OF WORK GOALS

Successive groups of junior (third-year) business administration students from the universities of Connecticut and Indiana in the United States attended a semester-long Program in European Studies at the Center for European Studies of Maastricht University, the Netherlands (Vunderink, 1992). In the context of a class in intercultural communication, we administered to them a questionnaire about their goals for an ideal job after graduation. We did the same with a matched population of Dutch business administration students at the same university. Table 9.1 shows the questionnaire.

The 22 items in the questionnaire include the 14 used in Hofstede's IBM studies, from which the country scores on the Individualism/Collectivism (Ind/Col) and Masculinity/Femininity (Mas/Fem) dimensions were derived (Table 1.1 and Hofstede, 1980, p. 239). The questionnaire was answered in 1989 and 1990 by four groups of U.S. students at Maastricht, a total of 89 respondents, 48 men and 41 women. Dutch business administration students completed the same questionnaire during regular classroom sessions in 1989 and 1990. Virtually all Dutch students can read English, but we wanted to test the effect of the questionnaire language on the answers. The pile from which the questionnaires were handed out to the Dutch students therefore contained alternating English and Dutch versions. In this way, the language in which the questionnaire was answered by the Dutch students was randomized.

In 1989, 71 English language and 77 Dutch language questionnaires were collected. The rankings of the 22 goals in the two language versions were strongly but not perfectly correlated (Spearman rho = .84***).[2] It was evident that the words chosen for the Dutch translation had in some cases carried a different emotional meaning to the respondents from the English words. In 1990, the experiment was repeated with an improved Dutch translation for six items. In that year, 58 English language and 48 Dutch language questionnaires were collected. The rankings of the goals in the two language versions had become more similar (rho = .92***); however, the overall mean scores for the two language versions still differed. The overall means were 2.50 for the Dutch version and 2.26

TABLE 9.1 Questionnaire for Students

This is an anonymous questionnaire, but we would like to know whether you are:
(1) a woman or (2) a man (please circle).

Imagine the job you would like to get after graduation. In choosing an ideal job,
how important would it be to you to (please circle one answer in each line across):

1 = of utmost importance
2 = very important
3 = of moderate importance
4 = of little importance
5 = of very little or no importance

1.	have sufficient time left for your personal or family life	1	2	3	4	5
2.	have challenging tasks to do, from which you can get a personal sense of achievement	1	2	3	4	5
3.	have little tension and stress on the job	1	2	3	4	5
4.	have good physical working conditions (good ventilation and lighting, adequate work space, etc.)	1	2	3	4	5
5.	have a good working relationship with your direct superior	1	2	3	4	5
6.	have security of employment	1	2	3	4	5
7.	have considerable freedom to adopt your own approach to the job	1	2	3	4	5
8.	work with people who cooperate well with one another	1	2	3	4	5
9.	be consulted by your direct superior in his/her decisions	1	2	3	4	5
10.	make a real contribution to the success of your company or organization	1	2	3	4	5
11.	have an opportunity for high earnings	1	2	3	4	5
12.	serve your country	1	2	3	4	5
13.	live in an area desirable to you and your family	1	2	3	4	5
14.	have an opportunity for advancement to higher level jobs	1	2	3	4	5
15.	have an element of variety and adventure in the job	1	2	3	4	5
16.	work in a prestigious, successful company or organization	1	2	3	4	5
17.	have an opportunity for helping other people	1	2	3	4	5
18.	work in a well-defined job situation where the requirements are clear	1	2	3	4	5
19.	have training opportunities (to improve your skills or learn new skills)	1	2	3	4	5
20.	have good fringe benefits (material advantages other than cash salary)	1	2	3	4	5
21.	get the recognition you deserve when you do a good job	1	2	3	4	5
22.	fully use your skills and abilities on the job	1	2	3	4	5

for the English version.[3] The Dutch students differentiated less between items on a 1-5 scale when answering in English.

For the comparison between the values of the Dutch and U.S. students, only the English language questionnaires have been used; they yielded the most conservative estimate for the national differences.[4] The total number of Dutch students who completed an English language questionnaire was 129: 102 male and 27 female.

Table 9.2 shows the overall comparison between the American and the Dutch students' mean scores on the 22 goals. The genders were more evenly represented in the U.S. group than in the Dutch group (U.S., 46% female, Dutch 21%). This difference has been controlled for by using as the country scores: (m + f)/2, the average between the mean scores of each country's males and females.

The bottom lines in Table 9.2 show that Americans scored an overall mean across all 22 goals of 2.02, and Dutch of 2.32. Americans therefore tended to score *everything* as more important than the Dutch did.[5] This is a response set that has to be controlled for; we eliminated it by standardizing across the 22 goals (Hofstede, 1980, pp. 77-80).

The Americans scored the following goals as relatively more important: earnings, advancement, and benefits. Marginally more important were serving their country, living in a desirable area, a good working relationship with their boss, and security of employment. The Dutch scored the following as relatively more important: freedom on the job, being consulted by their boss, and training opportunities. Marginally more important were making a real contribution to the success of their company, fully using their skills and abilities, and helping others.

In Table 9.3, standard scores are presented separately for men and women from the two countries. Consistent gender effects (male-female score difference of at least .05 points in the same direction in both countries) are found for some items. More important for men in both countries (with items in italics differentiating American from Dutch students) are *earnings, advancement, prestigious company,* and *benefits.* More important for women in both countries are having little tension and stress, an element of variety and adventure, a well-defined job situation where the requirements are clear, *fully using skills and abilities, security, helping others,* and good cooperation.

TABLE 9.2 Overall Comparison Between the Work Goal Importance Scores of American and Dutch Students

Work Goal	American (m + f)/2			Dutch (m + f)/2			Difference Standard Scores	
	Mean	Standard Score[a]	Rank	Mean	Standard Score[a]	Rank	US+	NL+
Advancement (14)[b]	1.45	−1.27	1	1.99	−.59	8	.68*	
Superior (5)	1.51	−1.14	2	1.92	−.71	5	.43§	
Challenge (2)	1.56	−1.03	3	1.82	−.88	4		
Variety (15)	1.64	−.86	4	1.78	−.95	2		
Cooperation (8)	1.66	−.81	5	1.79	−.94	3		
Conditions (4)	1.73	−.65	7	2.04	−.50	10		
Private time (1)	1.73	−.65	7	2.12	−.36	12		
Earnings (11)	1.73	−.65	7	2.46	.24	16	.89**	
Use skills (22)	1.77	−.54	9.5	1.76	−.98	1		.44§
Living area (13)	1.77	−.54	9.5	2.27	−.10	14	.44§	
Recognition (21)	1.87	−.33	11	2.00	−.57	9		
Security (6)	1.90	−.26	12	2.41	.15	15	.41§	
Contribute (10)	1.92	−.21	13	1.94	−.68	6.5		.47§
Benefits (20)	2.03	.03	14	2.66	.59	17	.56*	
Freedom (7)	2.08	.14	15	1.94	−.68	6.5		.82**
Training (19)	2.13	.26	16	2.08	−.42	11		.68*
Consulted (9)	2.22	.47	17	2.16	−.28	13		.75**
Company (16)	.50	1.09	18	2.79	.77	19		
Helping (17)	2.51	1.11	19	2.71	.67	18		.44§
Clarity (18)	2.66	1.46	20	3.19	1.53	20		
Stress-free (3)	2.83	1.83	21	3.30	1.71	21		
Serve country (12)	3.13	2.52	22	4.03	2.99	22	.47§	
Overall mean	2.02			2.32				
Standard deviation	.44			.57				

a. Scores range from 1 = *of utmost importance* to 5 = *of very little or no importance*.
b. Numbers in parentheses refer to the questions in Table 9.1.
For differences in standard scores, §*p* < .10, *p < .05, and **p < .01. The significance is based on a difference of means test, one-tailed, assuming equal group sizes of 54 (2 × the number of Dutch women) and a standard deviation of item scores within groups of .80 (this is the median value for all standard deviations found), taking account of the transformation of scores in the standardization process. The limits are § = .38, * = .52, and ** = .72.

TABLE 9.3 Work Goal Importance Standard Scores for American Versus Dutch Students According to Gender

Work Goal	American		Dutch		Gender Effect Consistent
	Male	Female	Male	Female	
Advancement (14)[a]	−1.34	−1.16	−.88	**−.32**	m+
Superior (5)	−1.13	−1.11	−.59	−.80	
Challenge (2)	−1.09	−.95	−.88	−.87	
Earnings (11)	−.81	−.46	−.16	**.60**	m+
Cooperation (8)	−.76	−.84	−.86	−.99	f+
Variety (15)	**−.58**	−1.11	−.88	−.99	f+
Private time (1)	−.44	**−.84**	−.47	−.26	
Use skills (22)	−.44	−.62	−.81	−1.11	f+
Living area (13)	−.44	−.62	−.40	**.17**	
Contribute (10)	−.44	**.03**	−.59	−.74	
Conditions (4)	−.39	**−.89**	−.63	−.37	
Recognition (21)	−.35	−.30	−.37	−.74	
Freedom (7)	−.30	**.57**	−.59	−.74	
Security (6)	−.16	−.35	.27	.05	f+
Benefits (20)	−.02	.08	.51	.65	m+
Training (19)	.16	.35	−.39	−.44	
Consulted (9)	.30	.63	−.11	−.44	
Company (16)	1.04	1.11	.61	.90	m+
Helping (17)	1.13	1.06	.81	.53	f+
Clarity (18)	1.55	1.33	**1.72**	1.32	f+
Stress-free (3)	**2.11**	1.49	1.76	1.63	f+
Serve country (12)	2.38	2.58	2.95	2.96	
For raw scores:					
Overall mean	2.09	1.94	2.34	2.31	
Standard deviation	.45	.45	.55	.61	

NOTE: Bold type indicates remarkably different scores. In the last column, gender effects have been marked as consistent if the male-female difference in standard scores is in the same direction in both countries and measures at least .05 points.
a. Scores range from 1 = *of utmost importance* to 5 = *of very little or no importance*.
b. Numbers in parentheses refer to the questions in Table 9.1.

The Americans (both men and women) tended to score more often in the direction of the men, the Dutch (men and women) more often in the direction of the women (except for "security," which was preferred by the women and by the Americans more than by the Dutch). The average of the absolute differences (i.e., differences regardless of their + or −

TABLE 9.4 Individualism and Masculinity Index Scores

	United States	*Netherlands*	*Difference*
IDV (students)	30	27	3
IDV (IBM)	91	80	11
MAS (students)	62	16	46
MAS (IBM)	62	14	48
	Male	*Female*	*Difference*
MAS (U.S. students)	69	54	15
MAS (Dutch students)	39	−11	50

sign) between the standardized scores of male and female Americans in Table 9.3 is .27, and that between male and female Dutch, .26.

INDIVIDUALISM AND MASCULINITY
SCORES FOR BOTH NATIONALITIES

The student data allow computation of country scores for Ind/Col and Mas/Fem, using the approximation formulas in the VSM 82 (Hofstede, 1982a). See Table 9.4.

The absolute IDV scores for the students are at another level (the student samples differ in many respects from Hofstede's IBM populations), but the difference between the United States and the Netherlands, or rather the lack of difference, is upheld. For Masculinity, the student scores are virtually identical to the IBM scores. This similarity should be considered as accidental; the consistency of the *difference* between the countries (48 versus 46) is what counts.

The lower part of Table 9.4 tests whether MAS scores by gender follow the expected pattern of a widening gap between the sexes for a more masculine country (Hofstede, 1991, p. 83). In both cases, men score as more masculine than women. Also, American women students score as more masculine than Dutch men. The gap between men's and women's scores in the Dutch data, however, is not smaller but larger than in the U.S. data. This is because the MAS Index scores are partly based on the importances of "advancement" and "earnings," for which Table 9.3 shows particularly large gaps between males and females in the Dutch sample. These gaps are a manifestation of the "Heine effect" (see Chapter 5, note 8), a delay in the entry of Dutch women into the business world that is also visible in the low percentage of women in the Dutch student samples in 1989 and 1990. It is a transitional phenomenon. Compare the position of the Netherlands in Tables 5.3 and 5.4.

IN-DEPTH INTERVIEWS

During the spring term of 1990, the first author studied one group of American students qualitatively. She attended parts of their program and social events and interviewed them extensively at the beginning and at the end of their stay. In addition, she administered a questionnaire developed for evaluating the learning process of American students abroad (Carlson & Widaman, 1988; for results, see Vunderink, 1992). For comparison purposes, she also interviewed 12 Dutch students, some of whom had spent an academic year studying in the United States. The information collected in her in-depth interviews represents the qualitative part of our study.

One of the obvious differences between the United States and the Netherlands is the latter's welfare system. Most American students at first considered the Dutch tax system—which makes the Dutch welfare system possible—as almost criminal. It robbed the Dutch of the opportunity to fulfill the goal of becoming rich. That Dutch people could have a different set of values, expressed in a willingness to pay higher taxes to maintain a welfare state, was hard for the Americans to understand.

Another area of differences consists of attitudes toward caring. One day, while talking about the United States with a group of students, the interviewer asked how they felt about the poorer part of the population in their country. One of them answered, "I don't know, that is not my world." Only the interviewer seemed shocked by that remark; none of the Americans present took issue with it. A Dutch student making the same remark would be condemned by others for insensitivity and selfishness, because caring for other people is one of the dominant values in Dutch society.

A related issue that came up especially at the end of the Americans' stay was what they saw as the relative lack of stress in the Netherlands. Several of the interviewees said that they had never been so relaxed, and that the Netherlands as a whole was a much more easygoing society than the United States. The women appreciated this aspect of Dutch society more easily than the men. In Table 9.3, a lack of stress was scored as extremely unimportant to the American male students but relatively more important to the American women. For the Dutch students, there was hardly any gender difference. American men feel they have to be tough and able to cope with as much stress as it takes to reach the top, but this applies less to the women. As Table 9.3 shows, the American women also attach a much greater importance than the men to having good physical working conditions and sufficient time for personal or family life, issues on which the Dutch again show smaller gender differences.

In the interviews, both the Dutch and the American students were asked to list the characteristics of a person they would regard highly. Most of the American students answered "someone who makes a lot of money, someone who has made it in his profession." Integrity, honesty, and using abilities to the fullest, whatever they are, were often mentioned by the Dutch and rarely by the Americans. Making a lot of money was rarely included in the Dutch list. This tallies with the questionnaire results about the goals for an ideal job (Table 9.2) showing that the greater importance of "an opportunity for high earnings" is what most distinguishes the answers by the Americans from those by the Dutch, where "fully use your skills and abilities on the job" is the most important goal for the Dutch.

The same difference is shown in the remark made by an accompanying American professor after he had interviewed a number of Dutch students for a place at the university of Indiana. He was surprised to find that the Dutch students did not have a clear picture of their future careers. At that age (around 22), Dutch students tend still to be working out what their personal skills and abilities are, who they are, and where they will fit in the society. They like to do well, but they do not aspire to be the best. They have not planned their careers in detail, as quite a few of the Americans have. The American students interviewed often remarked that in the Netherlands, people spent much more time in introspection than in the United States.

In Chapter 1, Table 1.2 of this book, it is suggested that failing in school is a minor accident in a feminine culture but a disaster in a masculine one. To be the best was very important to the American students. The student who is at the top of the class is a winner, and everybody wants to be associated with him or her. In the Netherlands, a student's position in class will not contribute to his or her social attractiveness. This tallies with another item from Table 1.2, the contrast between a modesty norm and an ambition norm.

DISCUSSION

The United States and the Netherlands score fairly close on four of Hofstede's (1991) five indexes of national culture; only on Masculinity is there a wide gap. The United States is among the top third most masculine countries, the Netherlands among the least masculine. We can therefore expect that adaptation problems of Americans in the Netherlands or of Dutch persons in the United States will be focused on the issues related to this dimension, like those summarized in Table 1.3.

Both the questionnaire study and the interviews show considerable differences in values between American and Dutch students. One could argue that the groups were not perfectly matched, because the Americans had opted to go overseas and were surveyed there, whereas the Dutch were surveyed in their home country. The Americans might thus represent a more enterprising sample. On the other hand, virtually all Dutch students have traveled abroad at that age; compared to the average American student, Dutch students are more cosmopolitan. It is unlikely, therefore, that this situational factor could have accounted for the value differences found.

The questionnaire study revealed that for the American students, earnings, advancement, and benefits were much more important goals in their ideal future jobs than for the Dutch. The first two are immediately related to the Masculinity dimension. Freedom, being consulted by their direct superior, and training were the goals on which the Dutch students scored much higher than the Americans. From these, "training" for a student is associated with another goal, "use of skills," which is also more frequently endorsed by the Dutch. In the interviews, the importance of using one's skills is related to the question "who you are," whereas the stress on material gain concerns the question "what you are." This distinction can be added as a new connotation to the Mas/Fem dimension: It expresses a nonmaterial versus a material view of the quality of life.

In the interviews the word "freedom" was frequently used, but with very different connotations between the two national cultures. The Dutch wanted to enjoy their freedom on the job; the Americans wanted a free market economy. Whereas the different connotations are particularly clear in this case, we suggest that in general, cultural differences lead to the same (or equivalent) words receiving different connotations. Words are symbols for which emotional meaning is culturally determined. "Money" as a symbol also has a very different emotional meaning in U.S. society than in Dutch society.

The importance of being consulted by one's direct superior in the Netherlands has been stressed in an eminent book by French anthropologist Philippe d'Iribarne (1989). He compared subsidiaries of the same French multinational corporation in France, the United States, and the Netherlands. He identified a different base philosophy (*logique*) in the three countries, rooted in centuries of history of each: honor in France, contractual relations in the United States, and consensus in the Netherlands. This distinction goes beyond the Mas/Fem dimension; it belongs to the idiosyncrasies of each society, to that part of the variance in cultures not explainable by any worldwide dimensions—although consensus seeking can be seen as a feminine way of settling disputes (Table 1.3). The American view of the working relationship as a contractual relationship explains the relative unimportance of freedom on the job and of being consulted by the boss, but "having a good working relationship with your direct superior" is scored as more important by the Americans than by the Dutch, showing that even within the contract, some dependence on the boss remains—if only his or her influence on one's further career.

The split of work goals according to gender (Table 9.3) proves that some of the key goals on which females and males differ (in both countries) also distinguish Americans and Dutch as national groups (regardless of gender): earnings, advancement, and benefits, as opposed to use of skills and helping others. In all these cases, the Americans' scores are closer to the men's scores and the Dutch scores are closer to the women's scores. This justifies the conclusion that the dimension on which the two countries primarily differ can be called "masculine" versus "feminine."

The scores for the two student groups on the Ind/Col and Mas/Fem dimensions showed that, as in the IBM studies, the Americans scored as slightly more individualist than the Dutch, but considerably more masculine. Female American students scored as more masculine than male Dutch students. A prediction that did not come true was that the gap in Masculinity scores between the genders would be larger in the United States than in the Netherlands, because of the low interest of the Dutch women in "advancement" and "earnings"—which we believe is shifting to a less extreme position.

This chapter has illustrated both quantitatively and qualitatively that American and Dutch students showed considerable value differences that could not be attributed to more Individualism on the American side but was clearly explained by a large distance on the Mas/Fem dimension.

NOTES

1. This is a slightly edited version of Hofstede and Vunderink (1994).
2. As in the other chapters, * stands for $p < .05$, ** for $p < .01$, and *** for $p < .001$.
3. The difference of the mean scores between the Dutch and the English language version, tested with the t test, is significant at $p = .05$, one-tailed.
4. The Spearman rank correlation between the U.S. and the Dutch student scores was .82*** for the English version and .80*** for the improved Dutch version.
5. The difference between the overall means for U.S. versus Dutch students, tested with the t test, is significant at $p = .05$, two-tailed.

PART III

CULTURE, SEXUALITY, AND RELIGION

10

COMPARATIVE STUDIES
OF SEXUAL BEHAVIOR

Sex as Achievement
or as Relationship?

Geert Hofstede

This chapter draws on existing comparative research to show that even sexual behavior is culturally constructed, and some of it relates to the national culture dimension of Masculinity/Femininity (Mas/Fem). Masculine cultures are less open about sexual issues than feminine ones. The sexual revolution in the United States in the 1950s may have had more impact in some other countries than in the United States itself. In feminine countries, marriage is less holy and partners are less dependent on each other. The concepts of sex and love are closer together. It is more accepted that women take an active role during sexual intercourse. Parenthood is more positively valued in feminine than in masculine cultures, and the well-being of children plays a more important

153

role in the parents' ways of arranging their lives. Abortion, contraception, masturbation, and homosexuality are more taboo in masculine than in feminine cultures. Teenage pregnancies in industrialized countries occur most in countries that combine weak Uncertainty Avoidance with Masculinity. Sex in masculine cultures is more felt as an achievement, in feminine cultures as a relationship.

THE CULTURAL CONSTRUCTION
OF SEXUALITY

Dear Ann Landers,

A 16-year-old Japanese girl from Tokyo will be staying with us for the next several months. This is her first visit to the United States. We have a hot tub and invited "Midori" to use it. I was amazed when she appeared in the tub totally nude. This shocked me because I always thought the Japanese were much more puritanical (and modest) than Americans.

Midori explained that Japanese families and close friends bathe together regularly in the nude—a custom centuries old. She cannot understand why we Americans wear bathing suits. When I mentioned the sexual implications, she looked puzzled and replied: "There is nothing sexual about bathing."

I am stumped. If Japanese males and females can bathe naked together without becoming sexually aroused, why can't we?—PUZZLED IN CALIF.[1]

Sexual norms differ from one country to another. More generally, the ways in which sex is practiced and experienced are not human universals. Sexuality is as much socially and culturally constructed as other aspects of human life (Caplan, 1987). Even theories of sexuality differ according to the nationality of their author. In the introduction to his unfinished *The History of Sexuality*, French philosopher Michel Foucault (1976) claims that the key issues in sexuality are *power* and *discourse*, but in French society and French philosophy, power and discourse are important concepts in understanding *any* phenomenon. If power would be the decisive factor in sex relations anywhere, we would expect the cultural dimension of Power Distance to be able to explain international differences—but this is not the case. France, by the way, scored quite high on Power Distance, but Foucault makes less of the difference between the sexuality of men and women than British authors do (Seidler, 1987, p. 84). In the IBM studies, France scored feminine and Britain masculine. British zoologist Richard Dawkins (1976) claims that behind human sexual behavior is a system based on the survival of the fittest genes. This is an invisible hand, a kind of market mechanism of DNA, an idea that strongly appeals in the Anglo-American world (Hofstede, 1991, chapter 6). Even the categories used in thinking about sex therefore are heavy with culture, but the cultural component in sexuality has attracted relatively few studies. "Sexuality has been the last domain (trailing even gender) to have its natural, biologized status called into question" (Vance, 1991, p. 880).

OPENNESS AND RESEARCH
ABOUT SEXUALITY

Norbert Elias (1968/1980, p. 230ff.) has described the considerable variation over the past five centuries in Europe of people's openness in discussing sexual issues, such as those between parents and their children or teachers and their students. He uses the example of the *Colloquia*, a collection of dialogues for instructing young people written by Erasmus of Rotterdam (1469-1536). In one of the dialogues, young Sophronius sees the girl Lucretia, a prostitute he has visited before, and manages to persuade her to change her way of life, promising her to find her a room with a decent woman and to look after her. Sophronius's action is presented as an eminent example of moral behavior.

Erasmus's *Colloquia* (written in Latin) were translated, reprinted, and used as reading material for young boys during three centuries. Only in the 19th century did they go out of fashion. Elias cites the German pedagogue Von Raumer in his 1857 *History of Pedagogy*: "How could they introduce such a book in numerous schools! . . . Erasmus pictures lust at its ugliest, and then adds something supposedly constructive. Such a book does the 'Doctor Theologiae' recommend to an eight year old boy, to benefit from its reading" (from Elias, 1968/1980, p. 232; translation by Geert Hofstede).

Elias attributes the inhibition in speaking about sexual issues that Von Raumer expresses to an advancing process of civilization in Europe, in which more and more rules for civilized behavior became internalized. This extreme taboo on discussing sex is often called "Victorian," after the regime of Queen Victoria of Britain (1819-1901), but it has lasted in much of the Western world well into the second half of the 20th century.

In the United States, a sexual revolution broke out in the 1950s, marked by such events as Kinsey's studies *Sexual Behavior in the Human Male* (Kinsey, Pomeroy, & Martin, 1948) and *Sexual Behavior in the Human Female* (Kinsey, Pomeroy, Martin, & Gebhard, 1953), but also by the introduction of the anticonception pill (1960), the creation of *Playboy* magazine, the musical *Hair* and the Broadway show *Oh! Calcutta*. Kinsey's research was followed by Masters and Johnson's study *Human Sexual Response* (sex in the laboratory; 1966) and Shere Hite's feminist *The Hite Report on Female Sexuality* (1979) and *The Hite Report on Male Sexuality* (1981).

Surprisingly, however, the sexual revolution may have had a more lasting effect outside the United States than inside.[2] Kinsey's work has been followed by local studies in other countries (for Britain, described in Stanley, 1995), but in the United States there has been a considerable backlash of conservative ideas, and the taboo on discussing sex in public has been lifted much less than in some European countries—especially the ones with more feminine cultures.

One would assume that the threat of AIDS would have led academics, governments, and the public to overcome taboos and study sexual behavior systematically (Tuzin, 1991), but this is not everywhere the case. After the various pioneering research projects on sexual behavior in the United States, there is still considerable resistance to further studies. A broad interview survey, "Sex in America" (Laumann, Gagnon, Michael, & Michaels, 1994; Michael, Gagnon, Laumann, & Kolata, 1994), designed explicitly in view of the fight against AIDS, met with strong resistance among conservative U.S. politicians. The Bush administration withdrew its financing, and, supported only by private funds, the study had to settle for a smaller scale than planned. It ended up surveying 3,400 respondents out of a population of 260 million.

Goldman (1994) reports on her experiences in studying children's sexual cognition in Australia, Great Britain, Sweden, and the United

States. Again strong resistance was met in the United States; she ended up with a "North American" sample—half U.S. and half Canadian.

The same resistance did not exist in the Netherlands. In this country, interview surveys of sexual behavior were held in 1968, 1981, and 1989; the last and most extensive covered a sample of 1,000 respondents out of a population of 15 million, representative for the ages 18 to 50 (Van Zessen & Sandfort, 1991).

All broad survey studies of sexual behavior so far have been conducted at the national, not at the intercultural, level. Hatfield and Rapson (1995) have collected the results of such national studies and put them side by side. This is often a frustrating task because these national survey studies are rarely cross-nationally compatible, and differences may as easily result from the way data are collected as from real properties of the respondent populations. For example, the U.S. and the Dutch studies mentioned above show different styles: The U.S. study focuses strongly on frequencies and numbers, whereas the Dutch includes more questions about motives and feelings.

Internationally designed comparative studies of sexual values and behavior (like the one by Goldman mentioned above) are rare. Differences in sexual behavior are sometimes implicit in cross-cultural studies on a broader range of topics; in this chapter, we will find several examples. Comparative studies explicitly addressing sexual issues always cover few countries, usually only two. When these are countries that, in the IBM studies, differed considerably on the Mas/Fem dimension but were similar on the three others, I have interpreted the differences found as related to Mas/Fem. This is the case when an English-speaking country (Australia, Britain, Ireland, United States) is compared with one of the Nordic countries, or to the Netherlands. As we saw in Table 1.2, among 53 countries the English speaking ones all scored masculine (from rank 7-8 in Ireland to 16 in Australia) and the northwestern European countries scored very feminine (from rank 47 in Finland to 53 in Sweden), but all scored relatively low on Power Distance and Uncertainty Avoidance and high on Individualism.

In spite of the sexual revolution of the 1950s, culturally masculine countries continue to manifest a stronger taboo on addressing sexual issues openly than culturally feminine ones. In the Netherlands, whatever taboo there was has been put aside in view of the need to fight

AIDS. To some Americans, the Dutch show a "lack of moral fibre."[3] The
Dutch in foreign eyes have always been rather unashamed about sex.
In a monograph published in 1911, German/Italian sociologist Robert
Michels wrote "Love life in the Netherlands is quite astonishing to a
foreigner: eroticism all over the place!"[4]

Michels was a pioneer of the systematic comparative study of sexual
behavior. He laid the foundations for a "comparative love science" (*Ver-
gleichende Liebeswissenschaft*, Michels, 1911, p. 33). His material, however,
had to remain limited to personal impressions. In the present chapter, I
will try to build up his science with more objective information.

The comparative cross-national studies of sexual and sex-related
behaviors referred to in this chapter were all found in the existing
literature. The reader should be warned that what the studies provided
are trends at the collective level that do not predict behaviors and
feelings of specific individuals in these countries. The studies point to
cultural and social forces in the particular societies, but individuals
have been affected by these forces to different extents. The conclusions
from this chapter, therefore, should not be used for stereotyping individuals.

SEX, LOVE, AND MARRIAGE

Data about values and demographics related to marriage were included in the massive public opinion surveys sponsored in the early
1980s by the European Value Systems Study Group (Ester, Halman, &
de Moor, 1993; Harding, Phillips, & Fogarty, 1986; Stoetzel, 1983; see
also Chapter 11). Originally, these surveys covered nine countries (Belgium, Denmark, France, Germany, Great Britain, Ireland, Italy, Netherlands, and Spain); later on, data from Norway, Canada, and the United
States were added, and the project was renamed World Values Survey.
In 1990, a second round was held, now covering 15 countries (the same
as before plus Iceland, Portugal, and Sweden, and not counting a
separate but smaller sample for Northern Ireland). Unfortunately, the
results are not easily accessible.

Halman (1991, p. 331) published some of the results of the first round
(early 1980s); see Table 10.1. The percentages of respondents cohabiting
(living together unmarried, whether or not with children) were still

TABLE 10.1 Survey Results Concerning Marriage From the World Values Survey (1981/1982)

Countries in Order of MAS	Factors in Marriage Success				
	Percentage Cohabiting	Income	Tastes	Sex	Approves of Single Mother
Italy	2	41	46	70	35
Ireland	1	55	39	67	20
Great Britain	2	47	51	74	31
Germany	5	33	52	52	24
United States	3	45	52	75	29
Belgium	2	39	40	61	30
Canada	5	41	51	74	34
France	4	41	40	70	61
Spain	0	37	45	56	36
Denmark	11	13	23	58	68
Netherlands	4	37	32	67	31
Norway	7	23	26	66	34
Spearman rank correlations with MAS	−.52*	.68***	.61**	.29	−.50*

SOURCE: Data are from Halman (1991, pp. 331, 335).
NOTE: $n > 1,000$ per country.
*$p < .05$. **$p < .01$. ***$p < .001$ (one-tailed).

small (a maximum of 11% in Denmark), but across the 12 countries they rank correlated −.52[*5] with the Masculinity score MAS. In the 1980s and 1990s, the phenomenon of cohabitation grew considerably (Ester et al., 1993, p. 99), especially in the feminine northwestern European countries. The institution of marriage is holier in masculine than in feminine countries. Among a list of 13 issues influencing the success of a marriage, the importance attached to "an adequate income" and to "tastes and interests in common" covaried most with MAS (rho = .68*** and .61**, respectively); both were judged more important in masculine countries. This suggests that in feminine cultures, marriage partners—and especially the wife—are seen and see themselves as less dependent on the other. The importance of a "happy sexual relationship" was rated high overall and did not correlate significantly with MAS.

In Chapter 5, I referred to the research of Buss (1989, 1994) about criteria for selecting a marriage partner. The criteria for brides, rated by men, that varied most between countries were the right age difference, wealth, industriousness, and *chastity* (no previous sexual experience). All four were strongly correlated with Collectivism.[6] Unlike the three other criteria, however, chastity in brides was even more strongly rank correlated (−.72***) with (1987) *GNP per capita*. Individualism and GNP per capita are closely related (rho = .68***), but it is not so much the individualism in a society that leads young people to put less weight on chastity, but simply increasing affluence. The mechanism, which has operated in all industrialized societies over the past one or two generations (for data from the Netherlands, see Ravesloot, 1995), probably is as follows. Increasing affluence provides women with more educational opportunities (in any society, if education first becomes available, parents give priority to boys who are not needed around the house). Girls start to move around more freely, and they get more opportunities to meet boys. Increasing affluence also gives people more living space and more privacy. Medical care and information improves, including information on contraception. Young people get more opportunities for sexual exploration, and sexual norms adapt to this situation. The assumption that behavior follows values is often naive; more often, values and norms follow modal behavior. "What people want and what they do, in any society, is to a large extent what they are made to want, and allowed to do" (Caplan, 1987, p. 25).

For the characteristics of a husband desired by women, preferred age difference and wealth are even more strongly correlated with Collectivism than for men's choices, industriousness more weakly, and chastity not at all, but the importance of chastity in husbands is again significantly negatively correlated with national wealth (GNP per capita).[7] The correlation of industriousness, wealth, and chastity with Collectivism can be understood by the fact that marriage in a collectivist society is a contract between families rather than between individuals. These will be the aspects that families can observe. If the marriage is arranged, individuals have little say at all in the choice of their partner. This does not mean that the marriage is less happy. Research in India has shown more marital satisfaction in arranged than in love marriages, and more in Indian love marriages than in American marriages (Yelsma & Athappilly, 1988). Dion and Dion (1993) have concluded that although cultural Individualism fosters the valuing of romantic love, certain aspects of individualism at the psychological level make developing intimacy problematic.

All correlations of partner preferences mentioned so far were with the Ind/Col dimension, not with the Mas/Fem dimension of national cultures. Chapter 5 revealed that correlations with Mas/Fem exist for the *differences between men's and women' desires*, in the cases of chastity and industriousness. For chastity, there is a significant multiple correlation with Uncertainty Avoidance *plus* Masculinity. Differences between men's and women's criteria for a partner point to a double moral standard (women should be chaste and industrious, men do not need to), and the gap in the moral standard is correlated with the culture's Masculinity.

Foa and colleagues (1987) studied to what extent the attitudes of young female and male hetero- and homosexuals in the United States ($n = 390$) and Sweden ($n = 179$) differentiated between *sex* and *love*. They used an ingenious method of asking their subjects to sort cards into two piles; no labels for the piles were imposed. Within each country, sex and love were seen as more different by men than by women. Among men, they were seen as most different by homosexuals and least by married heterosexuals, with single heterosexuals in between. Among women, the order was reversed: Sex and love were seen as most different by married heterosexuals, less by single heterosexuals, and least by lesbians. The perception gap between the sexes was smallest for married couples (who have to accommodate to the partner's attitude), larger for singles, and largest for homosexuals (who do not have to accommodate to the other sex at all). Much larger than the differences between these categories within the countries, however, were the differences between the two countries as a whole: All Swedish groups distinguished much less between sex and love than the corresponding U.S. groups, and there was no overlap between the answers from the two countries in this respect. All groups in the feminine culture, Sweden, came much closer to equating sex with love.

An anecdotal case of a two-country comparison of sexual behavior is found in the 19th-century Dutch literature. Gerrit Van de Linde, known as *De Schoolmeester* (the schoolmaster), was a theology student at Leyden University who fled from the Netherlands to Britain in 1834, after having fathered a child on the wife of a professor. In a letter (in rhyme)

to a Dutch friend who visited London that same year, Van de Linde
wrote:

> *If sometimes here your evil lust might start to vex and burn,*
> *postpone that business to Holland, after your return*
> *to see an English prostitute nobody will advise*
> *they lie between the sheets like marble, or like ice.*
> *to bring an English whore to life, while doing as-you-know,*
> *one has to lay another with a hiccup fit below.*
> (Van Deel et al., 1975, p. 63; English translation
> by Geert Hofstede)[8]

Van de Linde's poetical statement can be seen as the result of a comparative participant observation study of the sexual behavior of prostitutes in (masculine) Britain versus (feminine) Netherlands. The
assumption that in feminine cultures the norm is for women to take a
more active part in the coitus than in masculine cultures is not that
farfetched. In March, 1993, Janet L. Wolfe, American sexologist and
author of the book *What to Do When He Has a Headache* (Wolfe, 1992),
visited the Netherlands on a promotion visit. In an interview with
columnist Alice Fuldauer, Wolfe described how the men who consulted
her in the United States said they felt turned off when their partner took
the initiative. When Fuldauer cited Dutch research showing exactly the
opposite—Dutch men wanting their women to start (Vennix, 1989)—
Wolfe muttered "bullshit." The idea that norms for sexual interaction
may differ between countries obviously had never occurred to her.[9]

Wolfe's statement that American men do not want their partner to
take initiative is in conflict with the results of a research project in the
state of Hawaii (Hatfield & Rapson, 1993, p. 92) showing that both
dating men and married men wanted their partner to initiate sex more.
We may be dealing with different subsets of the U.S. population or even
with inconsistencies in feelings within the same population. A study by
Komarovsky (1976) among male U.S. students showed considerable
strain between egalitarian sex role norms on one side and a deeper need
for adhering to a traditional male role on the other.

The French women's magazine *Marie Claire* once contained an interview with a young woman from France who participated in a feminist

encounter group in the United States in the 1970s. The subject was "orgasm."

> When it was my turn, I told what I feel. I talk easily about sex, undoubtedly because I enjoy it easily. Sex for me is something joyful. Talking about it made me feel happy. Until the moment I stopped, and then the other women told me they did not believe me. I could not feel that way. Such things existed only in male erotic phantasies. . . . (Lebrun, 1988, p. 25; translation by Geert Hofstede)

Even orgasms have a cultural component. An impressionistic comparison of novels suggests to me that in the more feminine French culture, female sexuality, other things being equal, is more positively valued than in more masculine cultures.

As mentioned in Chapter 5, in extremely masculine cultures the men's *machismo*, or ostentatious manliness, is supposed to be complemented by a corresponding female behavior called *marianismo*, a combination of near-saintliness, submissiveness, and frigidity (Stevens, 1973). The terms are from Latin America and are especially used in Venezuela, Mexico, and Colombia. Women in this case are not supposed to enjoy sex; only men do. In less masculine cultures, such a double standard for the enjoyment of sex is unacceptable.

PARENTHOOD

The first round of the World Values Survey contained this question: "If a woman wants to have a child as a single parent but she doesn't want to have a stable relationship with a man, do you approve or disapprove?" In the last column of Table 10.1, the percentages "approve" are listed. Approval of single motherhood is negatively rank correlated with MAS (-.50*).

Parenthood as such is more valued in feminine cultures. The Nordic and other feminine countries have a reputation of being child-centered. Germany is masculine, and a frequent criticism by Germans themselves is that their society is *kindfeindlich*—hostile to children, who should be seen but not heard. Concerning Great Britain, a young Dutch professional working in an international company in London told me about his culture shock when his wife became pregnant. First one colleague and then another, when he told them, said "How long have you been trying?" The family doctor and another doctor started their consultation with "Do you want to keep it?" (personal communication). Both reactions, to a Dutch father and mother, are shocking.

In Chapter 5, I referred to the ideas of U.S. feminist Sandra Scarr (1996), who opposes maternity leave because it damages women's careers—a point of view that she expressed, of all places, in a conference in Sweden. The Swedes, obviously, retorted with "What about the children?" The United States is about the only industrial country in the world that has no legal provision for maternity leave. Swedish law even provides paternity leave.

Obviously, parenthood and careers for women can best be combined if there are two parents who both do take their share in housework and education. In Chapter 4, De Mooij showed a finding from consumer research (Eurodata Survey 1991) that across 16 European countries, who does most of the food shopping is strongly related to MAS[10]—it is the feminine countries where the men shop more frequently. Without being evenly shared, domestic and educational chores are, on average, less unequally distributed in less masculine cultures.

ABORTION, CONTRACEPTION, MASTURBATION, AND HOMOSEXUALITY

Abortion has been a debated issue in many countries as well as at international conferences. It has been both positively welcomed, as the ultimate way to avoid overpopulation of the world, and depicted as the ultimate evil. The link of opinions about abortion to religious attitudes is evident, and I shall come back to it in Chapter 12.

Halman (1991) has published data about the rejection of abortion in 12 countries from the World Values Survey 1981/1982. The scores are influenced by extreme rejection at that time in the Catholic countries Ireland and, to a lesser extent, Spain, but nevertheless the rank correlation between rejection of abortion and MAS was a significant .49*. The key question is whether a woman should have a choice to terminate an unwanted pregnancy. Masculine cultures are less likely to allow her this choice than are feminine ones. Public opinions about abortion are unrelated to the actual frequency with which abortion is practiced: Countries where abortion is illegal have their secret aborters, and actual abortions may be more frequent than in countries where abortion is permitted. The Netherlands, for example, with public abortion clinics, is supposed to have the world's lowest abortion rate.

The frequency of abortions obviously is related to the availability and use of *contraceptives*. The time when disseminating information about contraception was a crime (as it still was in some U.S. states in the 1950s) has nearly everywhere passed. The birth control pill, developed in the United States in 1956 by Gregory G. Pincus, who was inspired by feminist Margaret Sanger, has virtually disconnected sex from pregnancy for any woman affluent and intelligent enough to use it. Condoms have met a revival since the outbreak of AIDS around 1980. The World Values Survey did not, among all its questions, include one about attitudes to contraception, yet impressionistically, national attitudes still differ along the Mas/Fem dimension, as is visible, for example, in "safe sex" campaigns fighting AIDS. In feminine cultures like the Netherlands and the Nordic countries, contraceptives are easily available, awareness of the need for safe sex is promoted through very direct public advertising, and the use of condoms is demonstrated to young teenagers in the public school system. Many masculine cultures maintain taboos on information about and sometimes availability of contraceptives, even in the face of the AIDS threat.

The acceptance of masturbation is also more common in feminine than in masculine societies. The study "Sex in America" (Laumann et al., 1994; Michael et al., 1994) had a special question about "feeling guilty after masturbation." Of the respondents, 54% of men and 47% of women said they felt guilty (Laumann et al., 1994, p. 82). The Dutch study by Van Zessen and Sandfort (1991) reported 11 different feelings after masturbation (relaxed, comfortable, satisfied, energetic, active, sexually aroused, lonely, guilty, sad, tense, and awful). Of Dutch respondents, 6% of men and 7% of women answered they felt guilty. Because the questions in the two studies were not in the same format, the comparison is only suggestive. The Dutch again seem to be more matter of fact, and the Americans moralistic—even in the way in which the questions were asked. President Bill Clinton fired U.S. Surgeon General Joycelyn Elders for suggesting, at an international AIDS conference, that

TABLE 10.2 Rejection of Abortion and Homosexuality According to World
Values Survey (1981/1982)

Countries in	Percentage "Can Never Be Justified"	
Order of MAS	Abortion	Homosexuality
Japan		52
Italy	32	63
Mexico	73	
Ireland	79	59
Great Britain	32	43
Germany	32	42
South Africa		64
United States	44	65
Belgium	37	51
Canada	39	51
France	23	47
Spain	51	56
Denmark	23	34
Netherlands	32	22
Norway	19	50
Spearman rank correlation with MAS	.49*	.53*

SOURCE: For abortion, data are from Halman (1991, p. 340). For homosexuality, data are from
Inglehart (1990, p. 194). For Norway, data are from Halman (1991, p. 338).
NOTE: $n > 1,000$ per country.
*$p < .05$ (one-tailed).

children be taught how to masturbate as an integral component of safe
sex education (Abramson & Pinkerton, 1995, p. 149).

Masculinity is negatively related to the acceptance of homosexuality.
The World Values Survey contained a question concerning "to what
extent homosexuality can be justified." Inglehart (1990) has published
mean answer percentages to this question, including those for three
countries not listed by Halman (1991): Japan, Mexico, and South Africa.
Table 10.2 shows the percentages of respondents in 15 countries who
answered "never." They vary from 22% in the Netherlands to 73% in
Mexico, and the percentages rank correlate .53* with MAS.

Ross (1989) surveyed 600 homosexual men in Australia, Ireland,
Finland, and Sweden. Young homosexuals had more problems accept-

ing their sexual orientation in Ireland and Australia, less in Finland, and least in Sweden. Ross considers the societies in question as homophobic in this order; it is also the order of the countries on the Masculinity Index. Homosexuality tends to be felt as a threat to masculine norms and rejected in masculine cultures (Bolton, 1994); this goes with an overestimation of its frequency (Diamond, 1993). In feminine cultures, homosexuality is more often considered a fact of life.

In an earlier study, Ross (1983) had administered the Bem Sex Role Inventory (BSRI; Bem, 1974) to 163 Australian and 176 Swedish homosexual men, and to control groups of 98 Australian and 57 Swedish heterosexual men. The BSRI is a U.S. questionnaire that places respondents on two scales, one of masculine and one of feminine gender role acceptance. Australian heterosexuals, Swedish heterosexuals, and Swedish homosexuals did not differ in their position on the "masculinity" and "femininity" BSRI scales. Only the Australian homosexuals differed: They scored as masculine as the other three samples, but with a significantly higher feminine role acceptance. Ross (1983, p. 287) concludes that "gender role in homosexuals has a strong societal component": It is the antihomosexual Australian context that leads these homosexual men to identify more than other men with a feminine role. In the more accepting Swedish context, this identification process simply does not take place. Rossi (1965, p. 138) has argued that in the United States, a fear of latent homosexuality prevents men from showing their tender sentiments, making it impossible for them to see these as human rather than feminine.

Ross found some other differences. A questionnaire on sex role conservatism showed the two groups of Australians scoring much more conservative than the two groups of Swedes, but with a wider gap for homosexuals than for heterosexuals: Swedish homosexuals were less conservative than heterosexuals, but Australian homosexuals were considerably more conservative than Australian heterosexuals. A set of questions on attitudes toward parents showed that the two national groups did not differ in their attitude toward the father, but that the Swedes rated their mothers as significantly more "active" than the Australians. Finally, demographic questions showed the Swedes had become homosexually active earlier (age 19) than the Australians (age 21), suggesting that the latter had more resistances to overcome.

TEENAGE PREGNANCIES

The age at which women usually have their first pregnancy varies from country to country. Economic development in most cases leads to postponing marriage and childbirth. In some developed countries, however, teenage pregnancies of mostly unmarried girls of lower economic status are a social problem. Jones and colleagues (1986) have published an international study of this phenomenon that is an implicit source of comparative cross-national data on sexual behavior. They collected secondary data from 37 industrialized countries; for 30 countries, reliable figures for teenage pregnancies per year between 1971 and 1980 were available. From these, 22 overlap with the IBM set of countries.

Pregnancy rates per 1,000 women are given for the age ranges of below 20 and below 18. Jones and colleagues (1986, pp. 8-9) found that pregnancies below the age of 18 co-vary positively at the country level with the following:

■ The frequency of abortions among women aged 15-44
■ Maternal mortality
■ The percentage of the labor force in agriculture
■ Religiosity (people stating that God is important in their life).

They co-vary negatively with the following:

■ Policies favoring provision of contraceptives to young, unmarried women
■ Actual use of condoms by married people
■ Open attitudes in society about sex
■ Income equality in society (percentage of national household income going to those in the lowest 20%)
■ Per capita government expenditure on education.

In Chapter 12, I will come back to the link with religiosity. The analysis by Jones and colleagues shows that early teenage pregnancies are part of a broader cultural syndrome. It is extremely likely that this syndrome should somehow relate to the national culture indexes.

Surprisingly, across the 22 countries, none of the Hofstede indexes correlates directly with either the below 20 or the below 18 pregnancy rates. National wealth (1980 GNP per capita) rank correlates –.57***

TABLE 10.3 Teenage Fertility Below Age 18 (1979/1980; per 1,000 women)

Weak Uncertainty Avoidance		Strong Uncertainty Avoidance	
Countries in Order of MAS	Fertility	Countries in Order of MAS	Fertility
Ireland	23	Japan	2
Great Britain	41	Austria	41
United States	101	Italy	28
Australia	45	Switzerland	8
New Zealand	64	Germany (West)	21
Canada	46	Greece	80
Finland	18	Belgium	26
Denmark	16	Israel	32
Netherlands	10	France	25
Norway	29	Spain	37
Sweden	15	Portugal	59
Spearman rank correlation with MAS	.59**		−.49*

SOURCE: Data are from Jones et al. (1986, pp. 243-244), after Westoff, Calot, and Foster (1983).
$*p < .05. **p < .01$ (one-tailed).

with 1979/1980 pregnancies below 20, and −.49** with pregnancies below 18. The stronger correlation with the "below 20" rate shows that the retarding effect of economic development on marriage age is more universal than its effect on very early pregnancies. The "below 18" rates, however, are the more interesting ones as implicit indicators of sexual habits. These have been reproduced in Table 10.3.

We are mainly interested in the variance in pregnancy rates that cannot be attributed to differences in economic development. This means that we should focus on the two dimensions that do not logically relate to national wealth: Uncertainty Avoidance (UAI) and Mas/Fem (MAS). The combination of UAI and MAS in relation to sexual behavior appeared earlier as a correlate of the difference between bridegrooms and brides in their desire for chastity of the partner (Buss's research): In strong UAI, masculine cultures, the double moral standard was most pronounced.

Zero-order and multiple correlations of both UAI and MAS with below 18 pregnancies are virtually nil. If we split the 22 countries into "strong" and "weak" Uncertainty Avoidance,[11] however, the relationship becomes clear. Across the 11 strong UAI countries, below 18 pregnancies are significantly negatively correlated (−.49*) with MAS. Across the 11 weak UAI countries, the reverse is the case (.59**). This unique configuration suppresses the zero-order and multiple correlations. The interpretation is that in the strong UAI countries, the behavior of young girls is subjected to a more rigid social code, the more so if the culture is also more masculine (the combination that produced the double moral standard mentioned above). The extreme case is Japan, which has the fewest teenage pregnancies but a very high abortion rate (Jones et al., 1986, p. 10). In the weak UAI countries, social codes are more tolerant. In this case, if the culture is masculine, boys have things their way, leaving girls with teenage pregnancies. If the culture is feminine, the girls have things their way, and they are more careful. These countries are also the ones with the most open attitudes about sex and easy provision of contraceptives.

Table 10.3 shows that five out of the six weak Uncertainty Avoidance, masculine countries (Great Britain, United States, Australia, New Zealand, and Canada) had below 18 pregnancy rates of over 40 per 1000 women. Outside this group, only Greece, Portugal, and Austria scored over 40, and the first two of these in 1979/1980 were still quite poor. The combination of weak Uncertainty Avoidance with masculine values stands for frequent teenage pregnancies.

SEX AS ACHIEVEMENT, EXPLOITATION, OR RELATIONSHIP?

Remarkably, the combination of weak Uncertainty Avoidance and Masculinity is also the one that fosters the strongest need for achievement, according to David McClelland. McClelland (1961) was inspired by the anthropological study of folktales and tried to do something similar for modern nations. He turned to stories in the schoolbooks from which children learned to read. He and his team analyzed children's stories from a large number of countries. They classified these stories according to need for achievement, for affiliation, and for power. In *Culture's Consequences* (Hofstede, 1980, pp. 197, 287), I show that across 22 overlapping countries, McClelland's need for achievement measure correlates strongly with the combination of low UAI and high MAS (R = .73***).[12]

Sexual performance can be experienced as achievement, especially for the male partner; thus, the achievement motive will play a greater role in sexual activity in weak Uncertainty Avoidance, masculine countries than in others. This is supported by a study by Gibbons, Helweg-Larsen, and Gerrard (1995), who surveyed female and male adolescents, ages 13-15, in rural areas of the United States (n = 500) and Denmark (n = 224), about influences that lead young people to engage in risky behaviors. The Americans showed themselves more sensitive to social comparison, which is an essential component of achievement motivation. They reported comparing themselves to and being influenced by their peers more than the Danes. The Danes reported being influenced by their parents more than did the Americans.

The Gibbons survey covered four risky behaviors: smoking, drinking alcohol, sex, and use of drugs. Danes reported drinking alcohol much more than Americans (79% vs. 28%), smoking more (16% vs. 6%), and using more drugs (10% vs. 1%). There was no difference between the two countries in the percentages claiming to have had sex (12% for both), but Danish boys and in particular Danish girls reported more intention to have sex in the next year than their American counterparts. The most striking finding, however, was that although both country samples overestimated the percentage of their peers who engaged in each behavior, the Americans overestimated much more than the Danes. The sexually active Americans estimated that 67% of their peers had sex too; the sexually inactive Americans still thought that 45% of their peers had sex. For the Danes, the corresponding figures were 40% and 26%, respectively. For drinking, the Danes even *under*estimated their peers' involvement. The overestimation obviously plays a role in the social comparison process: By overestimating the number of peers who engage in some behavior, people develop psychological support for that behavior. If young people in a masculine culture overestimate risky behaviors more, they develop a stronger support for such behaviors.

Strong achievement motivation in teenage sexual relations leads to a need for "scoring"—and anecdotal impressions from especially U.S. articles, books, and films confirm that boys, and sometimes girls too, often think about sex in terms of scoring. Scoring is ego oriented: It is a lonely adventure in which the partner remains an object. Cultural masculinity contains an element of this ego boosting, more so than cultural femininity, which is primarily oriented toward establishing relationships. We can expect that girls in masculine cultures more often feel exploited than in feminine ones, and that they feel that their feelings do not count.

A three-country survey study (Sprecher & Hatfield, 1994; Sprecher, Hatfield, Cortese, Potapova, & Levitskaya, 1994) dealt with premarital sexual standards and consent to sexual intercourse among some 1,500 unmarried male and female college students in Japan, the United States, and Russia, median ages 20-21 years. Acceptance of premarital sex was most common in the U.S. sample and least common in the Japanese sample. Premarital sex was more accepted by men than by women in the United States and Russia, but there was no gender difference in this respect in Japan. Ninety percent of the American and Russian men but only 35% of the Japanese men claimed to be sexually experienced; among the women, the figures were 78%, 64%, and 58%, respectively. More Japanese women claimed experience than Japanese men, but this, according to the authors, may have been an artifact of the sampling: Men and women came from different universities. Other questions asked in the survey were about the occurrence of situations in which the respondent wanted sex but said no to the partner ("token resistance to sex") and situations in which the respondent did not want sex but said yes ("consent to unwanted sex"). Of the sexually experienced American women, 55% claimed to have at least once consented to unwanted sex, against 32% of the Russian and 25% of the Japanese women. Among men, the figures were 35%, 35%, and 30%, respectively. These percentages show a greater frequency of having felt exploited among U.S. women. A relationship with MAS cannot be proven, however, because Japan in the IBM studies scored more masculine than the United States. Russia did not figure in the IBM studies, but replications give it a MAS score in the middle or on the feminine side of the scale (Hofstede, Kolman, Nicolescu, & Pajumaa, 1996, p. 208). Other influences, in particular Japanese Uncertainty Avoidance and Collectivism, have certainly played a role: The three cultures differ on several dimensions simultaneously. In an older study comparing Japanese and British students aged 18-22 (Iwawaki & Eysenck, 1978), the differences in reported sexual experience between Japan and Britain were much larger than those between Japan and the United States in the Sprecher study, but in the meantime, Japanese society has become more affluent and considerably more individualistic.

Less frequent feelings of being exploited among women in a feminine culture are confirmed in a survey study by I. M. Schwartz (1993) about sexual experiences among U.S. and Swedish unmarried female students, ages 18-25. Of the respondents, 79% of Americans (*n* = 217) and 90% of Swedes (*n* = 186) claimed to be sexually experienced. The survey asked about their affective reactions to their first coitus. The mean age for first sex did not differ; it was 17 in both countries, with a 19-year-old partner. Swedes, however, reported a lower age of social acceptance for girls having sex (16) than Americans (19), and in general a greater acceptance of premarital sex, regardless of the existence of a love relationship. Americans significantly more than Swedes reported the following feelings: guilty, fearful, anxious, sorry, exploited, confused, and embarrassed. Swedes more than Americans reported that they used contraceptives (76% vs. 57%). Swedes had sex earlier in the relationship (31% within one month vs. 15% for Americans) and reported more sex partners in their lifetime (69% more than two, vs. 57% for Americans). From the period before their first sex, Swedes reported more experience in masturbation; Americans more with various other erotic activities, from kissing to fellatio.

A question that—as far as I know—Schwartz did not ask is who took the initiative for the first coitus: the boy or the girl. My impression is that in the Netherlands, it is quite frequently the girl. The Gibbons et al. (1995) finding about Danish girls of 13-15 years old reporting the intention to have sex in the next year points in the same direction.

These studies help to understand why sexual harassment is more an issue in, for example, the United States than in the Netherlands and the Nordic countries. Sex in a masculine culture is more likely to be experienced as exploitative, and in a feminine culture as a relationship. In the Dutch language, "sexual harassment" is translated as "unwanted intimacies," implying that there are wanted intimacies as well. In a survey feedback session in Denmark (Hofstede, Neuijen, Ohayu, & Sanders, 1990), a research partner and I discussed our finding that nobody among the Danish respondents thought that "a married man having sexual relationships with a subordinate" should be a reason for the man's dismissal. One female respondent explained this as follows: "Either she likes it, and then there is no problem. Or she doesn't like it, and then she will tell him to go to hell." There are two assumptions in this answer: (Most) Danish subordinates will not hesitate to speak up to their boss (small Power Distance), and (most) Danish bosses will "go to hell" if told so. In such a society, sexual harassment is unlikely to become a big issue.

The assumption of mutual consent to sex in a feminine culture is not a new phenomenon, caused by the emancipation of women. The theme has been present in Dutch prose and poetry since the Middle Ages. For example, a Dutch epigram from 1672, "Griet en Jan" (Maggie and Jack; notice the sequence), goes as follows:

> Beautiful love, my heart so sweet
> I'd like to—but I only need
> to if you wish. Then she replied:
> It's just a trifle, come aside.
> (From Den koddigen opdisser [1672],
> in Van Straten, 1992, p. 116.
> English translation by Geert Hofstede)[13]

A SUMMARY TABLE

Table 10.4 summarizes the differences in sexual norms and behaviors that this chapter found to be associated with a feminine versus a masculine national culture. The table should be read with care. First, as stated at the beginning of this chapter, these are societal trends and should not be used for the stereotyping of individuals. Second, the columns in the table are opposite poles, and actual cultures are likely to be somewhere in between. Third, the evidence cited is often from only a few countries. In particular, nearly all studies cited in this chapter, by the nature of the subject, are from industrialized, or even wealthy, countries. As we saw in Chapters 1 and 5, effects of Mas/Fem differences in wealthy countries do not necessarily appear in poorer countries. Fourth, sexual norms and behaviors also vary among subcultures inside countries. Having made all these provisos, I still want to defend the

TABLE 10.4 Differences in Sexual Norms and Behaviors Associated With the Masculinity/Femininity Dimension of National Cultures

Feminine Cultures	Masculine Cultures
Matter-of-fact attitudes about sexuality	Moralistic attitudes about sexuality
Weak taboo on addressing sexual issues openly	Strong taboo on addressing sexual issues openly
Existing taboos set aside in the interest of fighting AIDS	Existing taboos limit possibilities for fighting AIDS
Sex research focusing on experiences and feelings	Sex research focusing on numbers and frequencies
More unmarried cohabitation	Less unmarried cohabitation
Wife less dependent on husband	Wife more dependent on husband
Mothers rated more active by sons	Mothers rated less active by sons
Chastity equally unimportant or important for bride and groom	Chastity important for bride, not for groom
Little distinction between sex and love	Wide distinction between sex and love
Norm of woman's active participation in coitus	Norm of passive role of woman during coitus
Parenthood, including single parenthood, key element in parents' life	Parenthood, including single parenthood, secondary element in parents' life
Husbands do part of shopping for food	Wives do all food shopping
Abortion seen as the woman's decision	Abortion felt as a threat to society
Contraceptives and information freely available	Information on contraception limited
Masturbation associated with pleasure	Masturbation associated with guilt
Weak taboo on homosexuality; it is accepted as a fact of life	Strong taboo on homosexuality; it is perceived as a threat
If culture is strong in Uncertainty Avoidance, more teenage pregnancies	If culture is weak in Uncertainty Avoidance, more teenage pregnancies
Sex basically seen as relationship between partners	Sex easily associated with exploitation of partner
Adolescents sensitive to opinion of parents	Sex among adolescents seen as competitive achievement
Premarital sex socially acceptable at an early age; girls may take initiative	Premarital sex socially acceptable at a later age, or not at all
Girls do not report negative feelings about first sex	Girls report negative feelings about first sex
Girls report sex earlier in relationship and more partners	Girls report sex later in relationship and fewer partners
Girls report less petting but more masturbation	Girls report more petting but less masturbation
Unwanted intimacies are not such a big issue	Sexual harassment is a big issue

table because it indicates the broad range of possible cultural differences in sexuality and how different aspects are interrelated through the cultural context.

Culture includes values, and values imply judgment. The issues in this chapter are heavily value laden. They are about moral and immoral, decent and indecent behavior. The comparisons offered should remind us that morality is in the eye of the beholder, not in the act itself. There is no one best way, neither in social nor in sexual relationships: Any solution is best according to the norms that come with it. Women and men in one type of society are not necessarily "better off" than in another. Women from one culture may consider those from another as immoral or oppressed, but many of those others consider themselves as the moral ones, and usually, "the oppressed women like the oppressing men" (Bártová, 1976, p. 257).

The Japanese girl Midori with whom this chapter opened is a reminder that what is decent or indecent is relative. For a Japanese, "there is nothing sexual about bathing." Nakedness is not so shocking in Japan. "Even in mainstream publications, pictures of naked women are so common that United Airlines has been forced to ban some Japanese newsmagazines from its planes because of passenger complaints" (from a column by T. R. Reid in the *Honolulu Advertiser*, November 9, 1994; originally in the *Washington Post*). The complaints, mind you, were not about naked men; this is still a very masculine culture. The same column from which the above quotation is taken tells that what shocks Japanese in the behavior of Westerners is kissing in public, which is not done in Japan, not even between spouses. The prime rule for intercultural understanding is "suspend judgment." In Dutch, we say "count to ten first." Things will look different if you understand their cultural context.

OTHER CONTRIBUTIONS IN PART III

Part III consists of two more chapters. In Chapter 11, Verweij reports, from his comparative studies of religiosity in Western countries, how the Mas/Fem dimension emerged as a major predictor of secularization. Chapter 12 relates the subjects of sexuality and of religion. Both deal with the very roots of humanity. The chapter shows why it is not at all surprising that the same cultural syndrome, Masculinity versus Femininity, affects both fields.

NOTES

1. From Ann Landers's column in *The Honolulu Advertiser*, November 18, 1994. Permission to reprint granted by Ann Landers/Creators Syndicate.

2. History shows more cases where ideas developed in one country are so countercultural that they have most of their success abroad. An example is Buddhism, which originated in India but conflicted too much with the caste system and had to move to China and Southeast Asia to be widely adopted. A recent example is Statistical Quality Control, developed by J. M. Juran and W. E. Deming in the United States but popularized in Japan. The "obsessive" intolerance of errors it demands is countercultural in the United States.

3. The expression is from American columnist Walter Lacqueur, who also coined the term "Hollanditis," or Dutch disease, for the Dutch antinuclear stance.

4. *"Ganz verblüffend für einen Fremden ist das Liebesleben in Holland. Erotik allüberal!"* (English translation by Geert Hofstede).

5. As in other chapters, * stands for $p < .05$, ** for $p < .01$, and *** for $p < .001$. Tests are one-tailed.

6. Across 28 countries, the Spearman rank correlations with the Individualism Index (IDV) are age difference $-.75$***, wealth $-.70$***, industriousness $-.70$***, and chastity $-.57$***. For chastity, a similar association was obtained by Bond (see Chinese Culture Connection, 1987). Bond and his team of 24 researchers surveyed male and female students in 23 countries with a Chinese Value Survey. The value of "chastity in women" was at the collectivist pole of a dimension correlated with Ind/Col.

7. The Spearman rank correlation coefficient, across 28 countries, of women's preferences for chastity with GNP per capita was $-.53$***. The Spearman rank correlation coefficients of women's preferences with IDV were as follows: for age difference, $-.75$***, for wealth, $-.73$***, and industriousness $-.50$**.

8. The original is:

> *Zoo somtijds de booze lusten van het vleesch je hier mochten kwellen*
> *Zou ik je maar aanraden om dat grapjen tot in Holland uit te stellen*
> *Want de Engelsche publieke meisjens zal niemand je recommandeeren*
> *Ze liggen precies als bevroren monumenten in de veêren*
> *En om te maken dat een Engelsche hoer-vrouw, onder,*
> * je weet wel wat ik meen, een beetjen leeft*
> *Zou je er een andere onder moeten leggen die den hik heeft.*

9. From *NRC Handelsblad*, March 13, 1993. I commented in a letter to the editor, printed in *NRC Handelsblad*, April 8, 1993.

10. The Spearman rank correlation of "women main food shoppers" and MAS is .68**. Without the traditional countries Greece, Portugal, and Spain, it is .91***.

11. In assigning countries to the two groups, I put Finland (UAI = 59) with the weak and Switzerland (UAI = 58) with the strong Uncertainty Avoidance countries to keep the clusters (Nordic vs. Central European) intact.

12. McClelland collected stories from around 1925 and from around 1950. I found significant correlations with the 1925 data only. In *Culture's Consequences* (p. 171), I argued that the 1925 stories were more traditional and resembled better the anthropologists' folktales that McClelland tried to match; the post-World War II 1950 stories in most countries were modernized and internationalized.

13. The original is:

> *Zoete lieve meid, mijn hartje die zo zoet ziet,*
> *ik zou jou wel eens een reis, je weet wel, maar ik moet niet*
> *tenzij het is uw wil. Toen gaf zij hem bescheid*
> *en zei: 'Kom, doe het eens, 't is maar een kleinigheid.'*

11

THE IMPORTANCE OF FEMININITY IN EXPLAINING CROSS-NATIONAL DIFFERENCES IN SECULARIZATION[1]

Johan Verweij

A study of secularization (loss of religiosity) in Christian nations used the results of a secondary analysis of data from the 1990 European Values Survey across 14 industrialized countries, plus Canada and the United States. Country scores on eight variables expressing aspects of religiosity were computed and were correlated with eight country-level variables whose explanatory power was postulated on the basis of various existing theories. Surprisingly, Hofstede's Masculinity Index proved by far the strongest correlate of secularization, in the sense that more strongly Masculine cultures have remained less secularized. The study explains why this could be so, in spite of the paradoxical fact that within countries, women are consistently more religious than men.

INTRODUCTION

Secularization is a major issue in the sociology of religion (Tschannen, 1991; Wallis & Bruce, 1992, p. 8). The prevailing theory of secularization states that the role of institutionalized religion, in society in general and in the life of the individual person, has decreased with the development of modern industrial society (Berger, 1969; Dobbelaere, 1981; Giddens, 1993, pp. 457-486; Martin, 1978, p. 3; Wilson, 1982). However, there are large differences in secularization among nations in the Western world. Countries such as the Netherlands, Denmark, and France are far more secularized than, for example, Ireland, Spain, and Portugal (Halman & de Moor, 1993).

The United States, a modern society with a high level of religious involvement, poses the strongest challenge to the empirical tenability of the prevailing secularization theory (Brown, 1992, p. 35; Finke, 1992, pp. 149-151; Greeley, 1989; Hadden, 1987). Some authors want to explain the exceptional case of the United States by the "economics of religion." They argue that religious markets function like other markets: More competition between religious organizations should lead to more religious consumption (Stark & Iannaccone, 1994). Religious pluralism forces religious organizations to "produce efficiently a wide range of alternative faiths well adapted to the needs of consumers" (Iannaccone, 1992, p. 128). Cross-national research showed that people in religiously pluralistic countries, such as the United States and Canada, have high levels of church attendance (Iannaccone, 1991, p. 158).

Although this economic approach to religion has gained popularity—Warner (1993) even calls it a new paradigm—it is also increasingly criticized.[2] In this chapter, I want to join this debate by presenting some results of a study of secularization (Verweij, Ester, & Nauta, 1997)[3] that took institutional and cultural factors into account in addition to "economic" factors such as religious pluralism.

In this study, a secondary analysis was performed on data from the 1990 European Values Study (EVS), a representative cross-national interview survey of value patterns in the Western world (Halman & Vloet, 1994; see also Ester et al., 1993). Data were available for the following 16 countries: Belgium, Canada, Denmark, France, Great Britain, Germany (West), Iceland, Ireland, Northern Ireland, Italy, Netherlands, Norway, Portugal, Spain, Sweden, and the United States. Eight variables measuring aspects of religiosity were constructed:

1. church membership;
2. church attendance;
3. religious upbringing;
4. importance of religious rites at birth, marriage, and death;
5. confidence in the church's position on moral, family, spiritual, and national issues;
6. self-rated religiosity (being a religious person, belief in personal God, importance of God, religion as source of comfort and strength, takes time for prayer or meditation);
7. orthodoxy (belief in God, life after death, the devil, hell, sin, and resurrection)[4]; and
8. Christian worldview about the meaning of life, death, and suffering.

Each of the 16 countries received a single score on each of these variables. Subsequently, these scores were related to country characteristics such as modernization, religious pluralism, and Hofstede's (1991) dimensions of national culture.

While interpreting the results of this study, one must keep two things in mind. First, we only compared modern or fairly modern countries; therefore, the existence of a causal relationship between modernization and secularization cannot be tested. Second, by relating institutional and cultural factors to aggregated country data on religious variables derived from the behavior of individuals, we limit our analyses to secularization as a process of declining religious involvement in national societies as a whole.[5]

CROSS-NATIONAL DETERMINANTS OF SECULARIZATION

Modernization, the transition from a traditional agrarian based society to a modern (post)industrial society, is the classic explanation of secularization. All kinds of subprocesses of modernization, such as industrialization, differentiation, urbanization, rationalization, and democratization (Ester et al., 1993, p. 3), are supposed to have led to an erosion of the central role that religion and religious beliefs once played in society. Modernization encouraged rational and empirical thinking, which contradicts the belief in a supernatural being; it also led to the disappearance of the plausibility structures of religion, such as the neighborhood and the village (Wallis & Bruce, 1992). Proponents of the prevailing secularization theory put most emphasis on the process of societal differentiation, through which religion became only one institution among others and lost its overarching claims (Berger, 1969; Dobbelaere, 1993, p. 28; Wilson, 1996, p. 16). One of the founders of sociology, Émile Durkheim, referred to this process of differentiation as follows:

> If there is one truth that history teaches us beyond doubt, it is that religion tends to embrace a smaller and smaller portion of social life. Originally, it pervades everything; everything social is religious; the two words are synonymous. Then, little by little, political, economic, scientific functions free themselves from the religious function, constitute themselves apart and take on a more and more acknowledged temporal character. (Durkheim, 1893/1964, p. 169)

Unfortunately, no measures of functional differentiation have been developed yet. Because of the interrelatedness of differentiation with economic development, one uses Gross National Product (GNP) per capita (Jagodzinski & Dobbelaere, 1995, p. 83). This is a defendable choice if one considers technological and economical developments as the motor of modernization (Bax, 1988, p. 30).

Development of the Welfare State

Over time, churches had to transfer property, influence, and control to the state (Martin, 1978). Education, health care, and welfare became collective concerns, and this has "taken some of the tragedy, some of the magic and much of religion out of life" (De Swaan, 1988, p. 10). The reduced influence over such areas as education made it difficult for the church to ensure religious teachings (De Swaan, 1988, p. 83). Inglehart (1990, pp. 178-181) points to the high level of personal security in contemporary advanced societies, which reduces the individual dependence on arbitrary forces and diminishes the influence of traditional religious norms. This high level of security can be traced to the "postwar economic miracle and the rise of the welfare state" (Inglehart, 1990, p. 205). This variable was operationalized as the percentage of Gross National Product expended on social security provisions in 1990.

Religious Pluralism

A high level of religious pluralism should be positively related to the level of religious involvement because there is a large variety of religious products consumers can choose from, producers are more sensitive to the desires of the consumers, religious organizations deal more efficiently with their resources, and innovation is stimulated (Iannaccone, 1992, p. 129). The religious market theory predicts that, contrarily to the claims of the prevailing secularization theory, religion can still play a vital role in contemporary society (Stark, Finke, & Iannaccone, 1995, p. 431). Religious pluralism was measured by the Herfindahl index, which varies between 0 and 1 and measures the probability that "two people, selected at random from those claiming a religious affiliation, share the same religion" (Iannaccone, 1991, p. 166).[6]

State Regulation of Religion

Chaves and Cann (1992) argue that religious pluralism does not explain the high level of religious involvement in Catholic countries such as Spain and Italy, and that the relationship between the state and the church is more important than religious pluralism in explaining the level of church attendance. If there is a close relation between the state and religion, there is a large probability that religion will become identified with a particular side in a social or political conflict, "opening the door to secularity as a symbol of opposition" (Chaves & Cann, 1992, p. 276). They devised a scale that runs from 0 to 6 (from *none* to *a lot of* state regulation) and measures, among other things, whether there is a single officially designated state church, whether the state influences the appointment of church leaders, and whether there is a system of ecclesiastical tax collection (Chaves & Cann, 1992, pp. 280-281).

Catholics/Protestants

Besides the level of state regulation, Chaves and Cann found a substantial effect of the percentage of Catholics in a country (1992,

TABLE 11.1 Pairwise Correlations Between Religious Variables and Country Variables

	Church Membership		Church Attendance		Religious Upbringing		Importance of Rites of Passage	
	P^a	S^b	P	S	P	S	P	S
GNP per capita	.15	.32	−.63*	−.67*	−.68*	−.73*	−.40	−.51§
Expenditures on social security	−.18	−.16	−.32	−.42	−.28	−.21	−.44	−.58*
Level of state regulation	.40	.39	−.66*	−.72*	−.70*	−.59*	−.15	−.29
Percentage Catholics	−.27	−.40	.56*	.60*	.76*	.68*	.25	.35
Herfindahl index	.33	.42	−.14	−.10	−.07	.16	.13	.16
Uncertainty avoidance	−.24	−.35	.09	.32	.55*	.48§	.08	.13
Individualism	−.30	−.46§	−.06	.06	−.12	.00	−.13	−.18
Masculinity	.04	.07	.60*	.61*	.67*	.61*	.72*	.78*

a. P = Pearson correlation.
b. S = Spearman correlation.
§$p < .10$. *$p < .05$.

p. 285). The high level of religious involvement in Catholic countries would be explained by their low level of individualization compared to Protestant countries (Jagodzinski & Dobbelaere, 1995, pp. 80-84). Protestantism reduced religion to its most essential elements by divesting itself from mystery, miracle, and magic (Berger, 1969, p. 111). It narrowed the relationship between the sacred and the people to only one channel, the Word of God: "It needed only the cutting of this one narrow channel of mediation . . . to open the floodgates of secularization" (Berger, 1969, p. 112).

Cultural Dimensions

To explore more deeply the relationship between culture and religion, we decided to include three[7] of the four national culture dimensions of Hofstede (1991) in our analyses. Initially, we were especially interested in the variable Individualism/Collectivism because the process of individualization was supposed to have stimulated secularization

TABLE 11.2 Pairwise Correlations Between Religious Variables and Country Variables

	Confidence in the Church		Religiosity		Orthodoxy		Christian Worldview	
	P^a	S^b	P	S	P	S	P	S
GNP per capita	−.35	−.46§	−.43	−.47§	−.26	−.38	−.65*	−.69*
Expenditures on social security	−.65*	−.59*	−.60*	−.62*	−.68*	−.71*	−.53§	−.58*
Level of state regulation	−.68*	−.67*	−.61*	−.59*	−.63*	−.50§	−.59*	−.59*
Percentage Catholics	.40	.46§	.38	.30	.21	.14	.55*	.51*
Herfindahl index	−.50*	−.28	−.28	−.14	−.39	−.12	−.10	.03
Uncertainty avoidance	.38	.40	.18	.21	−.02	.06	.31	.27
Individualism	.07	.10	.04	.13	.25	.19	−.13	.02
Masculinity	.59*	.51§	.69*	.70*	.73*	.71*	.74*	.74*

a. P = Pearson correlation.
b. S = Spearman correlation.
§$p < .10$. *$p < .05$.

(by making religion a matter of free choice for the autonomous individual). As we will see later, however, the Masculinity/Femininity (Mas/Fem) dimension turned out to be one of the most important correlates of the level of religious involvement. Finally, we included the Uncertainty Avoidance Index. Religion reduces anxiety because it "helps in the acceptance of the uncertainties one cannot defend oneself against" (Hofstede, 1991, p. 110). We expect a high level of religious involvement in countries where the culture fosters a strong need to avoid uncertainty.

RESULTS

Tables 11.1 and 11.2 present the correlations between the eight religious variables and the country characteristics.[8] Overall, there are no large differences between the Spearman rank and the Pearson product moment correlations (the former are less sensitive to the impact of countries with an extreme value on one of the country characteristics). If we look only at the directions of the effects, most of the expectations

TABLE 11.3 Pairwise Correlations (Pearson) Between Country Variables
(before transformation)

	X1	X2	X3	X4	X5	X6	X7	X8	X9
X1	1.00								
X2	.03	1.00							
X3	.41	.42	1.00						
X4	−.72*	.07	−.62*	1.00					
X5	−.31	.49§	.54*	.13	1.00				
X6	−.47§	.18	−.29	.76*	.22	1.00			
X7	−.53§	.20	−.21	.77*	.24	.93*	1.00		
X8	.64*	−.26	−.11	−.40	−.50§	−.42	−.60*	1.00	
X9	−.25	−.51§	−.48§	.48§	−.24	.22	.19	.25	1.00

NOTE: X1 = GNP per capita 1990, X2 = expenditures on social security 1990, X3 = level of state regulation, X4 = percentage Catholics 1990, X5 = Herfindahl Index 1990, X6 = Power Distance Index, X7 = Uncertainty Avoidance Index, X8 = Individualism Index, and X9 = Masculinity Index.
§$p < .10$. *$p < .05$.

are confirmed. Religious involvement is lowest in modernized countries, strongly developed welfare states, countries with a close relationship between the church and the state, Protestant countries, religiously monopolistic countries, and countries with a low level of Uncertainty Avoidance or Masculinity. Not in agreement with the theory are (a) the inconsistent, and marginal, relation between Individualism/Collectivism and religious involvement, and (b) the reverse relationship between church membership and most of the country characteristics (compared with the other religious variables).[9]

Of all country characteristics, Masculinity correlates highest with four of the eight religious variables: importance of religious rites, religiosity, orthodoxy, and Christian worldview. The relationship between the state and the church is most important with respect to church attendance and confidence in the church; results differ for church membership and religious upbringing (depending on which of the two correlations one looks at). Except for church membership, Masculinity correlates significantly with all the religious variables. Besides Masculinity, the relationship between the state and the church, per capita GNP, expenditures on social security, and percentage of Catholics have significant correlations with at least three religious variables. Table 11.3 shows the intercorrelations between these variables.

It appears that for the study of secularization, Mas/Fem is the most important single country characteristic. It is especially related to the subjective side of religiosity, and somewhat less to institutionalized religious practices. Because countries with feminine cultures are predominantly Protestant, welfare states, and characterized by a close relationship between state and church (Table 11.3), we had to check whether the relationship between Masculinity and religious involvement could be spurious. This was not the case. A regression analysis of importance of religious rites, religiosity, orthodoxy, and Christian worldview on Masculinity and a second country characteristic showed that (a) with respect to religious rites and orthodoxy, Masculinity was the only variable with a significant effect ($p < .05$); (b) GNP per capita and Masculinity both had significant effects on Christian worldview ($p < .05$), and in all other combinations, Masculinity was the only variable with a significant effect; and (c) Masculinity lost its significance ($p = .06$) when orthodoxy was also regressed on expenditures on social security ($p = .19$) but remained the most important variable in all other combinations of two country characteristics.

Cross-national variations in secularization also can be explained by the effects of micro variables—by the composition of the different populations involved (Campbell & Curtis, 1994, p. 216).[10] It appeared, however, that for church attendance and religiosity, even if one controls for the effects of more than 20 sociodemographic variables and individual value orientations (such as postmaterialism and institutional trust), Masculinity still remained one of the most important country characteristics (Verweij et al., 1996). Surprisingly, only a few micro variables, such as age, gender, and moral permissiveness, had significant effects on religiosity or church attendance in 8 or more of the 16 countries involved (Verweij et al., 1996). In explaining religious involvement, therefore, one must look at variables at the country level.

DISCUSSION

Countries with a feminine culture are far more secularized than countries with a masculine culture. Hofstede himself points at the fact that the Jewish-Christian heritage seems to flourish best in masculine cultures. The more traditional interpretation of Christianity emphasizes the difference between men and women and the secondary, supporting role of women in religion and society. This becomes clear in the first book of the Bible (Genesis), in the story of the woman being made from Adam's rib: "This text gives clear priority to the male partner and defines the woman as 'a help meet' (i.e., appropriate) for him; it justifies a society in which there is male dominance" (Hofstede, 1991, p. 101). The Christian God has a masculine image, which makes Him more important and acceptable in masculine cultures (Hofstede, 1991, pp. 101-102).

Several authors refer to the patriarchal bias of traditional Christianity, founded on the Bible and expressed in religious beliefs, ethics, hymnody, language, practices, liturgy, and the writings of influential theologians (Daly, 1973, pp. 3-45; Ozorak, 1996, p. 17; Peek, Lowe, & Williams, 1991, p. 1207; Ruether, 1983, p. 22; Steiner-Aeschliman & Mauss, 1996, pp. 248-255). The masculine image of God as a great patriarch in Heaven confirms and supports a patriarchal society (Biezeveld, 1996, p. 29; Steiner-Aeschliman & Mauss, 1996, p. 249). A radical feminist theologian writes, "if God is male, then the male is God" (Daly, 1973, p. 19). Another feminist theologian has argued,

> Whereas ancient myth had seen the Gods and Goddesses as within the matrix of one physical-spiritual reality, male monotheism begins to split reality into a dualism of transcendent Spirit (mind, ego) and inferior and dependent physical nature. . . . Thus the hierarchy of God-male-female does not merely make woman secondary in relation to God, it also gives her a negative identity in relation to the divine. Whereas the male is seen essentially as the image of the male transcendent ego or God, woman is seen as the image of the lower, material nature. (Ruether, 1983, p. 54)

The masculine character of Christianity not only stimulated a patriarchal society but also has been supported by a male-dominated social structure (Peek et al., 1991, p. 1207). The images and values of a given society have been projected in religious dogmas and beliefs, obtaining an objective independent status, and these in turn justify the same social structures that gave rise to them (Daly, 1973, p. 13). This reciprocal relationship between religion and society's values might explain the impact of femininity on secularization: "Religious symbols fade and die when the cultural situation that gave rise to them and supported them ceases to give them plausibility" (Daly, 1973, p. 15). The cultural situation in the Western world has changed substantially since the 1950s, especially in the domain of family, marriage, and the relationship between men and women. Possibly there has been a shift from masculine to feminine values in certain countries of the Western world, going hand in hand with a declining religious involvement.

At least in most Christian churches, anybody can observe that at the individual level women participate more in the activities of the church than men, while these same churches treat them as inferior to men (Derks & Monteiro, 1996, p. 17; Ozorak, 1996, p. 17). Women are, in all aspects, more religious than men, and this is one of the few consistent cross-national findings (Verweij et al., 1996). There is a large variety of sociological and psychological explanations for women's higher religiosity, but none of these has been consistently supported or thoroughly tested (Hoge & Roozen, 1979; Walter, 1990, p. 85). Ozorak argues that most women she studied perceived, but did not accept, gender inequality in their religious faiths. To reduce their discomfort, they used several behavioral and cognitive coping strategies (Ozorak, 1996, pp. 21-23). Women, she affirms, experience their religion differently from men. They emphasize a personal relationship with a loving God whom they see as a friend and confident, whereas men see God rather as a cosmic ruler or judge (Ozorak, 1996, pp. 18-27). Women see care and connection as the greatest moral goods, whereas men put emphasis on independence and objectivity (Ozorak, 1996, p. 18): "Being less glorified or less well represented is only of critical concern if the religious community is perceived primarily in terms of its hierarchy. That perspective invites a zero-sum conception of power that requires losers in order to have winners. By contrast, a weblike perspective allows the possibility of a community without losers" (Ozorak, 1996, p. 27).

According to the workforce theory, gender differences in religiosity are related to gender differences with respect to participation in the labor market (Hoge & Roozen, 1979). The traditional role of women in the church fits a society in which men work as breadwinners outside the home and women stay at home and raise the family. The church in this case is women's only legitimate opportunity to widen their horizon beyond the home; for men, it competes with many other outdoor activities. In modernizing societies, women are less and less needed in the home and participate more and more in economic activities previously reserved for men. This leads to a reduction in the gender gap in religiosity.

Cross-national studies investigating the validity of this workforce theory show inconclusive results. Sometimes gender differences in religious involvement were reduced if one controlled for labor force participation (De Vaus & McAllister, 1987; Stoetzel, 1983, p. 92); other times they remained quite large (De Vaus, 1984; Verweij et al., 1996).

What the correlations between Femininity and secularization might show is that this process is modified by the dominant values in countries about gender roles. In more masculine societies, even if modernization occurs, women's roles and values continue to include the maintenance of at least part of their special religiosity, and men in these societies also continue more often to declare themselves religious, even if they leave most of the practicing of religion to their women. In more feminine societies, modernization implies that women who do the same things as men also value the same things; they lose their special roles and values in religious matters, and in this respect they become like men, who were never very religious anyway. It is evident that future research on the relationship between Masculinity/Femininity, gender, and secularization might produce fascinating results.

NOTES

1. This chapter summarizes several papers presented by the author at (inter)national conferences in 1995/1996. Thanks to Peter Ester and Rein Nauta, supervisors of the author's PhD dissertation, who coauthored some of it.

2. See, for example, discussions in the *Journal for the Scientific Study of Religion*, 1995 (34) and 1996 (35).

3. See this paper for detailed information about the operationalization (and cross-national comparability) of the religious variables and the country characteristics, the country scores on both kind of variables, and the analyses that were performed.

4. This was measured by a "Mokken" scale, named for a Dutch professor who empirically found a hierarchical order in political beliefs, in which every belief implies the previous ones.

5. Dobbelaere (1981, pp. 11-12) also distinguishes secularization as a process of laicization and secularization as a process of religious change. These processes take place at the level of society as well as at the level of the religious organization.

6. The higher the score on this index, the less religiously pluralistic a country.

7. To avoid problems of multicollinearity, we excluded Power Distance because for our 16 countries it correlated .93 with Uncertainty Avoidance (see Table 11.3).

8. Certain variables were transformed because it appeared that outliers had a serious effect on the relationships between the religious variables and the country characteristics: (a) the Individualism Index was raised to the square power, and (b) in

the case of church attendance and religious upbringing, GNP per capita was squared. Subsequently, we checked whether there were any curvilinear relations between the religious and country variables (by regressing all religious variables on each country characteristic and its square), but this was nowhere the case.

9. This probably is due to the high level of church membership in the Scandinavian countries (Protestant, religiously monopolistic, a high GNP per capita, a lot of state regulation of religion), where people automatically, from birth, belong to the state church.

10. Suppose, for example, that (a) old people go to church more often than young people and (b) in Portugal, there are more old people than in the Netherlands. In that case, the micro variable "age" could explain why the Netherlands is more secularized than Portugal.

12

RELIGION, MASCULINITY, AND SEX

Geert Hofstede

This last chapter connects the previous two; it argues that sexuality and the sacred in human history always have been closely linked. Religious beliefs follow values as much as the reverse, and like values, they vary along the masculine/feminine continuum. In Christian countries, the poles of the dimension correspond to a focus on God the Father on the masculine side, and a focus on one's fellow human beings on the feminine side. The existence of varieties of religiosity within the same Christian churches is shown, reflecting among other things value differences related to the Masculinity/Femininity (Mas/Fem) dimension. Christianity in the United States reflects masculine majority and feminine minority values. Non-Christian religions show some evidence of harboring the same kind of differences among their different currents. All religions have their do's and don'ts about sexuality. A main theme is their attitude toward sexual pleasure, which may be condoned for both genders, for men only, or not at all. The Mas/Fem dimension offers a framework to link values related to religion with values related to sexuality. The fact that the Mas/Fem dimension is associated with these two sensitive areas helps understand why it sometimes is treated as a taboo by writers and researchers.

FERTILITY AND THE SACRED

The Austrian village of Willendorf is famous for its "Venus," but this local beauty is some 25,000 years old: a small stone sculpture of a pregnant woman, without a face or arms but with exaggerated sexual parts—heavy hips, bottom, and bosom. Several more of such figures, dating from the upper Paleolithic period, have been found in Europe and Western Asia. The Cuevas de Tito Bustillo, a system of caves in Ribadesella, Asturias, northern Spain, are a picture gallery of Paleolithic art—wall paintings from about 14,000 years ago. As in other caves in Spain and France, there are wonderful pictures of hunted animals, but in one cave, the Sala de las Vulvas, there is a wall painted with female genitals. There must have been something sacred about these representations. Not much has changed in 14,000 years. In the Musée d'Orsay in Paris, there is a painting by Gustave Courbet, which he made in 1866 and called *L'Origine du Monde* ("The Origin of the World"). What it shows is a young woman's genital zone. Large standing stones representing male genitals—phalluses—are found in neolithic sanctuaries, for example in Portugal; they are about 5,000 years old.

Fertility rites are known from virtually all human civilizations (Schubart, 1941); they survive to the present day, such as in wedding ceremonies and in sanctuaries devoted to prayers for pregnancy. All religions celebrate the events of procreation: births, weddings, and deaths. In Judaism and most of Islam, circumcision of the male organ is a condition for being admitted to the religious community. In Hinduism, the architecture of temples models the lingam and yoni: phallus and vulva. Chinese philosophy and religious practices give strong importance to the complementarity of yang and yin, the male and female element.

Most or all religions contain do's and don'ts about love and sex. U.S. sociologist Peter Berger has written,

Every society is faced with the problem of providing for its physical procreation. This has meant, empirically, that every society has worked out more or less restrictive "programs" for the sexual activity of its members. . . . The problem of legitimation is to explain why the particular arrangement that has developed in a particular society . . . should be faithfully adhered to, even if it is at times annoying or downright painful. One efficient way of solving the problem is to mystify the institution in religious terms. (1969, p. 90)

The treatment in the same part of this book of religiosity and sexuality is therefore not so farfetched. In human history, religion and sex always have been closely associated. Religion is a way for humankind to influence the supernatural, to provide certainties beyond the unpredictable risks of human existence. Birth, marital fertility, and death figure foremost among these unpredictables. The artifacts of Willendorf and Ribadesella testify that the link between procreation and the supernatural already had been made at the dawn of human civilization.

RELIGION AND VALUES:
WHICH WAY CAUSALITY?

U.S. anthropologist Clifford Geertz has defined religion as follows: A religion is

(1) a system of symbols which acts to (2) establish powerful, pervasive, and long-lasting moods and motivations in men by (3) formulating conceptions of a general order of existence and (4) clothing these conceptions with such an aura of factuality that (5) the moods and motivations seem uniquely realistic. (1973, p. 90)

Religious beliefs are obviously linked with *values*. In *Culture's Consequences* (Hofstede, 1980), I defined a value as "a broad tendency to prefer certain states of affairs over others" (p. 19). Values are the components of the dimensions of national culture identified in *Culture's Consequences*. Geertz's "powerful, pervasive, and long-lasting moods and motivations" imply preferences for certain states of affairs over others. The question is, do religious beliefs determine values or vice versa? The common assumption, found among other places in public statements by politicians, is that values follow from religion.

Verweij (Chapter 11 and Verweij et al., 1997) analyzed data on secularization collected by the European (later World Values) Survey across 16 countries. He found that country scores on the Mas/Fem dimension were the best available predictor of a Christian country's degree of secularization: Countries with feminine values had secularized faster than those with masculine ones. This suggests that the direction of causality is from values to religion, not vice versa.

A similar conclusion was drawn in *Culture's Consequences* (p. 132), where a common "Latin" value pattern was shown to exist in countries once part of the Roman Empire, a value pattern established already in the first centuries A.D. In the 16th century A.D., when attempts at reformation shook Christian Europe, they succeeded only in countries outside the limits of the former Roman Empire; the Roman Catholic church maintained itself within the limits of the former empire. The presence or absence of a value pattern established by the Roman Empire in pre-Christian times was a decisive factor in the failure or success of the Reformation more than 1,000 years later.

Italian sociologist and economist Vilfredo Pareto (1848-1923) has distinguished *residues* and *derivations* in human sentiments. Residues represent underlying nonlogical general themes rooted in human instincts; derivations are their justifications in specific ideas and theories (Pareto, 1916/1976, p. 215ff). Religious doctrines are derivations; values are residues.

Christianity split many times. The most important schisms were between Eastern Orthodoxy and Roman Catholicism, and later between Catholicism and various Protestantisms. The other great world religions also underwent internal schisms, such as between Mahayana and Theravada in Buddhism and between Sunni and Shia in Islam. The spread of doctrines has been affected by military and political events, but also by the minds of the receivers. Local pre-existing values determined which doctrines were acceptable and which were not; moreover, doctrines were adapted when they moved to a new cultural environment. A place where this adaptation has been very visible is Middle and East Java, Indonesia. It successively underwent the influences of Hinduism, Buddhism, Islam, and Christianity, but the pre-existing values of nonaggressive Javanese mysticism were integrated into whatever religion was adopted (Mulder, 1980).

Once a particular current of a religion has been established in a country, it reinforces the values that led to its being adopted in the first place (Hofstede, 1980, p. 181). According to Berger (1969, p. 128), "religion might appear as a formative force in one situation and as a dependent formation in the situation following historically," but I think the reverse sequence has occurred with at least equal frequency: religion as dependent on pre-existing values first, and as a formative force later.

Berger explains the formation of human societies by three steps: externalization, objectivation, and internalization. Externalization is the impact on the world of the physical and mental activity of humans. Objectivation is the recognition of the products of this activity as "reality," external to its creators. Internalization is the reappropriation by humans of this reality into their subjective consciousness (Berger, 1969, p. 4). These steps can be recognized in the formation of religions. First, some people have developed mental images of the supernatural, images that reflect the human environment at the time of their first appearance (externalization). Second, these mental images have been institutionalized into specific religious beliefs and denominations (objectivation). Third, these institutionalized images have become part of people's subjective consciousness (internalization).

CHRISTIAN BELIEFS AND
THE MAS/FEM DIMENSION

The Masculinity pole of the Mas/Fem dimension, as it was found in the IBM studies, stands for a society in which men are supposed to be tough and women tender. The Femininity pole stands for a society in which both men and women can be tender. Because in all societies men traditionally have dominated in institutions outside the home, Masculinity has produced tougher and Femininity more tender societies. Berger's three steps of externalization, objectivation, and internalization can explain why tough societies will favor tough religions, with tough gods and tough rites; tender societies will develop tender religions, with tender gods and rites.

Christianity has always maintained a dialectic between tough/masculine and tender/feminine elements. Genesis, the first book of the Judeo-Christian Old Testament, codified in the fifth century B.C.E., is ambiguous about the equality or inequality of men and women. It contains two conflicting versions of the creation of humankind. The first, Genesis 1:27-28, states:

> So God created man in his own image, in the image of God created he him; male and female created he them. And God blessed them, and God said to them, Be fruitful, and multiply, and replenish the earth, and subdue it.[1]

This text suggests equal partnership and complementarity between the genders. The second version, Genesis 2:8ff., contains the story of the garden of Eden, in which God first put "the man" alone. Genesis 2:18 then states, "And the Lord God said, It is not good that the man should be alone: I will make him a help meet for him."

Then follows the story of the Woman made from Adam's rib. This text gives clear priority to the male partner and defines the woman as "a help meet" (i.e., appropriate) for him; it justifies a society in which there is male dominance.

In the Bible as a whole, the Old Testament reflects tougher values (eye for eye, tooth for tooth) and the New Testament more tender values (turn the other cheek). God in the Old Testament is majestic. The New Testament contains passages like the following poem:

> *Then shall the King say to those on his right:*
> *"Come, you whom my Father has blessed . . .*
> *For I was hungry and you fed me,*
> *I was thirsty and you gave me drink,*
> *I was a stranger and you entertained me,*
> *I was unclothed and you clothed me,*
> *I was ill and you looked after me,*
> *I was in prison and you visited me."*
> *Then the just will answer:*
> *"Lord, when did we . . . [do all these things]?"*
> *The King will answer them:*
> *"I tell you truly,*
> *in so far as you did it to one of these my brothers,*
> *even to the least of them, you did it to me."*
> *Then he will say to those on the left:*

"Begone from me, accursed ones, to the eternal fire
which has been prepared for the devil and his angels!
For I was hungry but you never fed me . . ."
(from *St. Matthew* 26:34-40; see Moffatt, 1949)

Jesus Christ can hardly be called a macho hero.[2] The Christian Gospel offers a choice of values for different positions on the Mas/Fem values scale. Catholicism has produced some very masculine, tough currents (Templars, Jesuits) but also some feminine, tender ones (Franciscans); outside Catholicism can be found groups with strongly masculine values (like the Mormons) and groups with more feminine values (like the Salvation Army). On average, however, countries with a Catholic tradition tend to maintain more masculine and those with Protestant traditions more feminine values. Many Protestant churches now practice equality between men and women in their leadership and clergy, whereas the Roman Catholic church strongly maintains the male prerogative to the priesthood.

In *Culture's Consequences* (p. 209), the Catholic/Protestant ratio in Christian countries was shown to be correlated with both Uncertainty Avoidance and Masculinity (more Catholicism in uncertainty avoiding and masculine countries). Verweij, in Chapter 11, found similar correlations on the basis of percentage of a country's population that was Catholic in 1990. Verweij's conclusions in Chapter 11 were that feminine Christian countries in the past decades have secularized more than masculine ones. In masculine Christian countries, people rate their religiosity higher and attach more importance in their lives to God, Christian rites, orthodoxy, and Christian worldviews. Verweij's study used data from the 1990 European/World Values Survey. The first, 1981/1982 round of the same survey already contained a large number of questions about religion. These included the claimed observance of the Ten Commandments, one by one. French sociologist Jean Stoetzel, who published an insightful analysis of the results across nine countries in 1983, divided the Commandments into three categories:

▦ Moral commandments: (4) honoring parents, (5) no killing, (7) no stealing, (8) no false witness, and (9) do not covet thy neighbor's goods
▦ Sexual commandments: (6) no adultery, (10) do not covet thy neighbor's wife

■ Purely religious commandments: (1) no other gods, (2) not using God's name in vain, and (3) keeping the Sabbath holy

Overall, the claimed observance was highest for the moral commandments and lowest for the religious commandments. For all three categories—moral, sexual, and religious—observance was correlated with the rated "importance of God in my life," both at the level of individual respondents and at the level of country means. The correlations were strongest, however, for the religious commandments and weakest for the moral commandments (Stoetzel, 1983, pp. 98-101). Across the nine countries, the "importance of God" was significantly correlated with the Masculinity Index (MAS; Hofstede, 1991, p. 102; rho = .70**[3]).

The moral and sexual commandments define relationships with fellow humans, whereas the religious commandments define relationships with God. In masculine countries, God is more important. If God is more important, the commandments that define a relationship with God are stressed as much as those that define relationships with fellow humans. If God is less important, which is the case in feminine countries, the moral commandments remain important, but the sexual and in particular the religious commandments carry less weight.

The 1981/1982 European Values Study also confirmed that women in all nine countries were more religious than men. Verweij, in Chapter 11, drew attention to the paradox in Christianity that in countries with a masculine culture, religious values are more strongly endorsed, but that these values are more practiced by the women than by the men.

Table 12.1 shows country comparisons on some other questions from the European/World Values Survey 1981/1982 that correlate with MAS. One question (Harding, Phillips, & Fogarty, 1986, question 262) referred to 17 "qualities which children can be encouraged to learn at home." "Religious faith" was positively correlated with MAS, but "politeness and neatness" and "feeling of responsibility" were *negatively* correlated with MAS. It seems that masculine cultures—which, as Verweij also showed, have remained more religious—put less stress on civil education. The 1990 European/World Values Survey contained a question "Generally speaking, would you say that most people can be trusted or that you can't be too careful in dealing with people?" Percentages answering "Can't be too careful" across 11 countries correlated $r = .66**$ with MAS.[4] If most people cannot be trusted, there is less reason for

TABLE 12.1 Survey Results From the World Values Survey (1981/1982)

	Percentage "Important for Child to Learn at Home"			
Countries in Order of MAS	Religious Faith	Politeness	Responsibility	Always Love Parents Regardless
Italy	22	37	46	79
Ireland	42	23	22	75
Great Britain	13	27	24	56
Germany	17	29	63	48
United States	39	37	44	72
Belgium	17	48	37	72
Canada	25	41	41	68
France	11	51	40	76
Spain	22	20	63	70
Denmark	8	51	63	35
Netherlands	14	42	55	39
Norway	11	60	64	47
Spearman rank correlations with MAS	.58*	−.62**	−.58*	.63**

SOURCE: Data are from Halman (1991, pp. 337, 340).
NOTE: $n > 1,000$ per country.
*$p < .05$. **$p < .01$ (one-tailed).

always being polite. "Feeling of responsibility" may contrast with the religious value of relying on God.

The last column of Table 12.1 is based on the choice between two statements (Harding et al., 1986, p. 259): (a) Regardless of what the qualities and faults of one's parents are, one must always love and respect them; and (b) One does not have the duty to respect and love parents who have not earned it by their behavior and attitudes. Masculine cultures to a much lesser extent think that parents have to *earn* their respect. Although the question refers to "parents," it is likely that the attitude toward the father played a major role in the choice of an answer. The answer does not mean that parents in feminine countries are really less respected; in Chapter 10, I referred to a study by Gibbons and colleagues (1995) in which adolescents in feminine Denmark reported more frequently being influenced by their parents than adolescents in masculine America.

TABLE 12.2 Differences in Religiosity Associated With the
Masculinity/Femininity Dimension of National Cultures

Feminine Cultures	*Masculine Cultures*
Appeal of "tender" religions and religious currents	Appeal of "tough" religions and religious currents
Men and women can be priests	Only men can be priests
In Christianity, greater affinity to Protestantism	In Christianity, greater affinity to Catholicism
In Christian countries, lower self-ratings of religiosity and of the importance of God in one's life	In Christian countries, higher self-ratings of religiosity and of the importance of God in one's life
Less importance attached to Christian rites, orthodoxy, and Christian worldviews	More importance attached to Christian rites, orthodoxy, and Christian worldviews
In Christian countries, more stress on relationship with fellow humans than with God	In Christian countries, more stress on relationship with God than with fellow humans
Most (other) people can be trusted	One cannot be too careful with other people
Children have to learn politeness and responsibility	Children have to learn religious faith
Parents have to earn their children's respect and love	Parents should always be loved and respected regardless of qualities and faults
Exemplarism and mysticism	Theism, traditionalism, and conversionalism

Table 12.2 summarizes the differences in religiosity found to be associated with feminine versus masculine cultures (the last lines represent a hypothesis that will be discussed later). The major conclusion from the summary is that among Christian countries, the tough, masculine societies endorse most strongly the importance of God—and other values derived from it. One could argue that this is obvious: The Christian God is the Father; He is masculine. Such a God appeals more to the population of a masculine society, including the women who were socialized to inequality of gender values. In a feminine society, the stress will be more on the importance of relationships with fellow humans than with God.

The New Testament of the Christian Bible carefully balances the importance of the relationships with God and with one's fellow humans. In one story Jesus is approached by a Pharisee with the question: "What is the greatest command in the Law?"

He replied, "You must love the Lord your God with your whole heart, with your whole soul, and with your whole mind. This is the greatest and chief command. There is a second like it: you must love your neighbor as yourself. The whole Law and the prophets hang upon these two commands." (St. Matthew 22: 37-40. Moffatt translation).

The comparison between Christian religiosity in more masculine and more feminine countries implies that the balance between these two commands is difficult to find. There are cultural imperatives which lead Christians in some countries to stress the first, and Christians in other countries to stress the second.

TOWLER'S "VARIETIES OF RELIGION"

One can question to what extent the answers on survey questions can reflect the essence of religiosity. Varieties of religiosity occur even within the same church. This became evident from a study with a different method. In 1963, John A. T. Robinson, then Anglican Bishop of Woolwich, England, published a little book *Honest to God*, containing critical ideas about traditional elements in Christian religion. As a result, he received about 4,000 spontaneous letters from mainly British readers (or nonreaders). These letters, some supportive, some critical, represent a unique source of information about styles of religiosity among the public at large. Robinson made his letter collection available to sociologist Robert Towler, who did an extensive content analysis (Towler, 1984). Towler found evidence of five different "varieties of religion" among the correspondents:

1. Exemplarism, with Jesus Christ as an example to follow;
2. Conversionism, based on a personal experience of having been saved from sin;
3. Theism, a sense of wonder and awe in the face of God's works in nature and the world;
4. Gnosticism, focusing on possession of secret knowledge about the spiritual world; and
5. Traditionalism, or uncritical acceptance of the teachings of the church whatever their content.

Had Towler's material covered more people from Asian cultures, at least one more variety would have been added:

6. Mysticism, focusing on a personal experience of unity with God.

The five British varieties of religiosity occurred within the same churches. The strong individualism in British culture, shown in the IBM studies, will encourage different individual beliefs and feelings. Towler's study shows what can be behind answers to survey questions about religiosity. The different varieties accommodate different and contrasting personal value systems, and cultural influences will make some of these varieties more or less popular among certain groups. Conversionism, theism, and traditionalism fit better within masculine (sub)cultures; exemplarism and mysticism in feminine ones. Gnosticism is probably unrelated to Mas/Fem.

RELIGIOSITY IN
THE UNITED STATES

In many studies of religiosity and secularization (but not in Verweij's study in Chapter 11), the United States figures as an exception: a country exposed to many of the forces that lead to secularization elsewhere, but nevertheless scoring high on all measures of religiosity (see Chapter 11). Surveys in the 1990s show that around 95% of Americans claim to believe in God. Peter Berger has suggested that U.S. churches have become secularized internally, but compared with other countries, they still occupy a more central symbolic position (Berger, 1969, p. 108).

Mainstream U.S. culture is quite masculine, and U.S. masculinity helps to understand the appeal of God the Father. The frequent revival movements that sweep the country often play on explicitly masculine sentiments. Pastoral worker Leanne Payne—who earlier wrote *The Healing of the Homosexual*—referred to a "growing cultural malady, already epidemic in proportions" that she called the "crisis in masculinity" (Payne, 1985, p. 11). The Promise Keepers, a men-only mass movement founded by football coach Bill McCartney in 1990, wanted to recruit 50,000 emissaries to local churches, people who would work to create "an environment of godly masculinity" (*The Economist*, June 8, 1995, p. 51). Conservative former judge Robert Bork, in his 1996 book *Slouching Towards Gomorrah*, blames the decay of Western culture on, among others, the feminists. Some antihomosexual and anti-abortion groups resort to terrorism.

Masculinizing authors and movements cater to the "moral majority" in the United States. U.S. political scientist Ronald Inglehart sees in the rise of these movements "a reaction to recent cultural change by groups who are less educated, have fewer resources, are less secure, and therefore more threatened by change" (1990, p. 179). He recognizes the same phenomenon in other countries, not only Western ones.

Not all of American Christianity is so masculine—this is a large country with a wide variation of subcultures. The Quakers, who nowadays find their membership mainly among intellectuals, are an example of culturally feminine values:

> Quakerism as a religion gives strong support to the sharing rather than the assertive life style . . . I found the emphasis on career muted among both men and women. . . . The life goal was to develop a certain character and to live in a simple, harmonious way rather than to achieve a career of great significance. It is the only society I have ever entered in America in which the first question asked of a man is not "What do you do?," but "Who are you?" . . . Though they realized of course that it was necessary to have an occupation and to earn money, that was not the most salient or valued feature of a person's life, as it is nearly everywhere else in contemporary America. (McClelland, 1975, pp. 108-109; also quoted in Ruether, 1983, p. 102)

In American settler history, the victims of the infamous Puritan trials in Salem, Massachusetts, in 1692 were not only supposed witches but also Quakers. Already in those days, Puritans and Quakers represented opposite forms of Christianity. What guarantees that they will both survive is "another culture that runs even deeper in America: the culture of freedom" ("America and Religion," 1995).

MAS/FEM AND
NON-CHRISTIAN RELIGIONS

So far, the relationship between masculinity and religiosity has been demonstrated across Christian countries only. Outside the Christian world, there are also tough and tender religions. Buddhism in masculine Japan is very different from Buddhism in feminine Thailand. Some young men in Japan follow Zen Buddhist training aiming at self-development by meditation under a tough master. A vast number of young men in Thailand spend some time as Buddhist monks, serving and begging. Young Thai women specialize in economic-entrepreneurial activities (Kirsch, 1985, p. 302), which is not the case in Japan. The syncretist Caodai religion of Vietnam recognizes a Father God and a Mother Goddess; it has male and female clergy (except at the top, which is male), but it strictly separates men and women in its sanctuaries, or even builds separate sanctuaries. I have no Masculinity Index scores on Vietnam, but I assume its culture to be fairly feminine.

In Islam, Sunni is a more triumphant version of the faith than Shia, which stresses the importance of suffering, following the founder Ali, who was persecuted. In the IBM studies, Iran, which is predominantly Shia, scored more feminine than the predominantly Sunni Arab speaking countries (Table 1.2).

Gender role divisions in the vast majority of religious institutions are traditionally quite rigid. The interesting thing is to see what happens after countries have become affluent, freeing women for tasks outside the home. In Christianity, the Roman Catholic church sticks strongly to traditional gender roles, but many Protestant churches have started admitting women to the priesthood, although not always wholeheartedly—in the Anglican church, the ordination of women threatens to be a cause for schism. Feminist Christian theologies try to create a theological base for a new gender role division (e.g., Ruether, 1983), but so far they remain a marginal phenomenon.

Non-Christian religions rarely have been exposed to affluence in society, except for Judaism, which shows the same division between traditional and modern currents as Christianity does. In Islam, modernity leads to less segregation of women and men during religious services, but there is no question yet of women being admitted to leadership roles.

RELIGIOUS ATTITUDES
ABOUT SEXUALITY

Pareto, whom we met earlier in this chapter, has identified six classes of "residues," of which the "sex residue" is one. He wrote:

The sex residues are manifested in phenomena which are similar to those termed "religious"; they may therefore be properly classified as a whole with religious phenomena. . . . Among ancient peoples and primitive peoples today, the sex organs and sexual acts are simply part of a general fetishism. For us moderns . . . though other fetishisms have disappeared or become weak, the sex fetishism endures. . . . In many Christian countries, it is possible to blaspheme Christ as much as one pleases, and no court of law will effectively intervene. But the courts will deal swiftly with anyone exhibiting an obscene postcard. . . . If we consider, one the one hand, the immense power of the church . . . and on the other, the insignificance of the results achieved in suppressing sexual immorality, we gain some idea of the tremendous strength of the sex residue, and realize how ridiculous are these pygmies of our day who imagine they can repress it. (Pareto, 1916/1976, p. 237)

Human sexuality always has two purposes: One is procreation, the other is pleasure. In fact, the latter, at least in the modern era, is much more general than the former, which is fortunate in a world threatened by overpopulation (Abramson & Pinkerton, 1995, pp. 17-18).

Different religions have taken different positions toward the pleasure side of sex. Christianity from its beginning has been uneasy about it and rejected sex for pleasure. St. Paul, in the Christian New Testament, is ambivalent about marriage. He was a bachelor himself and writes that he would like all men to be like himself, but it was "better to marry than to burn" (I. Corinthians 7:7-9). According to Foucault (1984a, p. 48; 1984b, p. 239), the Christian attitude to sex contrasted with the prevailing morality in the Greek and Roman civilizations, in which the early Christian church developed. Although the Greeks and Romans recognized dangers in excess of sexual pleasure, they did not consider pleasure evil in itself. The Romans did try to control sexual excesses by legal procedures, as they did for other aspects of their society. The Roman attempt at regulation probably inspired the Church of Rome's later belief that it could control sex by prohibition.

Augustinus (354-430) established the church's position that since Adam and Eve's fall from grace, all sexual activity is sinful, even if it is necessary for procreation (Schubart, 1941). The church thereby condemned a force it would never be able to control and established a perennial cult of sinfulness around it. This could be seen as "the source of its strength. As long as men and women continued to sin, they continued to need the grace of the sacraments only available through the Church" (Warner, 1976, p. 153). Augustinus also institutionalized celibacy for priests, which over the church's history was not always very well kept and had to be reconfirmed several times. It certainly contributed to the church's negative stance on sex: An organization led for centuries by unmarried and possibly frustrated men is very unlikely to take a positive view of others' pleasures.

The cult of the Virgin Mary in Roman Catholicism and Eastern Orthodoxy confirms the sinfulness of sex. In the Roman Catholic church, the cult was gradually elaborated and refined. In the New Testament of the Christian Bible, Mary was not a central figure. Jesus' birth is mentioned in only two of the four Gospels, and only St. Matthew (1:18) suggests that Mary had been "pregnant by the Holy Spirit" when she gave birth to Jesus. The church later affirmed that Mary had always remained a virgin; finally, Pope Pius IX in 1854 proclaimed the dogma of the Immaculate Conception, declaring that Mary had been entirely free of sin, implying that her own mother, too, had given birth to her without sexual intercourse. The cult of the Virgin is a masculine construction, declaring all other women sinful by implication and allowing men to blame their temptations on these women. There is a "powerful undertow of misogyny in Christianity, which associates women with the dangers and degradation of the flesh" (Warner, 1976, p. 225).

Marriage in Catholicism is considered a sacrament with the purpose of procreation. The prohibition of contraception and abortion is still a central dogma of the Roman Catholic church. The church leaders' tenacity in maintaining it, at a time when fewer and fewer of their flock respect it, and when overpopulation has become the number one world survival problem, is amazing, unless one realizes the strong common underlying values of religious and procreative behavior. Christian tradition knows seven deadly sins: anger, envy, gluttony, greed, lust, pride, and sloth, but in practice the first association of "sin" is with lust. Catholic bishops and U.S. television preachers are not fired for their greed or pride, but publicity about sexual adventures is their undoing.

Protestant Christian churches, when they split from Rome around the 16th century, did away with celibacy. Protestant churches as a rule do not consider marriage a sacrament, put less stress on procreation, and accept divorce (Ravesloot, 1995, p. 71). They tend not to take a position on sexual pleasure. Orthodox Islam accepts sexual pleasure for men but considers sexual pleasure in women a danger.

Currents in Hinduism have taken a very positive attitude to sexual pleasure, as manifested by the *Kamasutra* and the erotic temples of Khajuraho and Konarak in India (Abramson & Pinkerton, 1995, p. 196). The very explicit reliefs at Konarak—even the unavoidable elephants are copulating—shocked the Victorian British rulers when the temple was excavated from the sand. There have been other currents in Hinduism too, and it is difficult to associate the temples with a particular set of values. In Japanese and Thai Buddhist tradition, there is a place for prostitutes for men's sexual pleasure. In Thailand, the profession of prostitute carries less of a stigma than in the West (Kirsch, 1985, p. 312).

RELIGIONS, SEXUALITY, AND MAS/FEM DIFFERENCES

Chapter 10 showed sexuality to be partly culturally constructed and to vary with the Mas/Fem dimension in the sense that in masculine cultures, sex is experienced more as performance, and in feminine cultures as relationship. Chapter 11 showed Christian religiosity to vary with Mas/Fem, and in the earlier part of the present chapter, I interpreted this as a dialectic in religious thinking, in which people in tough, masculine cultures stress the belief in God the Father, while those in feminine cultures stress the relationship with their fellow human beings. The religious justification for the latter is "insofar as you did this to one of your brothers or sisters, even to the least of them, you did it to Christ." The tender values appear to last longer than their religious inspiration, so that these cultures continue caring for their fellow human beings after having become quite secularized (according to survey questions about religiosity).

The cultural constructions of sexuality and of religion therefore have a common theme: the existence of a masculine versus feminine continuum for the ways in which the culture handles these basic aspects of humanity. The position of a culture on this continuum is reflected in religious practices with regard to sexuality, especially its pleasure element. Masculine religions will either reserve pleasure to men or deny it to both genders; feminine religions will be silent on the subject or value sexual pleasure positively for men and women.

TABOOS AS ULTIMATE VALUES

As the title of this book puts it, there is a taboo about describing cultures in terms of "masculine" and "feminine." The taboo affects those who write and do research about cultural differences; Chapters 1 and 4 contain examples. The taboo exists primarily in masculine cultures. It is fed from the same concerns that lead to a stress on political correctness in writing about gender and to vigilance against sexual harassment.

"Taboo" is a Polynesian word. *Webster's Ninth New Collegiate Dictionary* (1990) defines "taboo" as an adjective as "1. forbidden to profane use or contact because of supposedly dangerous supernatural powers. 2a. banned on grounds of morality or taste. 2b banned as constituting a risk." Taboos reveal what is sacred. Taboos are about ultimate values, values that are not open to argument. Religion and sexuality are the main areas in which societies maintain taboos. The fact that the Mas/Fem dimension relates to both explains why this is a taboo dimension.

Nations in the world have become more and more interdependent, and violence has become a less and less effective way of resolving international problems. There is no substitute for listening to and talking with others, and for trying to understand the reasoning and motives of people whose mental programs differ. This means understanding one's own mental programs, including the taboos of one's culture, because taboos that some hold and others do not indicate values gaps to be bridged for a common future.

NOTES

1. All quotations are from the authorized version of the Holy Bible published by the British and Foreign Bible Society in 1954.

2. There have been attempts to change that. The musical *Jesus Christ Superstar* is a case. The Dutch newspaper *De Volkskrant* on June 26, 1997, reported that the Vatican has commissioned Brazilian designer Claudio Pastro to make a new portrait of Jesus, in which the face will not only be less European but also will not convey suffering, but "silent triumph." This looks like the masculinization of Christ.

3. As in the other chapters, * stands for $p < .05$, ** for $p < .01$, and *** for $p < .001$. One-tailed tests are used.

4. Not in Table 12.1; this was found with the help of the *DECOR* database at the Institute for Research on Intercultural Cooperation (IRIC), Maastricht and Tilburg, the Netherlands. Independent of this finding, the statement "most people can be trusted" already had been included in the new formula for MAS in IRIC's Values Survey Module 1994 (VSM 94).

REFERENCES

Abramson, P. R., & Pinkerton, S. D. (1995). *With pleasure: Thoughts on the nature of human sexuality*. New York: Oxford University Press.

Adebayo, A. (1988). The masculine side of planned parenthood: An explanatory analysis. *Journal of Comparative Family Studies, 19,* 55-67.

America and religion: The counter-attack of God. (1955, July 8). *The Economist*, p. 25.

Anderson, C. A. (1989). Temperature and aggression: Ubiquitous effects of heat on occurrence of human violence. *Psychological Bulletin, 106,* 74-96.

Anderson, C. A., & Anderson, K. B. (1996). Violent crime rate studies in philosophical context: A destructive testing approach to heat and Southern culture of violence effects. *Journal of Personality and Social Psychology, 70,* 740-756.

Arbose, J. (1980). The changing life values of today's executive. *International Management, 35*(7), 12-19.

Arrindell, W. A., Hatzichristou, C., Wensink, J., Rosenberg, E., van Twillert, B., Stedema, J., & Meijer, D. (1997). Dimensions of national culture as predictors of cross-national differences in subjective well-being. *Personality and Individual Differences, 23,* 37-53.

Bank, J., & Vinnicombe, S. (1995). Strategies for change: Women in management in the United Arab Emirates. In S. Vinnicombe & N. L. Colwill (Eds.), *The essence of women in management* (pp. 122-141). London: Prentice Hall.

Barnett, R. C., & Baruch, G. K. (1987). Social roles, gender, and psychological distress. In R. C. Barnett, L. Biener, & G. K. Baruch (Eds.), *Gender and stress* (pp. 122-143). New York: Free Press.

Barnett, R. C., & Rivers, C. (1996). *She works/he works: How two-income families are happier, healthier, and better off.* San Francisco: HarperCollins.

Baron, R. M., & Kenny, D. A. (1986). The moderator-mediator variable distinction in social psychological research: Conceptual, strategic, and statistical considerations. *Journal of Personality and Social Psychology, 51,* 1173-1182.

Bártová, E. (1976). Images of the woman and the family. In H. Ornauer, A. Sicińacski, & J. Galtung (Eds.), *Images of the world in the year 2000: A comparative ten-nation study* (pp. 255-278). The Hague, Netherlands: Mouton.

Bax, E. H. (1988). *Modernization and cleavage in Dutch society: A study of long term economic and social change.* Groningen, Netherlands: Groningen University Press.

Bem, S. L. (1974). The measurement of psychological androgyny. *Journal of Consulting and Clinical Psychology, 42,* 155-162.

Berger, P. L. (1969). *The sacred canopy: Elements of a sociological theory of religion.* Garden City, NY: Doubleday/Anchor.

Berger, P. L., & Luckmann, T. (1967). *The social construction of reality: A treatise in the sociology of knowledge.* Garden City, NY: Doubleday/Anchor.

Best, D. L., & Williams, J. E. (1993). A cross-cultural viewpoint. In A. E. Beall & R. J. Sternberg (Eds.), *The psychology of gender* (pp. 215-248). New York: Guilford.

Best, D. L., & Williams, J. E. (1994). Masculinity/Femininity in the self and ideal self descriptions of university students in fourteen countries. In A. M. Bouvy, F. J. R. van de Vijver, P. Boski, & P. Schmitz (Eds.), *Journeys into cross-cultural psychology* (pp. 297-306). Lisse, Netherlands: Swets & Zeitlinger.

Best, D. L., Williams, J. E., & Briggs, S. W. (1980). A further analysis of the affective meanings associated with male and female sex-trait stereotypes. *Sex Roles, 6,* 735-746.

Biezeveld, K. (1996). *Spreken over God als vader, Hoe kan het anders?* [Talking about God as Father: Is there an alternative?]. Baarn, Netherlands: Ten Have.

Billing, Y. D., & Alvesson, M. (1989). *Køn, ledelse, organisation: et studium af tre forskellige organisationer* [Gender, leadership, organization: A study of three different organizations]. Copenhagen: Jurist- og Økonomforbundets Forlag.

Bjorklund, D. F., & Kipp, K. (1996). Parental investment theory and gender differences in the evolution of inhibition mechanisms. *Psychological Bulletin, 120,* 163-188.

Blake, R. R., & Mouton, J. S. (1964). *The managerial grid.* Houston, TX: Gulf.

Bolton, R. (1994). Sex, science and social responsibility: Cross-cultural research on same-sex eroticism and sexual intolerance. *Cross-Cultural Research, 28*(2), 134-190.

Bond, M. H. (1991). Chinese values and health: A cultural-level examination. *Psychology and Health, 5,* 137-152.

Bork, R. H. (1996). *Slouching towards Gomorrah: Modern liberalism and American decline.* New York: HarperCollins.

Broverman, I. K., Vogel, S. R., Broverman, D. M., Clarkson, F. E., & Rosenkrantz, P. S. (1972). Sex-role stereotypes: A current appraisal. *Journal of Social Issues, 28,* 59-78.

Brown, C. G. (1992). A revisionist approach to religious change. In S. Bruce (Ed.), *Religion and modernization: Sociologists and historians debate the secularization thesis* (pp. 31-58). Oxford, UK: Clarendon.

Burkholder, R., Moore, D. W., & Saad, L. (1996, March). *Gender and society: Status and stereotypes. An international Gallup Poll report.* Princeton, NJ: The Gallup Organization World Headquarters.

Buss, D. M. (1989). Sex differences in human mate preferences: Evolutionary hypotheses tested in 37 cultures. *Behavioral and Brain Sciences, 12,* 1-14.

Buss, D. M. (1994). Mate preferences in 37 cultures. In W. Lonner & R. Malpass (Eds.), *Psychology and culture* (pp. 197-201). Needham Heights, MA: Allyn & Bacon.

Campbell, A., Converse, E., & Rodgers, W. L. (1976). *The quality of American life: Perceptions, evaluations, and satisfactions.* New York: Russell Sage Foundation.

Campbell, R. A., & Curtis, J. E. (1994). Religious involvement across societies: Analyses for alternative measures in national surveys. *Journal for the Scientific Study of Religion, 33,* 215-229.

Caplan, P. (Ed.). (1987). *The cultural construction of sexuality.* London: Tavistock.

Carlson, J. S., & Widaman, K. F. (1988). The effects of study abroad during college on attitudes toward other cultures. *International Journal of Intercultural Relations, 12,* 1-17.

Chaves, M., & Cann, D. E. (1992). Regulation, pluralism, and religious market structure. *Rationality and Society, 4,* 272-290.

The Chinese Culture Connection. (1987). Chinese values and the search for culture-free dimensions of culture. *Journal of Cross-Cultural Psychology, 18*(2), 143-164.

Cleary, P. D. (1987). Gender differences in stress-related disorders. In R. C. Barnett, L. Biener, & G. K. Baruch (Eds.), *Gender and stress* (pp. 39-72). New York: Free Press.

Cohen, J. (1992). A power primer. *Psychological Bulletin, 112,* 155-159.

Cohen, J., & Cohen, P. (1983). *Applied multiple regression/correlation analysis for the behavioral sciences* (2nd ed.). Hillsdale, NJ: Lawrence Erlbaum.

Coltrane, S. (1988). Father-child relationships and the status of women: A cross-cultural study. *American Journal of Sociology, 93,* 1060-1095.

Daly, M. (1973). *Beyond God the Father: Toward a philosophy of women's liberation.* Boston: Beacon.

Dawkins, R. (1976). *The selfish gene.* New York: Oxford University Press.

De Mooij, M. (1994). *Advertising worldwide* (2nd ed.). Hemel Hempstead, UK: Prentice Hall.

De Swaan, A. (1988). *In care of the state: Health care, education and welfare in Europe and the USA in the modern era.* Cambridge, UK: Polity.

De Vaus, D. A. (1984). Workforce participation and sex differences in church attendance. *Review of Religious Research, 25,* 247-256.

De Vaus, D. A., & McAllister, I. (1987). Gender differences in religion: A test of the structural location theory. *American Sociological Review, 52,* 472-481.

Derks, M., & Monteiro, M. (1996). Met wijsheid opent zij haar mond: Vroomheid, visie en vrouwelijkheid [With wisdom she opens her mouth: Piety, vision and femininity]. In M. Cornelis, M. Derks, M. Monteiro, & J. Strous (Eds.), *Vrome vrouwen: Betekenissen van geloof voor vrouwen in de geschiedenis* [Pious women: The meaning of faith for women in history] (pp. 9-26). Hilversum, Netherlands: Verloren.

Diamond, M. (1993). Homosexuality and bisexuality in different populations. *Archives of Sexual Behavior, 22*(4), 291-310.

Diener, E. (1984). Subjective well-being. *Psychological Bulletin, 95,* 542-575.

Diener, E. (1994). Assessing subjective well-being: Progress and opportunities. *Social Indicators Research, 31,* 103-157.

Diener, E., & Diener, M. (1995). Cross-cultural correlates of life satisfaction and self-esteem. *Journal of Personality and Social Psychology, 68,* 653-663.

Diener, E., Diener, M., & Diener, C. (1995). Factors predicting the subjective well-being of nations. *Journal of Personality and Social Psychology, 69,* 851-864.

Dion, K. K., & Dion, K. L. (1993). Individualistic and collectivistic perspectives of gender and the cultural context of love and intimacy. *Journal of Social Issues, 49*(3), 53-69.

d'Iribarne, P. (1989). *La logique de l' honneur: Gestion des entreprises et traditions nationales* [The logic of honor: Management and national traditions]. Paris: Seuil.

Dobbelaere, K. (1981). Secularization: A multi-dimensional concept. *Current Sociology, 29,* 1-213.

Dobbelaere, K. (1993). Church involvement and secularization: Making sense of the European case. In E. Barker, J. A. Beckford, & K. Dobbelaere (Eds.), *Secularization, rationalism and sectarianism: Essays in honour of Bryan R. Wilson* (pp. 19-36). Oxford, UK: Clarendon.

Draguns, J. G. (1990). Normal and abnormal behavior in cross-cultural perspective: Specifying the nature of their relationship. In J. W. Berry, J. G.

Draguns, & M. Cole (Eds.), *Nebraska Symposium on Motivation, 1989: Cross-cultural perspectives*. Lincoln: University of Nebraska Press.

Dunlap, R. E., Gallup, G. H., Jr., & Gallup, A. M. (1993). *Health of the planet: Results of a 1992 International Environmental Opinion Survey of citizens in 24 nations*. Princeton, NJ: The George H. Gallup International Institute.

Durkheim, E. (1964). *The division of labor in society*. New York: Free Press. (Original work published 1893)

Elias, N. (1980). *Über den Prozeß der Zivilisation: Soziogenetische und psychogenetische Untersuchungen* (Vol. 1). (On the process of civilization: Sociogenetic and psychogenetic studies.) Frankfurt am Main: Suhrkamp. (Original work published 1968)

Emerson, T. (1995, August 28). The rights of woman. *Newsweek*, pp. 20-26.

Emmons, R. A. (1986). Personal strivings: An approach to personality and subjective well-being. *Journal of Personality and Social Psychology, 51*, 1058-1068.

Endicott, K. (1992). Fathering in an egalitarian society. In B. S. Hewlett (Ed.), *Father-child Relations: Cultural and biosocial contexts* (pp. 281-295). New York: Aldine de Gruyter.

Ester, P., Halman, L., & de Moor, R. (Eds.). (1993). *The individualizing society: Value change in Europe and North America*. Tilburg, Netherlands: Tilburg University Press.

Eurobarometer. (1991, December). *Life styles in the European Community: Family and employment within the twelve*. Brussels: Commission of the European Communities.

Euromonitor. (1997). *Consumer Europe 1997*. London: Author.

Finke, R. (1992). An unsecular America. In S. Bruce (Ed.), *Religion and modernization: Sociologists and historians debate the secularization thesis* (pp. 145-169). Oxford, UK: Clarendon.

Fioravanti, M., Gough, H. G., and Frère, L. J. (1981). English, French and Italian adjective check lists: A social desirability analysis. *Journal of Cross-Cultural Psychology, 12*, 461-472.

Fleishman, E. A., Harris, E. F., & Burtt, H. E. (1955). *Leadership and supervision in industry*. Columbus: Ohio State University, Bureau of Educational Research.

Foa, U. G., Anderson, B., Converse, J., Urbansky, W. A., Cawley, M. J., Muhlhausen, S. M., & Tornblom, K. Y. (1987). Gender-related sexual attitudes: Some cross-cultural similarities and differences. *Sex Roles, 16*(9-10), 511-519.

Ford, C. (1985). Women in management: The revolution that never happens. *Unilever Magazine, 56*(2), 14-18.

Foucault, M. (1976). *The history of sexuality: Vol. 1. An introduction*. Harmondsworth, Middlesex, UK: Penguin.

Foucault, M. (1984a). *The history of sexuality: Vol. 2. The use of pleasure* (R. Hurley, Trans.). Harmondsworth, Middlesex, UK: Penguin.

Foucault, M. (1984b). *The history of sexuality: Vol. 3. The care of the self* (R. Hurley, Trans.). Harmondsworth, Middlesex, UK: Penguin.

Galtung, J. (1996). *Peace by peaceful means: Peace and conflict, development and civilization.* London: Sage.

Garver, J. B., Jr., Payne, O.G.A.M., & Canby, T. Y. (1990). *National Geographic atlas of the world* (6th ed.). Washington, DC: National Geographic Society.

Geertz, C. (1973). *The interpretation of cultures: Selected essays.* New York: Basic Books.

Gherardi, S. (1995). *Gender, symbolism, and organizational cultures.* London: Sage.

Gibbons, F. X., Helweg-Larsen, M., & Gerrard, M. (1995). Prevalence estimates and adolescent risk behavior: Cross-cultural differences in social influence. *Journal of Applied Psychology, 80*(1), 107-121.

Giddens, A. (1993). *Sociology.* Oxford, UK: Polity.

Gilligan, C. (1982). *In a different voice: Psychological theory and women's development.* Cambridge, MA: Harvard University Press.

Goldman, J.G.D. (1994). Some methodological problems in planning, executing and validating a cross-national study of children's sexual cognition. *International Journal of Intercultural Relations, 18,* 1-27.

Goldstein, A. P. (1994). *The ecology of aggression.* New York: Plenum.

Gough, H. G., & Heilbrun, A. B., Jr. (1980). *The Adjective Checklist Manual.* Palo Alto, CA: Consulting Psychologists Press.

Greeley, A. M. (1989). *Religious change in America.* Cambridge, MA: Harvard University Press.

Hadden, J. K. (1987). Toward desacralizing secularization theory. *Social Forces, 65,* 587-611.

Halman, L. (1991). *Waarden in de Westerse Wereld: een internationale exploratie van de waarden in de westerse samenleving* [Values in the Western world: An international exploration]. Tilburg, Netherlands: Tilburg University Press.

Halman, L., & de Moor, R. (1993). Religion, churches and moral values. In P. Ester, L. Halman, & R. de Moor (Eds.), *The individualizing society: Value change in Europe and North America* (pp. 37-65). Tilburg, Netherlands: Tilburg University Press.

Halman, L., & Vloet, A. (1994). *Measuring and comparing values in 16 countries of the Western world* (Documentation of the European values study 1981-1990 in Europe and North America). Tilburg, Netherlands: WORC.

Harding, S., Phillips, D., & Fogarty, M. (1986). *Contrasting values in Western Europe.* London: Macmillan.

Harris, M. (1981). *America now: The anthropology of a changing culture.* New York: Simon & Schuster.

Hatfield, E., & Rapson, R. L. (1993). *Love, sex and intimacy: Their psychology, biology, and history.* New York: HarperCollins College Publishers.

Hatfield, E., & Rapson, R. L. (1995). *Love and sex: Cross-cultural perspectives.* New York: Allyn & Bacon.

Helgesen, S. (1995). *The web of inclusion.* New York: Doubleday.

Hendrix, L. (1994). What is sexual inequality? On the definition and range of variation. *Cross-Cultural Research, 28,* 287-307.

Hewlett, B. S. (1992). Husband-wife reciprocity and the father-infant relationship among Aka pygmies. In B. S. Hewlett (Ed.), *Father-child relations: Cultural and biosocial contexts* (pp. 153-176). New York: Aldine de Gruyter.

Hite, S. (1979). *The Hite report on female sexuality.* New York: Knopf.

Hite, S. (1981). *The Hite report on male sexuality.* New York: Knopf.

Hofstede, G. (1980). *Culture's consequences: International differences in work-related values.* Beverly Hills, CA: Sage.

Hofstede, G. (1982). *VSM 82: Values Survey Module-1982 and scoring guide.* Maastricht, Netherlands: Institute for Research on Intercultural Cooperation.

Hofstede, G. (1983). Dimensions of national cultures in fifty countries and three regions. In J. B. Deregowski, S. Dziurawiec, & R. C. Annis (Eds.), *Expiscations in cross-cultural psychology* (pp. 335-355). Lisse, Netherlands: Swets & Zeitlinger.

Hofstede, G. (1986). Cultural differences in teaching and learning. *International Journal of Intercultural Relations, 10,* 301-320.

Hofstede, G. (1989). Women in management—A matter of culture. In *International Management Development Review, 5* (pp. 250-254). Brussels: Management Centre Europe.

Hofstede, G. (1991). *Cultures and organizations: Software of the mind.* London: McGraw-Hill.

Hofstede, G. (1993). *Images of Europe.* Valedictory address, University of Limburg, Maastricht.

Hofstede, G. (1994). *VSM 94: Values Survey Module 1994-manual.* Maastricht, Netherlands: Institute for Research on Intercultural Cooperation.

Hofstede, G. (1996). Gender stereotypes and partner preferences of Asian women in masculine and feminine cultures. *Journal of Cross-Cultural Psychology, 27,* 533-546.

Hofstede, G., & Bond, M. H. (1988). The Confucius connection: From cultural roots to economic growth. *Organizational Dynamics, 16*(4), 4-21.

Hofstede, G., Kolman, L., Nicolescu, O., & Pajumaa, I. (1996). Characteristics of the ideal job among students in eight countries. In H. Grad, A. Blanco, & J. Georgas (Eds.), *Key issues in cross-cultural psychology* (pp. 199-216). Lisse, Netherlands: Swets & Zeitlinger.

Hofstede, G., Neuijen, B., Ohayv, D. D., & Sanders, G. (1990). Measuring organizational cultures: A qualitative and quantitative study across twenty cases. *Administrative Science Quarterly, 35,* 286-316.

Hofstede, G., & Vunderink, M. (1994). A case study in Masculinity/Femininity differences: American students in the Netherlands vs. local students. In A. M. Bouvy, F.J.R. van de Vijver, P. Boski, & P. Schmitz (Eds.), *Journeys into cross-cultural psychology* (pp. 329-347). Lisse, Netherlands: Swets & Zeitlinger.

Hoge, D. R., & Roozen, D. A. (1979). Research on factors influencing church commitment. In D. R. Hoge & D. A. Roozen (Eds.), *Understanding church growth and decline, 1950-1978* (pp. 42-68). New York: Pilgrim.

Hoppe, M. H. (1990). *A comparative study of country elites: International differences in work-related values and learning and their implications for management training and development.* Unpublished doctoral dissertation, University of North Carolina at Chapel Hill.

Hoppe, M. H. (1993). The effects of national culture on the theory and practice of managing R & D professionals abroad. *R & D Management, 23*(4), 313-225.

Iannaccone, L. R. (1991). The consequences of religious market structure: Adam Smith and the economics of religion. *Rationality and Society, 3,* 156-177.

Iannaccone, L. R. (1992). Religious markets and the economics of religion. *Social Compass, 39,* 123-131.

Inglehart, R. (1990). *Culture shift in advanced industrial society.* Princeton, NJ: Princeton University Press.

Inkeles, A. (1997). *National character: A psycho-social perspective.* New Brunswick, NJ: Transaction Publishing.

Inkeles, A., & Levinson, D. J. (1969). National character: The study of modal personality and sociocultural systems. In G. Lindzey & E. Aronson (Eds.), *The handbook of social psychology* (2nd ed., Vol. 4, pp. 418-506). Reading, MA: Addison-Wesley.

Inter/View International.(1995). *European Media and Marketing Survey 1995.* Amsterdam: Author.

Iwawaki, S., & Eysenck, H. J. (1978). Sexual attitudes among British and Japanese students. *The Journal of Psychology, 98,* 289-298.

Jacobs, J. A. (1992). Women's entry into management: Trends in earnings, authority, and values among salaried managers. *Administrative Science Quarterly, 37,* 282-301.

Jagodzinski, W., & Dobbelaere, K. (1995). Secularization and church religiosity. In J. W. van Deth & E. Scarbrough (Eds.), *The impact of values* (pp. 76-119). Oxford, UK: Oxford University Press.

Jones, E. F., Forrest, J. D., Goldman, N., Henshaw, S., Lincoln, R., Rosoff, J. I., Westoff, C. F., & Wulf, D. (1986). *Teenage pregnancy in industrialized countries.* New Haven, CT: Yale University Press.

Kanter, R. M. (1977). *Men and women of the corporation.* New York: Basic Books.

Kanter, R. M. (1983). *The change masters: Innovation and entrepreneurship in the American corporation.* New York: Simon & Schuster.

Katz, M. M., & Konnor, M. J. (1981). The role of the father: An anthropological perspective. In M. E. Lamb (Ed.), *The role of the father in child development* (2nd ed., pp. 155-185). New York: Wiley.

Kelly, A. (1978). *Girls and science: An international study of sex differences in school science achievement.* Stockholm: Almqvist & Wiksell.

Kenrick, D. T. (1994). Evolutionary social psychology: From sexual selection to social cognition. In M. P. Zanna (Ed.), *Advances in experimental social psychology* (Vol. 26, pp. 75-121). Orlando, FL: Academic Press.

Kinsey, A. C., Pomeroy, W. B., & Martin, C. E. (1948). *Sexual behavior in the human male*. Philadelphia: Saunders.

Kinsey, A. C., Pomeroy, W. B., Martin, C. E., & Gebhard, P. H. (1953). *Sexual behavior in the human female*. Philadelphia: Saunders.

Kirsch, A. T. (1985). Buddhist sex roles/culture of gender revisited. *American Ethnologist, 12*, 302-320.

Komarovsky, M. (1976). *Dilemmas of masculinity: A study of college youth*. New York: Norton.

Laumann, E. O., Gagnon, J. H., Michael, R. T., & Michaels, S. (1994). *The social organization of sexuality*. Chicago: University of Chicago Press.

Lebrun, M. (1988, January). Les surdouées du plaisir [Supergifted for pleasure]. *Marie Claire*, pp. 25-28.

Lynn, R. (1991). *The secret of the miracle economy: Different national attitudes to competitiveness and money*. Exeter, UK: Social Affairs Unit.

Lynn, R., & Martin, T. (1995). National differences for thirty-seven nations in extraversion, neuroticism, psychoticism and economic, demographic and other correlates. *Personality and Individual Differences, 19*, 403-406.

Mant, A. (1979). *The rise and fall of the British manager* (Rev. ed.). London: Pan Books.

Marsh, H. W., & Myers, M. (1986). Masculinity, femininity, and androgyny: A methodological and theoretical critique. *Sex Roles, 14*, 397-430.

Martin, D. (1978). *A general theory of secularization*. Oxford, UK: Basil Blackwell.

Masters, W. H., & Johnson, V. E. (1966). *Human sexual response*. Boston: Little, Brown.

Matsumoto, D., & Fletcher, D. (1996). Cross-national differences in disease rates as accounted for by meaningful psychological dimensions of cultural variability. *Journal of Gender, Culture, and Health, 1*, 71-82.

McClelland, D. C. (1961). *The achieving society*. Princeton, NJ: Van Nostrand Reinhold.

McClelland, D. C. (1965). Wanted: A new self-image for women. In R. J. Lifton (Ed.), *The woman in America* (pp. 173-192). Boston: Houghton Mifflin.

McClelland, D. C. (1975). *Power: The inner experience*. New York: Irvington.

Merritt, A. (in press). Culture in the cockpit: Do Hofstede's dimensions replicate? *Journal of Cross-Cultural Psychology*.

Mesquida, C. G., & Wiener, N. I. (1996). Human collective aggression: A behavioral ecology perspective. *Ethology and Sociobiology, 17*, 247-262.

Meyer, J. (1994). *Roze en blauwe wolken: een longitudinaal onderzoek naar seksetypering door ouders in de eerste levensjaren van hun kind* [Pink and blue clouds: A longitudinal study of gender typing by parents in their child's first years]. The Hague, Netherlands: VUGA.

Michael, R. T., Gagnon, J. H., Laumann, E. O., & Kolata, G. (1994). *Sex in America: A definitive survey.* Boston: Little, Brown and Company.

Michalos, A. C. (1991). *Global report on student well-being: Vol. 1. Life satisfaction and happiness.* New York: Springer-Verlag.

Michels, R. (1911). *Die Grenzen der Geschlechtsmoral: Prolegomena, Gedanken und Untersuchungen* [The limits of sexual morality: Literature review, considerations and research]. München, Germany: Frauenverlag.

Miller, E. M. (1994). Paternal provisioning versus mate seeking in human populations. *Personality and Individual Differences, 17,* 227-255.

Mills, A. J. (1989). Gender, sexuality and organization theory. In J. Hearn, D. L. Sheppard, P. Tancred-Sheriff, & G. Burrell (Eds.), *The sexuality of organization* (pp. 29-44). London: Sage.

Moffatt, J. (1949). *The New Testament: A new translation.* London: Hodder & Stoughton.

Motowidlo, S. J. (1984). Does job satisfaction lead to consideration and personal sensitivity? *Academy of Management Journal, 27,* 910-915.

Motowidlo, S. J., Packard, J. S., & Manning, M. R. (1986). Occupational stress: Its causes and consequences for job performance. *Journal of Applied Psychology, 71,* 618-629.

Mulder, N. (1980). *Mysticism and everyday life in contemporary Java* (2nd ed.). Singapore: Singapore University Press.

Myers, D. G., & Diener, E. (1995). Who is happy? *Psychological Science, 6,* 10-19.

Myers, M., & Gonda, G. (1982). Utility of the masculinity-femininity construct: Comparison of traditional androgyny approaches. *Journal of Personality and Social Psychology, 43,* 514-522.

Near, J. P., & Rechner, P. L. (1993). Cross-cultural variations in predictors of life satisfaction: An historical view of differences among West European countries. *Social Indicators Research, 29,* 109-121.

Nisbett, R. E., & Cohen, D. (1996). *Culture of honor: The psychology of violence in the South.* Boulder, CO: Westview.

Odom, G. R. (1989). *Mothers, leadership, and success.* Houston, TX: Polybius.

Organisation for Economic Cooperation and Development [OECD]. (1995). *Literacy, economy and society: Results of the first Adult Literacy Survey.* Paris: Author.

Osgood, C. E., Suci, G. J., & Tannenbaum, P. H. (1957). *The measurement of meaning.* Urbana: University of Illinois Press.

Ozorak, E. W. (1996). The power, but not the glory: How women empower themselves through religion. *Journal for the Scientific Study of Religion, 35,* 17-29.

Pareto, V. (1976). *Sociological writings* (D. Mirfin, Trans.; selected and introduced by S. E. Finer). Oxford, UK: Basil Blackwell. (Original work published 1916)

Parkhurst, J. T., & Asher, S. R. (1985). Goals and concerns: Implications for the study of children's social competence. In B. B. Lahey & A. E. Kazdin

(Eds.), *Advances in clinical child psychology* (Vol. 8, pp. 199-228). New York: Plenum.

Payne, L. (1985). *Crisis in masculinity*. Westchester, IL: Crossway.

Peek, C. W., Lowe, G. D., & Williams, L. S. (1991). Gender and God's word: Another look at religious fundamentalism and sexism. *Social Forces, 69,* 1205-1221.

Peterson, M. F., & Smith, P. B. (1997). Does national culture or ambient temperature explain cross-national differences in role stress? No sweat! *Academy of Management Journal, 40,* 930-946.

Ravesloot, J. (1995). Courtship and sexuality in the youth phase. In M. Du Bois-Reymond, R. Diekstra, K. Hurrelmann, & E. Peters (Eds.), *Childhood and youth in Germany and the Netherlands: Transitions and coping strategies of adolescents* (pp. 41-71). Berlin: Walter de Gruyter.

Reader's Digest. (1991). *Eurodata 1991*. London: Author.

Renshaw, P. D., & Asher, S. R. (1983). Children's goals and strategies for social interaction. *Merrill-Palmer Quarterly, 29,* 353-374.

Roberts, J. M., & Sutton-Smith, B. (1971). Child training and game involvement. In E. M. Avedon & B. Sutton-Smith (Eds.), *The study of games* (pp. 465-487). New York: Wiley.

Robinson, J.A.T. (1963). *Honest to God*. London: SCM Press.

Rohner, R. P. (1986). *The warmth dimension: Foundations of parental acceptance-rejection theory*. Beverly Hills, CA: Sage.

Roland, A. (1988). *In search of self in India and Japan*. Princeton, NJ: Princeton University Press.

Roper, M. (1994). *Masculinity and the British organization man since 1945*. Oxford, UK: Oxford University Press.

Rosenberg, B. G., & Sutton-Smith, B. (1959). The measurement of masculinity and femininity in children. *Child Development, 30,* 373-380.

Rosenberg, B. G., & Sutton-Smith, B. (1960). A revised conception of masculine-feminine differences in play activities. *Journal of Genetic Psychology, 96,* 165-170.

Rosenberg, B. G., & Sutton-Smith, B. (1964). The measurement of masculinity and femininity in children: An extension and revalidation. *Journal of Genetic Psychology, 104,* 259-264.

Rosenberg, B. G., Sutton-Smith, B., & Morgan, E. (1961). The use of opposite sex scales as a measure of psychosexual deviancy. *Journal of Consulting Psychology, 25,* 221-225.

Ross, M. W. (1983). Societal relationships and gender role in homosexuals: A cross-cultural comparison. *The Journal of Sex Research, 19,* 273-288.

Ross, M. W. (1989). Gay youth in four cultures: A comparative study. *Journal of Homosexuality, 17*(3-4), 299-314.

Rossi, A. S. (1965). Equality between the sexes: An immodest proposal. In R. J. Lifton (Ed.), *The woman in America* (pp. 98-143). Boston: Houghton Mifflin.

Rotton, J. (1986). Determinism redux: Climate and cultural correlates of violence. *Environment and Behavior, 18*, 346-368.

Ruether, R. R. (1983). *Sexism and God-talk: Toward a feminist theology*. Boston: Beacon.

Salzburg Seminar. (1990). *The Salzburg Seminar 1990 program*. Salzburg, Austria: Author.

Sandemose, A. (1938). *En flygtling krydser sit spor* [A fugitive crosses his own track]. Copenhagen: Gyldendals Bogklub. (Danish translation; original work published in Norwegian, 1933)

Scarr, S. (1996). Family policy dilemmas in contemporary nation-states: Are women benefited by "family-friendly" governments? In S. Gustavsson & L. Lewin (Eds.), *The future of the nation state* (pp. 107-129). Stockholm: Nerenius & Santérus.

Schieman, C. A. (1985). Vrouwen en hogere managementfuncties [Women and higher management jobs]. *Harvard Holland Review, 2*(Spring), 75-82.

Schubart, W. (1941). *Religion und eros* [Religion and eros]. München, Germany: Beck.

Schwartz, D. C. (1968). On the ecology of political violence: "The long hot summer" as a hypothesis. *The American Behavioral Scientist, 11*, 24-28.

Schwartz, I. M. (1993). Affective reactions of American and Swedish women to their first premarital coitus: A cross-cultural comparison. *Journal of Sex Research, 30*(1), 18-26.

Schwartz, S. H. (1994). Beyond individualism and collectivism: New cultural dimensions of values. In U. Kim, H. C. Triandis, C. Kagitçibasi, S.-C. Choi, & G. Yoon (Eds.), *Individualism and collectivism: Theory, method, and applications* (pp. 85-199). Newbury Park, CA: Sage.

Schwartzman, H. B. (1978). *Transformations: The anthropology of children's play*. New York: Plenum.

Seidler, V. J. (1987). Reason, desire, and male sexuality. In P. Caplan (Ed.), *The cultural construction of sexuality* (pp. 82-111). London: Tavistock.

Spence, J. T. (1991). Do the BSRI and the PAQ measure the same or different concepts? *Psychology of Women Quarterly, 15*, 141-165.

Spence, J. T., & Helmreich, R. L. (1983). Achievement-related motives and behaviors. In J. T. Spence (Ed.), *Achievement and achievement motives* (pp. 7-74). San Francisco, CA: Freeman.

Sprecher, S., & Hatfield, E. (1994). *Premarital sexual standards among U.S. College students and a comparison with those of Russian and Japanese students.* Unpublished manuscript, Illinois State University, Department of Sociology and Anthropology, Normal.

Sprecher, S., Hatfield, E., Cortese, A., Potapova, E., & Levitskaya, A. (1994). Token resistance to sexual intercourse and consent to unwanted sexual intercourse: College students' dating experiences in three countries. *Journal of Sex Research, 31*(2), 125-132.

Stanley, L. (1995). *Sex surveyed 1949-1994: From mass-observation's "Little Kinsey" to the National Survey and the Hite Reports*. London: Taylor & Francis.

Stark, R., Finke, R., & Iannaccone, L. R. (1995). Pluralism and piety: England and Wales, 1851. *Journal for the Scientific Study of Religion, 34*, 431-444.

Stark, R., & Iannaccone, L. R. (1994). A supply-side reinterpretation of the "secularization" of Europe. *Journal for the Scientific Study of Religion, 33*, 230-252.

Statham, A. (1987). The gender model revisited: Differences in the management styles of men and women. *Sex Roles, 16*, 409-429.

Steiner-Aeschliman, S., & Mauss, A. L. (1996). The impact of feminism and religious involvement on sentiment toward God. *Review of Religious Research, 37*, 248-259.

Stevens, E. P. (1973). Marianismo: The other face of machismo in Latin America. In A. Pescatello (Ed.), *Female and male in Latin America* (pp. 90-101). Pittsburgh, PA: University of Pittsburgh Press.

Stoetzel, J. (1983) *Les valeurs du temps présent: une enquête européenne* [Present-day values: A European survey]. Paris: Presses Universitaires de France.

Sullivan, M. J., III. (1991). *Measuring global values: The ranking of 162 countries*. New York: Greenwood.

Sutton, C. D., & Moore, K. K. (1985). Executive women—20 years later. *Harvard Business Review, 63*(5), 42-66.

Sutton-Smith, B. (1971). Play preference and play behavior: A validity study. In R. E. Herron & Sutton-Smith (Eds.), *Child's play* (pp. 73-75). New York: Wiley.

Sutton-Smith, B., & Rosenberg, B. G. (1959). *Play and Game List*. Bowling Green, OH: Bowling Green State University. (I.B.M. Form I.T.S. 1100 A 6140)

Sutton-Smith, B., & Rosenberg, B. G. (1960). Manifest anxiety and game preference in children. *Child Development, 31*, 515-519.

Sutton-Smith, B., & Rosenberg, B. G. (1961). Impulsivity and sex preference. *Journal of Genetic Psychology, 98*, 187-192.

Sutton-Smith, B., Rosenberg, B. G., & Morgan, E. (1963). Development of sex differences in play choices during preadolescence. *Child Development, 34*, 119-126.

Tannen, D. (1990). *You just don't understand: Women and men in conversation*. New York: Morrow.

Taylor, A. R., & Asher, S. R. (1984). Children's goals and social competence: Individual differences in a game-playing context. In T. Field, J. L. Roopnarine, & M. Segal (Eds.), *Friendships in normal and handicapped children* (pp. 53-78). Norwood, NJ: Ablex.

Taylor, A. R., & Asher, S. R. (1985). *Goals, games, and social competence: Effects of sex, grade level and sociometric status*. Paper presented at the Biennial Meeting of the Society for Research in Child Development, Toronto, Canada.

Taylor, C. L., & Jodice, D. A. (1983). *World handbook of political and social indicators* (3rd ed., Vols. 1-2). New Haven, CT: Yale University Press.

Terman, L. M., & Miles, C. C. (1936). *Sex and personality*. New York: McGraw-Hill.

Towler, R. (1984). *The need for certainty: A sociological study of conventional religion*. London: Routledge & Kegan Paul.

Tschannen, O. (1991). The secularization paradigm: A systematization. *Journal for the Scientific Study of Religion, 30*, 395-415.

Tuzin, D. (1991). Sex, culture and the anthropologist. *Social Science and Medicine, 33*, 867-874.

UNICEF. (1995). *The state of the world's children*. New York: Oxford University Press.

United Nations Development Project. (1996). *Human development report 1996*. New York: Oxford University Press.

Van Baren, F., Hofstede, G., & Van de Vijver, F. (1995). *Knowledge of and attitudes to biotechnology: The influence of national cultures* (Report to the European Commission). Maastricht, Netherlands: Institute for Research on Intercultural Cooperation.

Van de Vliert, E., Kluwer, E. S., & Lynn, R. (1998). *Citizens of warmer countries are more competitive and poorer: Culture or chance?* Unpublished manuscript.

Van de Vliert, E., Nauta, A., & Huismans, S. E. (n.d.). *Polity, economy and culture as triggers of political strikes: A 98-nation study*. Unpublished manuscript.

Van de Vliert, E., Schwartz, S. H., Huismans, S. E., Hofstede, G., & Daan, S. (in press). Temperature, cultural masculinity and domestic political violence: A cross-national study. *Journal of Cross-Cultural Psychology*.

Van de Vliert, E., & Van Yperen, N. W. (1996). Why cross-national differences in role overload? Don't overlook ambient temperature! *Academy of Management Journal, 39*, 986-1004.

Van Deel, T., Eyssens, H., Geerts, D., De Geus, P., Mathijsen, M., & Welsink, D. (1975). *"De Schoolmeester": brieven, gedichten, toelichtingen* ["De Schoolmeester": Letters, poems, explanations] (2nd rev. ed.). Amsterdam: University of Amsterdam, Department of Dutch Literature, Werkgroep CML.

Van der Togt, J. J. W., & Van de Vliert, E. (1998). *Concern for others and for oneself: Predicting group effectiveness in organizations*. Unpublished manuscript.

Van Rossum, J. H. A. (1996). Why children play: Do Dutch boys and girls value similar goals in playing games that U.S. children do? *International Play Journal, 4*, 51-58.

Van Rossum, J. H. A., & Timmer, B. S. (1985). Sex-typing and sex-role identity in play and games preference in 7, 9, and 11 year old children. *Psychologica Belgica, 25*, 47-72.

Van Straten, H. (Ed.). (1992). *Razernij der liefde: Ontuchtige poëzie in de Nederlanden van Middeleeuwen tot Franse tijd* [Love's folly: Libertine poetry in the Netherlands from the Middle Ages to the Napoleonic occupation]. Amsterdam: Arbeiderspers.

Van Zessen, G. J., & Sandfort, T. (1991). *Seksualiteit in Nederland* [Sexuality in the Netherlands]. Amsterdam: Swets & Zeitlinger.

Vance, C. S. (1991). Anthropology rediscovers sexuality: A theoretical comment. *Social Science and Medicine, 33,* 875-884.

Veenhoven, R. (1984). *Conditions of happiness.* Dordrecht, Netherlands: Reidel.

Veenhoven, R., with Ehrhardt, J., Sie Dhian Ho, M., & De Vries, A. (1993). *Happiness in nations: Subjective appreciation of life in 56 nations 1946-1992.* Rotterdam, Netherlands: Erasmus University, RISBO.

Vennix, P.A.M. (1989). *Seks en sekse: verschillen in betekenisgeving tussen vrouwen en mannen* [The meaning of sex and gender: Different interpretations by women and by men]. Delft, Netherlands: Eburon.

Vennix, P., & Bullinga, M. (1991). *Sekserollen en emancipatie: Veranderingen in de kijk op "mannelijkheid" en "vrouwelijkheid"* [Gender roles and emancipation: Changed views on masculinity and femininity]. Houten, Netherlands: Bohn Stafleu Van Loghum.

Verhulst, F. C., Achenbach, T. M., Ferdinand, R. F., & Kasius, M. C. (1993). Epidemiological comparisons of American and Dutch adolescents' self-reports. *Journal of the American Academy of Child and Adolescent Psychiatry, 32,* 1135-1144.

Verweij, J., Ester, P., & Nauta, R. (1997). Secularization as an economic and cultural phenomenon: A cross-national analysis. *Journal for the Scientific Study of Religion, 36,* 307-322.

Vunderink, M. (1992). *Twenty-four Americans in Maastricht: A study in cultural differences* (Working Paper 92-2). Maastricht, Netherlands: Institute for Research on Intercultural Cooperation.

Waldron, I., Nowotarski, M., Freimer, M., Henry, J. P., Post, N., & Witten, C. (1982). Cross-cultural variation in blood pressure: A quantitative analysis of the relationships of blood pressure to cultural characteristics, salt consumption and body weight. *Social Science and Medicine, 16,* 419-430.

Wallis, R., & Bruce, S. (1992). Secularization: The orthodox model. In S. Bruce (Ed.), *Religion and modernization: Sociologists and historians debate the secularization thesis* (pp. 8-30). Oxford, UK: Clarendon.

Walter, T. (1990). Why are most churchgoers women? A literature review. *Vox Evangelica, 20,* 73-90.

Warner, M. (1976). *Alone of all her sex: The myth and cult of the Virgin Mary.* London: Picador.

Warner, R. S. (1993). Work in progress toward a new paradigm for the sociological study of religion in the United States. *American Journal of Sociology, 98,* 1044-1093.

Webster's ninth new collegiate dictionary. (1990). Springfield, MA: Merriam-Webster.

Weinreich-Haste, H. (1979). What sex is science? In O. Hartnett, G. Boden, & M. Fuller (Eds.), *Sex-role stereotyping: Collected papers* (pp. 168-181). London: Tavistock.

Westoff, C. F., Calot, G., & Foster, A. D. (1983). Teenage fertility in developed nations 1971-1980. *Family Planning Perspectives, 15,* 105-130.

Williams, J. E., & Best, D. L. (1977). Sex stereotypes and trait favorability on the adjective check list. *Educational and Psychological Measurement, 37,* 101-110.

Williams, J. E., & Best, D. L. (1982). *Measuring sex stereotypes: A thirty nation study.* Beverly Hills, CA: Sage.

Williams, J. E., & Best, D. L. (1990a). *Measuring sex stereotypes: A multination study.* Newbury Park, CA: Sage.

Williams, J. E., & Best, D. L. (1990b). *Sex and psyche: Gender and self viewed cross-culturally.* Newbury Park, CA: Sage.

Wilson, B. (1982). *Religion in sociological perspective.* Oxford, UK: Oxford University Press.

Wilson, B. (1996). Religious toleration, pluralism, and privatization. In P. Repstad (Ed.), *Religion and modernity: Modes of co-existence* (pp. 11-34). Oslo, Norway: Scandinavian University Press.

Wilson, M. S., Hoppe, M. H., & Sayles, L. R. (1996). *Managing across cultures: A learning framework* (Technical Report 173). Greensboro, NC: Center for Creative Leadership.

Wolfe, J. L. (1992). *What to do when he has a headache: How to rekindle your man's desire.* London: Thorsons.

Woodburn, J. (1988). African hunter-gatherer social organization: Is it best understood as a product of encapsulation? In T. Ingold, D. Riches, & J. Woodburn (Eds.), *Hunters and gatherers I. History, evolution and social change* (pp. 31-64). Oxford, UK: Berg.

World Bank. (1992). *World development report 1992.* New York: Oxford University Press.

World Bank. (1994). *World development report 1994.* New York: Oxford University Press.

World Bank. (1996). *World development report 1996: From plan to market.* New York: Oxford University Press.

Yelsma, P., & Athappilly, K. (1988). Marital satisfaction and communication practices: Comparisons among Indian and American couples. *Journal of Comparative Family Studies, 19,* 37-54.

Zandpour, F., Campos, V., Catalano, J., Chang, C., Cho, Y. D., Hoobyar, R., Jiang, S. F., Lin, M. C., Madrid, S., Scheideler, H., & Osborn, S. T. (1994, September/October). Global reach and local touch: Achieving cultural fitness in TV advertising. *Journal of Advertising Research,* pp. 35-63.

Zandpour, F., & Harich, K. R. (1996). Think and feel country clusters: A new approach to international advertising standardization. *International Journal of Advertising, 15,* 325-344.

AUTHOR INDEX

227

SUBJECT INDEX

ABOUT THE AUTHORS

Willem A. Arrindell is Lecturer in the Department of Clinical Psychology at the University of Groningen, the Netherlands, where he obtained his MA and PhD degrees. The fact that he was born on Curaçao, Netherlands Antilles, led him to undertake a comparative study of emotional distress in Dutch and Antillean subjects (*Personality and Individual Differences, 6*, 725-736). From 1991 to 1996, he fulfilled a postdoctoral fellowship of the Royal Netherlands Academy of Arts and Sciences. He has published more than 70 papers in the areas of applied psychological measurement, test development, and cross-cultural clinical psychology. He is coeditor (with C. Perris and M. Eisemann) of *Parenting and Psychopathology*.

Deborah L. Best is Distinguished Professor and Chair of the Department of Psychology at Wake Forest University in Winston-Salem, North Carolina. She received her BA and MA degrees from Wake Forest University and her PhD from the University of North Carolina at Chapel Hill. Her primary research interests are in developmental, cognitive, and personality psychology. With John E. Williams, she published the books *Measuring Sex Stereotypes* (Sage, 2nd edition, 1990) and *Sex and Psyche: Gender and Self Viewed Cross-Culturally* (Sage, 1990), as well as having authored more than 50 papers. She served as Treasurer of the International Association of Cross-Cultural Psychology for 8 years and is currently Associate Editor of the *Journal of Cross-Cultural Psychology*.

Marieke de Mooij is President of her own consultancy firm, Cross Cultural Communications Company (CCCC), at Badhoevedorp, the Netherlands, specializing in international marketing and communications strategy development. CCCC cooperates with the market research company Inter/View International of Amsterdam, the Netherlands. De Mooij is Associate Professor at the University of Navarra, Pamplona, Spain, and has lectured on cross-cultural marketing in many countries of Europe, Asia, and North America. She is the author of *Advertising Worldwide* (1994) and of *Global Marketing and Advertising: Understanding Cultural Paradoxes* (Sage, 1998).

Geert Hofstede is Emeritus Professor of Organizational Anthropology and International Management at Maastricht University, the Netherlands. He cofounded the Institute for Research on Intercultural Cooperation (IRIC) at Maastricht and Tilburg Universities. He holds an MSc degree in Mechanical Engineering from Delft Technical University and a PhD in Social Psychology from the University of Groningen. He worked in industry in roles varying from production worker to director of human resources, as well as in international business schools and research institutes (IMD, Lausanne; INSEAD, Fontainebleau; EIASM, Brussels). His best known books are *Culture's Consequences* (Sage, 1980) and *Cultures and Organizations: Software of the Mind* (1991). The latter has been translated into 14 other languages.

Michael H. Hoppe is Senior Program and Research Associate at the Center for Creative Leadership, an executive development firm headquartered in Greensboro, North Carolina. A native of Germany, he previously lived and worked in Austria and Greece. His past and current activities were and are concentrated on the development and growth of individuals and organizations, increasingly from an intercultural perspective. He holds graduate degrees from the University of Munich, Germany, and from the State University of New York, Albany, and received his PhD in adult education and organizational development from the University of North Carolina at Chapel Hill. His dissertation research on international differences in work-related values and learning in 19 countries constituted the first large-scale follow-up study on Hofstede's *Culture's Consequences.*

Evert Van de Vliert is Professor of Organizational and Applied Social Psychology at the University of Groningen, the Netherlands, and Past President of the International Association for Conflict Management. He worked as an organizational consultant before and after receiving his PhD degree from the Vrije Universiteit Amsterdam. Professor Van de Vliert is the author or coauthor of more than 100 papers, two books, and four coedited books, including *Complex Interpersonal Conflict Behaviour: Theoretical Frontiers* (1997) and *Using Conflict in Organizations* (Sage, 1997).

Jacques H. A. Van Rossum is a Senior Staff Member of the Department of Human Movement Behavior of the Faculty of Human Movement Sciences at the Vrije Universiteit Amsterdam, the Netherlands. He studied developmental psychology at the University of Nijmegen and obtained his PhD in Human Movement Sciences at the Vrije Universiteit Amsterdam, in the area of children's motor learning. His primary research interests are in motor development and sports psychology. He has edited and coedited two books on motor development and published more than 60 papers. In recent years, he has focused on talent development in sports. He is Consulting Editor of *High Ability Studies* and an adviser to various Dutch sports associations and to the Dutch Olympic Committee. During the academic year 1995-1996, he was a Visiting Professor of Sports Psychology at the Free University of Brussels, Belgium.

Johan Verweij studied political science at the universities of Nijmegen and of Amsterdam, the Netherlands. At the time of this research he was working at the Social and Cultural Planning Office

of the Goverment of the Netherlands. He was involved in preparing
a chapter for the World Culture Report, to be submitted to the United
Nations Educational. Scientific, and Cultural Organization in 1998.
At present he is finishing his PhD at the Faculty of Social Sciences at
Tilburg University, the Netherlands, with a thesis on cross-national
differences in secularization.

Mieke Vunderink is a Research Associate at the Institute for Research on Intercultural Cooperation (IRIC) in Maastricht, the Netherlands. She received her BA degree in Psychology from the Vrije
Universiteit Amsterdam and her MA in Cross-Cultural Developmental Psychology from the University of Utrecht, both in the Netherlands. In 1990, she did an in-depth study of the experiences of
American students during an overseas study semester in Maastricht.
She joined IRIC in 1993 and is currently involved in a research project
on African values.

John E. Williams is Emeritus Distinguished Professor of Psychology
at Wake Forest University in Winston-Salem, North Carolina. He
holds a BA degree from the University of Richmond and MA and PhD
degrees from the University of Iowa. Prior to working at Wake Forest
University, he was on the faculties at Yale University and the University of Richmond. He has authored more than 90 scholarly papers in
personality, social, and developmental psychology, and his three
books include *Measuring Sex Stereotypes* (Sage, 2nd edition, 1990) and
Sex and Psyche: Gender and Self Viewed Cross-Culturally (Sage, 1990),
both written jointly with Deborah L. Best. For 5 years, he served as
Editor of the *Journal of Cross-Cultural Psychology*; in 1996-1997, he was
a Fulbright Professor in India.

CPSIA information can be obtained at www.ICGtesting.com
Printed in the USA
BVOW071402171212

308416BV00001B/127/A